DATED

Habitats, Environments, and Human Behavior

Studies in Ecological Psychology and Eco-Behavioral Science from the Midwest Psychological Field Station, 1947-1972

Roger G. Barker
and Associates

Habitats, Environments, and Human Behavior

Jossey-Bass Publishers
San Francisco • Washington • London • 1978

HABITATS, ENVIRONMENTS, AND HUMAN BEHAVIOR
Studies in Ecological Psychology and Eco-Behavioral Science from the Midwest Psychological Field Station, 1947-1972
by Roger G. Barker and Associates

Copyright © 1978 by: Jossey-Bass, Inc., Publishers
433 California Street
San Francisco, California 94104
&
Jossey-Bass Limited
28 Banner Street
London EC1Y 8QE

Library of Congress Catalogue Card Number LC 77-82912

International Standard Book Number ISBN 0-87589-356-2

Manufactured in the United States of America

JACKET DESIGN BY WILLI BAUM

FIRST EDITION

Code 7749

The Jossey-Bass
Social and Behavioral Science Series

Preface

◆◇◆◇◆◇◆◇◆◇◆◇◆◇◆◇◆◇◆◇◆◇◆◇◆◇◆◇◆◇◆◇

Some years ago I made a weekly train trip from Champaign to Carbondale in Illinois. For long stretches the tracks and the highway were parallel, separated by only a few hundred feet and straight as taut strings. Strung on these twin cords at eight- to twelve-mile intervals were small towns. The train made few stops; its fifty-five-mile-per-hour speed swished and clanged viewers in the parlor car through most of the towns in a minute or two (past a blur of grain elevators, oil depots, the station, the mainstreet crossing, and a few people watching us flash by) to slide, again, into the quiet, almost uninhabited countryside.

There were almost always automobiles in view on the highway, pacing the train or slowly winning or losing the race with it. Over half-hour and hour periods, I would not infrequently make friends with a green sedan and its lone driver or with a pickup truck and its windswept children in the open bed. Out in the country, the races were fair and square, but in the towns the automobiles were invariably in trouble. Even before a town was visible from the car window, the vehicles on the highway would slip behind, as if encountering soft sand, and within

the towns they encountered more difficulty, sometimes completely stalling before the flying train swept me beyond viewing
distance. But often after the town was left behind, a highway
friend would reappear, gaining slowly, as if aided by an extra
pull from the trailing vacuum of the train, and reestablish his
ceded place in the race.

These occurrences raised a question: What happened to
the motorists in the towns? How did the towns delay my highway friends who were obviously bent on keeping up with the
train? I could make some guesses: rough streets, speed zones,
traffic congestion, pedestrian crossings, detours around street
carnivals, traffic lights, one-way lanes for street repairs. Perhaps
the pickup truck with the children was seduced to a short stop
by a hamburger stand or a Saturday farmers' market. It was
surely by means such as these that the towns intervened in the
behavior of my motoring friends. No mystery at all. But latent
in my mind were questions that became explicit later: If a town
exercises such strong control over people within so small a part
of its whole domain as a single highway, to what degree does it
take overall charge of its inhabitants? To what degree do people
live their own lives in towns, and to what degree do they carry
out the towns' programs and policies?

At the time, however, I only asked, "What do people do
in these towns? How do they live their lives? How do they raise
their children?"

In the years since then, I and my colleagues have systematically studied towns and parts of towns, with special reference
to them as habitats for children. Herbert F. Wright and I established the Midwest Psychological Field Station of the University
of Kansas in Oskaloosa, Kansas in 1947; it operated until 1972.
The rationale for the station was stated in the original application for support:

> This research aims to describe in concrete
> detail the conditions of life and behavior of all the
> children of a community. This is an aspect of child
> behavior which has received little attention from
> scientists, yet it is one that is of great importance

for an understanding of acculturation and personality formation.

Although we know a great deal about how children behave under relatively controlled, standardized conditions, such as intelligence- and personality-testing situations, we know little about the nature of the situations that actually confront children in their daily lives and how they react to them. Preoccupation by investigators with behavior under controlled conditions has crowded out concern with naturally occurring situations and with the interrelations between them and behavior. We do not know in concrete detail how parents, teachers, and other adults and children behave toward children, we do not know what pressures and demands are made upon children, we do not know how they respond: what successes, failures, frustrations, and happinesses children actually experience.

Over the years we have dealt with this problem in some major publications: *One Boy's Day* (Barker and Wright, 1951), *Midwest and Its Children* (Barker and Wright, 1955), *The Stream of Behavior* (Barker, 1963b), *Big School, Small School* (Barker and Gump, 1964), *Ecological Psychology* (Barker, 1968), and *Qualities of Community Life* (Barker and Schoggen, 1973). And during these years, too, we have considered special issues in shorter papers, published in books and journals for specialized groups, and in books that are now out of print. We present some of these papers here. Our intention has been to clarify some issues for old hands, to provide an overview of ecological psychology and eco-behavioral science for neophytes, and to sketch the course of development of our conception of an eco-behavioral science with fewer of the procedural details than the original publications required. A number of the chapters are extensively revised and shortened versions of original papers. Routine statistical technicalities relating to reliability and significance measures that are available in the original publications have been omitted.

Fourteen of the nineteen chapters are products of the

twenty-five years of research at the Midwest Field Station, three contributions report work done at other institutions by former research assistants after they left the Field Station, and two papers were prepared after the station closed; however, all the work issued directly from the Field Station program.

The data of the Field Station studies were secured in Oskaloosa, Kansas and in Leyburn, Yorkshire, England, code named Midwest (MW) and Yoredale (YD), respectively. These towns are rural business and government centers of about 1,000 population; they were chosen for detailed study because we wished to take our new look within communities that appeared likely to differ in ways of interest to us but that still would be within the same general cultural frame.

Although we began the research with a concern for the living conditions of children and their consequences for the immediate behavior and long-term development of the children, we soon made two discoveries: (1) the children of the towns could not be effectively considered apart from the other inhabitants and (2) our concerns could not be elucidated in terms of psychology alone. *Habitats, Environments, and Human Behavior* discusses these discoveries.

The extensive archival materials collected at the Midwest Psychological Field Station during its twenty-five years of operation have been deposited in the Spencer Research Library of the University of Kansas.

Acknowledgments

Financial support of the research reported in all chapters except Nine, Eleven, Twelve, and Nineteen is acknowledged in the original publications. Chapter Nine is based on a project funded in part by Research Grant No. 714 from the Vocational Rehabilitation Administration, U.S. Department of Health, Education and Welfare (HEW). Preparation of Chapter Eleven and the research reported therein was supported by Research and Training Center No. 4 (RT-4), Texas Institute for Rehabilitation and Research and Baylor College of Medicine, funded by the Rehabilitation Service Administration, HEW. The writing of

Chapters Twelve and Nineteen and editorial preparation of the book was aided by the Grace Medes Fund of the University of Kansas Endowment Association.

Permission to reprint materials has been received from Herbert F. Wright (Chapter Two), Edwin P. Willems (Chapter Five), Harper & Row (Chapter Six), *Journal of Extension* (Chapter Thirteen), University of Nebraska Press (Chapter Fourteen), Chronical Guidance Publications (Chapter Sixteen).

Oskaloosa, Kansas   Roger G. Barker
September 1977

Contents

◆◆◆◆◆◆◆◆◆◆◆◆◆◆◆◆◆◆◆◆◆◆◆◆◆◆◆◆◆◆◆

Contents

The Authors

Roger G. Barker is professor of psychology, emeritus, University of Kansas. He received the Ph.D. degree in psychology from Stanford University in 1934. His regular academic appointments have been at Harvard University (1937-1938), University of Illinois (1938-1942), Stanford University (1942-1946), Clark University (1946-1947), and University of Kansas (1947-1972). In 1954 he established the satellite station reported in this study in Leyburn, Yorkshire, England.

Barker is author, co-author, or editor of several books including *One Boy's Day* (with H. F. Wright, 1951), *Midwest and Its Children* (with H. F. Wright, 1955), *The Stream of Behavior* (1963), *Big School, Small School* (edited with P. V. Gump, 1964), *Ecological Psychology* (1968), and *Qualities of Community Life* (with P. Schoggen, 1973).

Barker's fellowships and honors have included General Education Board Fellow, University of Iowa; Fellow, Center for Advanced Study in the Behavioral Sciences, Stanford; Distinguished Scientific Award, American Psychological Association; Kurt Lewin Award, Society for the Psychological Study of

Social Issues; G. Stanley Hall Award, Division of Developmental
Psychology, American Psychological Association.

Roger Barker and his wife Louise live in Oskaloosa, Kansas (site of the Midwest Psychological Field Station) where they
have resided for twenty-nine years.

Louise S. Barker, chief field worker and assistant administrator
from the inception of the Field Station to its close.

Clifford L. Fawl, professor of psychology, Nebraska Wesleyan
University. He was research assistant at the Field Station
for several years and occasional interim administrator of
Midwest when work was in progress in Yoredale.

Paul V. Gump, professor of psychology, University of Kansas.
After a temporary research appointment at the Field
Station, he accepted the opportunity to become a regular
staff member of the station and the university.

Lauro S. Halstead, associate professor of rehabilitation and
community medicine, Baylor College of Medicine, and
attending physician, Texas Institute for Rehabilitation
Research.

Arthur Johnson, extension director, Jefferson County, Kansas;
an early supporter of the Field Station.

Dan D. M. Ragle, research associate and instructor in continuing
education, University of Kansas. He was director of statistical and computer operations for the Field Station.

Maxine F. Schoggen, counselor in human development, North
York Hospital, Toronto. She was a skilled field worker
and data analyst, creative critic, and protector of research
standards at the Field Station.

Phil Schoggen, professor of psychology, York University, Toronto. He was research assistant, research associate, and
finally associate director of the Field Station.

Allan W. Wicker, associate professor of psychology, Claremont Graduate School. He served as an independent observer of the Field Station.

Edwin P. Willems, professor of psychology, University of Houston, and professor of rehabilitation, Baylor College of Medicine. He was research assistant and interim program director at the Field Station.

Herbert F. Wright, professor of psychology, emeritus, University of Kansas. As co-founder of the Field Station and co-director during the first seven years of operation, he had a major influence on its conceptions and techniques.

Habitats, Environments, and Human Behavior

*Studies in Ecological Psychology
and Eco-Behavioral Science
from the Midwest Psychological
Field Station, 1947-1972*

Part 1

From Ecological Psychology to Eco-Behavioral Science

◆◆◆ ◆◆ ◆◆ ◆◆ ◆◆ ◆◆ ◆◆ ◆◆ ◆◆ ◆◆ ◆◆ ◆◆ ◆◆ ◆◆ ◆◆ ◆◆◆

The Midwest Psychological Field Station was established with the aim of studying the everyday behavior and psychological situations of the children of the town of Midwest. We came to the task as scientists with training and experience in experimental and child psychology. With this background, we set out to record the behavior and circumstances of individual children, with the intention of generalizing our findings in terms of distributions of a variety of measures of each of the 119 children in the town. We thought of this as ecological psychology,

1

as opposed to experimental and clinical psychology; our research plans differed from those of most other psychologists in that we forsook the laboratory and clinic for the "natural" habitats of our subjects.

We had much to learn about the methods and concepts required for an ecological psychology, but still we had no doubt that the general laws of psychology would apply. We were slow to discover that psychology is not enough when one seeks to explicate behavior that occurs in reading classes, grocery stores, and worship services, that an extraindividual behavior science is essential. We resisted the evidence of our data. Our prolonged use of the term ecological psychology *for both individual and extraindividual studies is a symptom of our recalcitrance. In fact, one book (Barker, 1968) that dealt with what we now see as eco-behavioral science was titled* Ecological Psychology. *But at last the data triumphed, and we saw that to fully elucidate behavior and its environment both ecological psychology and eco-behavioral science are required.*

Issues we met in the course of our discoveries are presented in Part One. The first two chapters consider fundamental issues of ecological psychology, the next two deal with problems of eco-behavioral science, and the final chapter argues that the latter science is distinct from psychology and requires special facilities and procedures.

Roger G. Barker   *1*

Stream of
Individual Behavior

◆━◆◆━◆◆━◆◆━◆◆━◆◆━◆◆━◆◆━◆◆━◆◆━◆◆━◆◆━◆◆━◆◆━◆◆━◆◆━◆◆━◆◆━◆◆━◆

We quickly made a discovery and encountered difficulties when we initiated our study of the everyday lives of the children of Midwest by attempting to record their behavior and environments individually. We discovered that behavior and environment are inexorably continuous in time, that they are relentlessly ongoing from sunrise to sunrise with no gaps whatsoever. This was not new to us as laypersons, of course, but our experiences in laboratories and clinics, where both behavior and environment are expertly arranged in discrete segments (interviews, experiments, tests), did not prepare us for this feature of ecological psychology. We came with no methods of recording the unbroken behavior stream, no concepts and techniques for identifying its parts and pieces, and no systems for analyzing its attributes. These lacks confronted us with great difficulties; we

Revision of chapter "The Stream of Behavior as an Empirical Problem," Barker (1963b, pp. 1-22).

3

had to devise methods and concepts, techniques, and systems of analysis, from the ground up.

In fact, the temporal dimension is among the most prominent of behavior's manifold characteristics, and many parts of the behavior stream have been identified and described, encompassing such diverse phenomena as an alpha wave, a maze-learning trial, a psychotic episode, a five-minute segment of behavior, a game of marbles, and an answer to a pollster's question. But despite its salience, when we began our research little was known about the disposition of these and the multitude of other happenings along behavior's temporal axis undisturbed by intrusions from investigators.

Units and Tesserae

We found that the stream of behavior can be divided into an infinite number of parts of two types. One type, here called *behavior units,* consists of the inherent segments of the stream of behavior. The boundaries of behavior units occur at those points of the behavior stream where changes occur independently of the operations of the investigator. Alpha waves, psychotic episodes, and games of marbles are behavior units. Behavior units enter psychology when investigators function as transducers, observing and recording behavior with techniques that do not influence its course. When a child is observed to sit on a rock (Lewin, 1935, p. 83), to refuse to say "please" (Stern, 1938, p. 499), or to make a "house" (Isaacs, 1933, p. 168) in the ordinary course of his life, without instigation or direction by the observer, behavior units are observed.

All sciences devise techniques for exploring the natural units of their phenomena. Here we find x-ray analyses, electrical, magnetic, and resonance techniques, and photographic recording. A primary concern of geographers, geologists, and oceanographers, for example, is with the naturally occurring, unrearranged surface of the earth.

The other parts of the behavior stream may be appropriately called *behavior tesserae.* Tesserae are the pieces of glass or marble used in mosaic work; they are created or selected by the mosaic maker to fulfill his artistic aims. Similarly, behavior tesserae are fragments of behavior that are created or selected by the investigator when he functions as an operator, arranging conditions in accordance with his scientific aims. Maze-learning trials, five-minute segments of behavior, and answers to pollsters' questions are behavior tesserae. They occur when there is input to the behavior stream from the investigator and feedback from the behavior stream to the investigator. When an investigator directs a subject to "Define orange," "Tell me what you see on the card," or "Judge which of these weights is the heavier," he destroys the natural units of the behavior stream and imposes behavior tesserae in their place. Behavior tesserae are produced by experiments and also by tests, questionnaires, and interviews, in other words, by all methods that require the subject to undertake actions at the behest of the investigator. Behavior tesserae are produced, too, by research methods that divide the behavior continuum into predetermined time periods or number-of-occurrence segments. In these cases, the beginning and the end points of the selected parts of the behavior stream are established by the technical requirements of the investigator, and they coincide only by chance with the inherent units of the behavior continuum. When an investigator tallies the occurrence of aggressive behavior in a sample of one-minute observations of a child, or records a child's first fifty utterances during a period of observation, he disregards the intrinsic structure of the behavior stream and selects parts from it that fit his research design.

Research methods that ignore or destroy existing structures and select or create new ones are standard techniques and of great value in most sciences. Chemists, biologists, and geologists grind and macerate, compound, synthesize, and rearrange their substances in order to make important analyses. The imposition of alien tesserae on the material of a science is dramatically illustrated by the way geographers and geometers divide the surface of the earth. About one hundred years ago, geodetic surveyors came to eastern Kansas with measuring rods and a plan. They divided the landscape into the surprising lattice of geometric squares called *sections*. These are geographical tes-

serae. They are true and useful regions, but they had no existence until the surveyors came with geometry and a design in
their heads and staked out the section boundaries. The tesserae,
themselves, tell nothing directly about the topography of this
part of the earth.

At about the time the surveyors came to Kansas, scientific psychologists moved into the field of behavior and began
staking off alien tesserae on its surface. In this task, they were
tough-minded, like the surveyors; they allowed few natural features of the behavioral terrain to interfere with the structures
imposed by their experiments, tests, questionnaires, and interviews. They imposed a geometry on behavior, a geometry
grounded on the axioms of experimental design and statistical
methods, a geometry that reveals nothing directly about the
behavioral surface on which it is imposed. Tesserae have dominated psychological research over the ensuing years, so that
psychology is surely one of the few sciences that has little more
knowledge than laypersons about the occurrence in nature of
many of its phenomena: of talk, of fear, of problem-solving
efforts (and their successes and failures), of laughter, of frustration, of being disciplined, of anger, of achievement, of cooperation, of play, of being teased.

It is true that some phases of behavior stream ecology
have not been neglected. Most systematists of psychology are
concerned implicitly or explicitly with the temporal dimension
of behavior; they refer to behavior's "patent continuities" (Allport, 1937, p. 5), to its "continuous and connected process"
(Ladd, 1898, p. 136), to its "orderly, continuous whole"
(Dewey, 1891, p. 86), to its "continuous, flowing activity"
(Stern, 1938, p. 78), to its "ceaseless movement" (Watson,
1924, p. 161), to its "organized process extending through
time" (Angyal, 1941, p. 348), to its "sequential character"
(Leighton, 1959, p. 18), to its "continuous change" (White,
1952, p. 328). And some systematists give a fundamental place
to the building blocks, to the units, of the behavior stream; for
example, Murray (1959), Parsons (1959), Muenzinger (1939),
Tolman (1929), and Miller, Galanter, and Pribram (1960) have
emphasized the problem of behavior stream units. For these and

other systematists we have studied, behavior stream units are theoretical constructs; their identification and their disposition within the behavior stream are not presented as empirical problems. But for ecological psychology the structure of the behavior stream is a central research task.

Units of the Stream of Behavior

There are two grounds for identifying and classifying behavior units; one is their structural-dynamic characteristics, the other their material-content properties. These two bases for identifying and classifying behavior units are illustrated in the following specimen record.

Brett Butley, seven years two months of age on July 5, 1957, was a member of the Upper Infants Class of the Yoredale County School. The morning "break" occurred at 10:30. After having a glass of milk supplied by the school and peeling an orange he had brought from home, Brett wandered into the school yard where much noisy activity was in progress. Some nine-year-old girls were running about trailing long strips of aluminum foil, boys the same age were administering the Yorkshire Bumps to any of their mates they caught, a vigorous game of chain tag charged helter-skelter over the crowded yard, and four of Brett's classmates played a quiet game of cricket in one corner. Brett appeared to weigh the possibilities as he ate his orange; he finally walked to the cricket game and asked Norman Stephenson, the bowler, if he could play. Brett stood watching the game as he finished eating his orange. Then the record, which was made at the time, continues (see Table 1):

This is a segment of Brett's behavior, which, however, continued minutes, hours, days, even years, before and after the actions described. The question to be determined is whether this is one or several units of Brett's behavior continuum, or if it is a behavior tessera, that is, an arbitrary behavior fragment containing no complete behavior unit. The analyst of the record identified the units marked along the record, namely "eating orange" (the terminal part of a long unit that overlapped with a number of previous units), "noting hurt child," "watching

Table 1. Behavior Record, Brett Butley

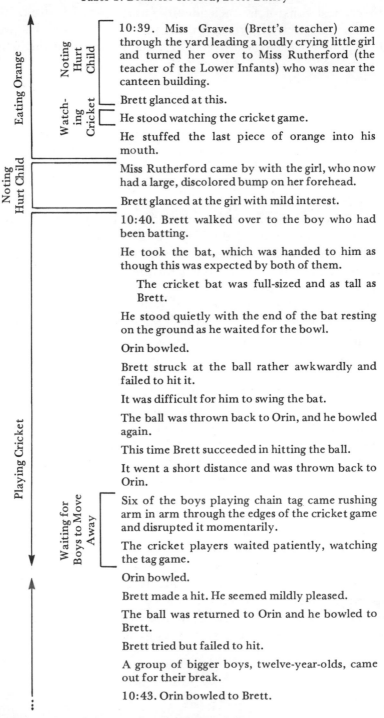

10:39. Miss Graves (Brett's teacher) came through the yard leading a loudly crying little girl and turned her over to Miss Rutherford (the teacher of the Lower Infants) who was near the canteen building.

Brett glanced at this.

He stood watching the cricket game.

He stuffed the last piece of orange into his mouth.

Miss Rutherford came by with the girl, who now had a large, discolored bump on her forehead.

Brett glanced at the girl with mild interest.

10:40. Brett walked over to the boy who had been batting.

He took the bat, which was handed to him as though this was expected by both of them.

    The cricket bat was full-sized and as tall as Brett.

He stood quietly with the end of the bat resting on the ground as he waited for the bowl.

Orin bowled.

Brett struck at the ball rather awkwardly and failed to hit it.

It was difficult for him to swing the bat.

The ball was thrown back to Orin, and he bowled again.

This time Brett succeeded in hitting the ball.

It went a short distance and was thrown back to Orin.

Six of the boys playing chain tag came rushing arm in arm through the edges of the cricket game and disrupted it momentarily.

The cricket players waited patiently, watching the tag game.

Orin bowled.

Brett made a hit. He seemed mildly pleased.

The ball was returned to Orin and he bowled to Brett.

Brett tried but failed to hit.

A group of bigger boys, twelve-year-olds, came out for their break.

10:43. Orin bowled to Brett.

Table 1 (Continued)

Watching Cricket	Brett hit the ball energetically. One of the big boys reached out and caught the ball as it was thrown to Orin. The big boy then bowled rather gently to Brett. Brett tried but missed. The big boy evidently intended to bowl, and Orin moved to the batter's position. Orin took the bat from Brett. Brett appeared to make no objection. 10:44. He stood passively with his fingers in his mouth watching as the game continued.

cricket game," "noting hurt child," "playing cricket," "waiting for boys to move away," "watching cricket game" (the beginning of a unit that extended beyond this part of the record). It is clear that the analyst performed the task of unitizing Brett's record in terms of a structural-dynamic behavior unit; the material-content properties vary widely within units he identified. For example, within the unit "playing cricket," there were intervals when Brett was quiet, when he was energetic, when he failed, when he succeeded, when he was pleased, and when he was patient. Each of these was a naturally occurring part of Brett's behavior stream and could legitimately have been identified as a behavior unit; but this was not done in the present case.

Structural-Dynamic Units: Behavior Episodes. The structural-dynamic units identified by the analyst are called *behavior episodes*; they have three defining properties.

1. Constant Direction. This is the basic criterion of a behavior episode; behavior is unidirectional from the beginning of an episode to its termination in the goal of the action. Identifying an episode in the stream of behavior requires, in the first place, diagnosing the goal to which the person is moving. Research by Dickman (1963) supports the view that the direction-

ality of behavior, the end to which it is moving, is almost as immediately perceived as visual form or auditory pattern.

2. Occurrence Within the Normal Behavior Perspective. The second defining attribute of an episode serves to delimit the segment of the behavior stream within which directionality is apprehended. The phenomenon of behavior directedness is a prime example of the inside-outside problem, as Floyd Allport (1955) called it, namely, that although the attributes of the component parts of a superordinate, enclosing unit may differ widely, they are all congruent with the attributes of the over-arching unit. Thus, the characteristics of the cells that comprise an organ often differ greatly among themselves, but they conform to the encompassing characteristics of the organ. This is true, too, of the directions of the parts of an episode and of the whole episode: The parts may have different directions, yet the direction of each coincides with the direction of the episode. For example, within the episode "going to school," the direction of each of the included parts "finding coat," "telling mother goodbye," and "getting bicycle" coincides with that of "going to school," yet the direction of "finding coat" is not equal to that of "telling mother goodbye." Directionality, which determines the beginning and the end points of a behavior episode, is itself dependent on the extent of the behavior stream segment within which directionality is determined. To escape from this paradox, it is necessary to define the behavior stream segment within which units are discriminated. This is what the episode criterion of normal behavior perspective does; it specifies the behavior stream segment within which direction is to be determined. It is equivalent to the description of the general size and range of a physical object by its perceptibility. For example, atoms are so small they are below the limen of visibility, the largest protozoan can just be seen by the "naked eye," and stars of the sixth magnitude can be seen in peripheral vision. This criterion eliminates from consideration short units that usually "run off" with no or only vague awareness of the person himself, or of others observing him (for example, "stepping down first step" as part of "getting bicycle"), and it eliminates long units that occur outside the limits of ordinary perception (for example, "getting an education"). The behavior

perspective criterion designates, by means of a perceptual coordinate, the span of the behavior continuum within which the primary episode criterion of directionality is to be applied.

3. Equal Potency Throughout Episode Course. The third defining characteristic of a behavior episode is that the whole episode has more potency than any of its parts and, conversely, that if any part of a behavior sequence with constant direction exceeds or equals the whole in potency, that part becomes a separate episode. The assumption behind this criterion is that when a part of a behavior stream, such as "finding coat," equals or exceeds in potency the whole directed unit ("going to school"), the part takes precedence over the whole within the behavior perspective of the person and in the total dynamics of the continuing behavior.

However abstract these criteria may appear, they provide defining characteristics that make it possible for independent analysts to agree not only on those points in the behavior stream where directionality changes but also on directional units of the same size and with the same beginning and end points. Reliability studies have shown that agreement in identifying episodes of behavior, as defined by the three criteria, is within the 72 percent to 87 percent range. Details of the reliability of episode identification and of various episode ratings are presented in *Midwest and Its Children* (Barker and Wright, 1955) and *Recording and Analyzing Child Behavior* (Wright, 1967).

Content Units. Parts of the stream of behavior with particular content properties are as numerous as behavior's myriad attributes. In Brett's record, we find periods of eating, walking, success, waiting, pleasure, failure, vigor, and passivity, among others; each of these could have been identified as a unit in terms of its content properties.

Research Methodology

In scientific research, behavior units (both episode and content units) are discovered, and behavior tesserae are designed. Discovery and design require different methods and encounter different difficulties. These different methods and difficulties have undoubtedly influenced the amount and the nature of research on the behavior stream; some of them are as follows.

Recording the Stream of Behavior. Much of the behavior stream is so sensitive to external conditions that special arrangements and precautions are required to avoid distorting it by the means used to observe and record it. Behavior units are revealed by gentle, open-minded, receptive methods. Such methods are in many respects more difficult to devise and apply than the controls that behavior tesserae demand. Some indication of how frequently research methods disturb behavior is indicated by those in common use. Tests, interviews, questionnaires, and experiments are designed precisely to destroy the naturally occurring conditions of the subject's life and to substitute for them the new, especially arranged situations that will elicit the behavior tesserae in which the investigator is interested.

The most adequate ecological behavior data at the present time are provided by verbal narrative records made by trained observers and by sound and motion pictures (or television tapes). Photographic records have both shortcomings and advantages. For the understanding of behavior and its context, both more and less are often needed than the lens and film are able to record. Behavior always occurs with reference to only a portion of the multiplicity of things and events surrounding the person. But behavior-and-context forms a pattern, a figure, against a neutral background; the former can be selectively seen and described by an observer but not by a camera, so after a film is made the task remains of selecting what is significant from the vast amount of material. But behavior-and-context is often not limited to immediately contiguous areas which are all the camera sees; what is behind the camera and out of the limited range of its lens is lost. The advantages of the filmed record lie in the preservation of details that are lost in verbal accounts and the opportunity the film provides the investigator to go back and "look again"; these are crucial advantages for some investigations. And for some studies the context beyond the camera's range is not important.

A verbal narrative has certain technical advantages as a

system for recording individual behavior. Some of these advantages derive from a narrative's own characteristics as behavior: It is continuous, as behavior is continuous, and in this respect is isomorphic with the behavior continuum. Also, language has symbol systems for directed behavior and for representing single and multiple channels of action. The vast number of temporal, relational, and linking terms and the vaster number of terms describing behavior attributes make language invaluable for recording behavior. Literary language has been suspect as a tool for science, and the effort to achieve greater precision via formulae, graphs, numbers, meter readings, photographs, and so on continues. However, rich, descriptive language is at the present time the recording medium par excellence of the stream of behavior, and it appears likely to remain so. We have called detailed narrative accounts of the stream of behavior *specimen records*. They have many of the values of biological specimen for scientific studies.

The Problem of Verification. Science continually searches for independent evidence of the adequacy of its methods and proof of its discoveries. In the case of tesserae, external checks and criteria are usually available at many points in the investigative process. The basic technical problem is to select from or introduce into the behavior stream the tesserae required to answer the questions the investigator brings to behavior. This requires firm, tough-minded, affirmative methods. The passwords are *control* and *selection*: control of the investigator's input to the behavior stream, selective sensitivity to the feedback from the behavior stream. If the problems the investigator brings to behavior are adequately formulated, this includes the operations required to select or create the necessary tesserae. An important part of the work on research design and experimental methods in psychology deals with general principles of establishing adequate tesserae. Some of these are formal and theoretical, such as those concerned with sampling; others are empirical, such as methods for pretesting interview questions, for validating test items, and for establishing maze reliability. All of them provide some independent evidence of the adequacy of the behavior tesserae used by the investigator through reference to theories or criteria external to the tesserae themselves.

There are no similar external criteria available for re- search on behavior units; the behavior stream itself decrees the boundaries and the properties of its own parts. The only empiri- cal evidence that behavior units actually exist and are self- generated, inherent divisions of the behavior stream (not prod- ucts of the methods used by the investigator) is obtained by replicating the observations and analyses.

Problems of Analysis. Behavior tesserae have greater har- mony with the theoretical and mathematical *zeitgeist* of pres- ent-day science than do behavior units. It has been a triumph of modern psychology to devise behavior tesserae that fit the con- ceptual and methodological canons of modern science. But here are the behavior episode units of eight-year-old Mary Ennis on the morning of May 12, 1949, between 7:58 and 8:12 (see Chapter Six):

- Looked for sweater.
- Talked to mother about beads.
- Brushed hair.
- Played with baby brother.
- Showed off skirt.
- Talked to mother about some money.
- Searched for a new half-dollar.
- Joked with mother about a key.
- Helped mother fold diapers.
- Talked baby talk to mother.
- Talked to mother about baby brother's bath.

How does one conceptualize and measure such phenomena? Can one do more than verbally describe them in ever-greater de- tail? Is their seeming disorganized complexity beyond the reach of quantitative and theoretical science? These queries can chal- lenge one's scientific endeavor, or they can forewarn one to turn away from the inherent units of Mary's ongoing behavior stream to devise or select tesserae that fit the assumptions of the available analytical tools.

To an important degree, stream of behavior research has

been limited by the domination of psychology by methods of analysis that require independence of the behavioral items entering the analysis. This condition is usually met by behavior tesserae obtained from different individuals. Such tesserae can be ordered or measured on one or a number of dimensions and then dealt with in terms of frequency distributions and their parameters. The central assumption of these methods—namely, independence of the events that enter the distributions—is, of course, strictly false, so far as units of the behavior stream are concerned. Any manipulation of behavior stream data to conform to the requirements of these methods destroys one of the stream's essential features, namely, that it is an interdependent, structured system.

The Problem of Representativeness. The stream of behavior and its environmental channel involve multiple units with multiple attributes. To include only a few of the units and attributes in an analysis, can, in effect, be as destructive of naturally occurring behavior and its conditions as it would be to actively intervene and impose tesserae or to dismantle the units in the process of analysis. Established research standards are very clear about the disturbing effects of biased sampling of subjects, and situational representativeness is also essential for the correct portrayal of nature. In research on the stream of behavior, behavior stream representativeness is also necessary; the isolation of a single behavior unit, class of unit, or unit attribute from the whole pattern can, in effect, distort the reality of behavior as surely as can direct interference with the behavior stream. This means that length of behavior stream records is important. A long record reduces the danger of biased selection of behavior units; a record covering 100 units rather than 50 is equivalent to using a larger rather than a smaller population sample, and the danger of false interpretation of the meaning of behavior units is reduced when they are placed in a context of behavior long enough to make the inclusive-included relations clear.

The Behavior Stream: A Tractable Problem

Some behavior sciences have not found the behavior stream as formidable as psychology has found it. The empirical study of behavior units and their temporal arrangement is a central issue in history, in linguistics, and in music, and it is prominent in the performing arts: in music, dance, drama. Laypersons, too, find the structure of the behavior stream to be a manageable phenomenon, and they have much practical knowledge of it. Those few psychologists who have studied it, find that the stream of behavior is not a formidable datum, that it occurs in bursts, pauses, and pieces of many sorts that can be described and evaluated for both scientific and practical purposes.

Herbert F. Wright   **2**

Psychological Habitat

◆◆◆◆◆◆◆◆◆◆◆◆◆◆◆◆◆◆◆◆◆◆◆◆◆◆◆◆◆◆◆◆◆

One might propose, for the sake of standardization and objectivity, to describe the surroundings of a person as they are perceived by people in general. This one can do efficiently with the help of a standard dictionary to establish what the surroundings mean. A Midwest child could see his or her mother and interact with her as no more or less than a "female parent," as the dictionary says she is, although this seems improbable. It is not improbable that the child will see her and interact with her at a given time as a person in a good mood or a bad mood who is presently helpful or hindering, bossy, protective, or generous.

Margaret Reid's mother urges some noodles on Margaret in the setting "home meal" in Midwest. The mother smiles and is gentle but very insistent. It seems clear that Mrs. Reid is behaving nurturantly from her point of view, and it might be that she is behaving in a nurturant way from the dictionary's or Midwest's point of view and from the observer's point of view. But more has to be added if we are to describe adequately Mar-

From section titled "Psychological Habitat" in Wright (1967, pp. 25-31).

garet's psychological habitat at the time. We have to tell how Mrs. Reid is behaving from Margaret's point of view. As Margaret sees it, is the behavior of the mother nurturant? Or, as the urging and insistence might suggest, is it not nurturant, but dominating? Or both? Or neither? The critically important parts of the psychological environment are in just such alternative characteristics of physical and social facts as they are perceived by the person. An adequate description of psychological habitat, then, has to heed these properties within a frame of reference that includes some form of the question "What does the person see and how does he or she see it?"

One thing to be said for inquiry of this kind is that we practice it daily with confidence in the information it yields. We identify casually the thing others notice or do not notice, and we see within limits how others look at, feel about, or "take" things, recognizing often that the viewpoint of another differs from our own. We see, within limits, what the actions of Y mean to X. Our belief in the correctness of such observation is strengthened by our finding that, very much more often than not, X sees our own behavior as we do. We often observe with confidence also the characteristics of "things in general" as they are for another person. Even when it appears to us that the "actual" circumstances of X are favorable, we may see that "as far as he is concerned" his situation as a whole is confused or unhappy or threatening; and the reverse can occur. In these cases, too, we generally act in relation to X as much in terms of his situation as we think it to be for him as in terms of what we know about the "actual" state of affairs.

The ability to see what another sees in his habitat is a necessity of social intercourse. It alone enables us to deal with our associates on the basis of their goals, obstacles, paths, and values, and, thereby, to adapt ourselves appropriately to the actions of others. Errors do occur in observation of circumstances as they are perceived by our associates. Doubtless they are frequent on the level of conditions that go with very long behavior units and deeper motives. If only for reliability purposes, therefore, it becomes important that the research here is concerned with comparatively short behavior units that correspond to intentions of the person. A starting base in common perception for reliable observing of environmental contexts is implied by the fact that, in the long run of minute-by-minute social interplay with others, we do generally adapt ourselves appropriately to their actions, which means that we must generally deal with them on the basis of their goals, obstacles, paths, and values, which is possible only in the degree that we do observe what they see in their situations.

How one observes the parts of another's habitat as the other sees them is yet another problem for studies of social perception that cannot be discussed in any detail here. But we should like to note, only as cues to such observation, the present behavior of the person, the sequential context of the behavior, and the characteristics of present behavior settings and objects.

One may observe that a dog is a threatening or fearsome creature in the eyes of Joe Ward, of Midwest, in part because one now sees Joe run from the dog (the present behavior cue), in part because one saw the dog bite Joe an hour earlier (the sequential context cue), and in part because one notes that the dog is big and fierce by common Midwest standards (a behavior object cue). The present behavior probably is the most sensitive indicator. We observe that, as a child sees it, a thing is liked because he approaches it, disliked because he withdraws from it, funny because he laughs at it, or sad because it makes him cry. This lead alone obviously puts us in a circle. We get the characteristics of the environmental object from the behavior that we want to understand by relating it to the object. Fortunately, however, the present behavior cue generally does not stand alone; settings or behavior objects and sequence indicators provide stimulus information that is in some degree independent. One is moderately safe anywhere in asserting that a swarm of bees nearing a boy on his way to school is perceived by him to be menacing and dangerous even if, at the time, one can observe little or nothing of the boy's behavior. And, going by sequential context, one who momentarily loses sight of the same boy at home with his mother can have some confidence that, to him, her mood is unhappy if one knows that a minute before, he found her weeping over bad news. The behavior cue is needed to check other cues, which, nonetheless, can be independently revealing.

Observation of another's situation in terms of what that other perceives in it can be devoid of rational inference, in the sense that one deliberately weighs criteria and deduces their consequences. It can be essentially direct. One may observe at once, without deliberation of any kind, that one or another aspect of a situation is now seen to be good, bad, indifferent, threatening, inviting, hot, cold, or whatever. As these examples suggest, however, such observation may always involve inference on some level. Nevertheless, it seems correct to generalize that the process of observing the facts with which we are now concerned does not differ in principle from observation of other complex phenomena.

We have not meant to imply that one who uses methods of observation and analysis from without can hope to break into the consciousness of a person and to come out with a description that duplicates its content through the shortest period of time. Only novelists, who are free to improvise and to fill in another's experience with their own, are in a good position to do this. Our aim has been only to represent the public side of private experience to the extent of exhibiting some properties that parts of a person's habitat have because they are objects of perception.

The relevant content of molar behavior includes by definition all of the conditions that make a difference to action by the person. Let alone the difficulties in apprehension of conscious experience from without, one cannot assume that these conditions are all represented in conscious experience. It would be superfluous to review here the common reasons for holding that many are not. Proof that an object or condition has entered the habitat of a person is established, in any event, by effectiveness rather than by awareness; whatever has effects on the molar behavior of the person exists in his psychological habitat. One can even doubt that the person is continually aware of habitat parts that derive from present behavior settings. It seems safe to say that Raymond Birch, whose mother works in the

Midwest County Courthouse, can traverse unerringly all of the corridors in this largest building of Midwest with his thoughts preempted by things that completely exclude the walls to his left and right. Yet the walls must continually make a difference to his behavior at the time. Otherwise, he would not continually avoid them. He must be less continually aware of them. Midwest children at school do not think to themselves all of the time, "I must not talk out loud without permission, I must not talk out loud without permission, I must. . . ." Yet talking out loud without permission is a fairly rare exception to a rule of the Midwest school setting. The children "conform" to the rule and thereby demonstrate its effectiveness for most of the time while the teacher who embodies it is present. But we outrightly doubt that they are aware of the rule through the whole of this time.

It is common practice in psychology to test the behavioral effectiveness of an observed condition in the situation of a person without any reference to private experience or to perception. One can do this in the case of the rule against talking out loud, for example, by observing the children both with and without the teacher in the room. On the same basis, one can compare the effects on behavior of different conditions and can use the observed differences in behavior to find by deduction the psychological properties of these conditions. This procedure, too, is common and probably offers the only available means of determining the particular characteristics of some facts in the context of behavior. It is no less true that the primary conditions in relation to which a person behaves at a given time are structured by and get their psychologically relevant properties from the processes of perception. Adequate effort to describe these conditions requires, therefore, a frame of reference and specific methods that enable one to identify these properties with the greatest possible clarity and directness.

There can be no getting around the fact that some "screening" and bias stemming from the standpoint of the observer can never be entirely escapable. All that a psychologist has to report on the parts of Midwest as they are seen by its children obviously will have to be accepted or rejected as *his* perceptions of what the children see. Psychology, where it undertakes representation of this kind, is enormously worse off as a descriptive discipline than many other sciences; but its position outside the facts is not unique in principle. An ideal view of a plant or a rock is biased and imperfect. This is true even of the view that reduces either plant or rock to proton-electron aggregates as nearly ultimate realities; for these, to face the paradox of all searching investigation, are in fact only inventions by the observer. Ultimately, the only advantage on the side of being "scientific" that one investigation can have over another lies not in any corner it has on reality, but in its better intersubjective tests. It follows that, however they stack up against the "true facts," descriptions of psychological habitat and of behavior should at least be as objective as reporting in this area will allow. Our case here will have to rest on the degree to which the findings on both habitat and behavior show internal consistency and otherwise make sense.

The greatest present need of research to describe psychological habitat is for adequate concepts by which to identify and relate different habitat conditions. In the absence of such concepts, one of two unsatisfactory alternatives must be chosen. The first is to link behavior directly with nonpsychological facts, that is, with the physical and social conditions that only supply raw materials for the habitats of individual persons. This has been attempted in correlational studies of behavior and age or sex, of behavior and climate, of behavior and social class or caste, and of behavior and urban or rural life. It should not be surprising that the correlations obtained in these studies are generally low and often contradictory, for it is known that lawfulness and stability are to be found only in relationships between events and facts of the same order. Modern physics, for example, does not use in its derivations biological, economic, or psychological quantities. The best one can expect from linking behavior directly with nonpsychological conditions is an indication of where some psychological truth may lie.

There remains the alternative of bridging the gap between behavior and nonpsychological habitat with the wisdom of common sense and art, in the manner of the novelist or the biographer. One can go beyond a statistical correlation of behavior with birth order, for example, and describe the psychological habitat of, say, an only child in terms of his loneliness, the overindulgence of his parents, and the oppressiveness of an atmosphere that is overcharged with adult interests and standards. Representation of this kind has been condemned as subjective. The objective way out has often been seen as just that of relating behavior to nonpsychological facts. But it may be asked whether, for the purposes of understanding molar behavior, the facts of this order are rightly to be accepted as objective.

Objective conditions are generally held to be the ones that actually exist, unviolated by the biases or special viewpoint of the observer, in the context of the phenomena under investigation. It is by no means clear that, for example, social class or race or climate, as these are defined and measured by the sociologist, the anthropologist, and the meteorologist, do actually exist for a child in the relevant determining context of his behavior. On the other hand, it is clear that conditions vaguely identified by words such as *loneliness, parental overindulgence,* and the *oppressiveness of adult standards* do exist in the contexts of behavior as coercive facts. A primary task of ecological psychology where it is concerned with psychological habitat is the one of conceptualizing such facts with enough precision that they can be related to behavior in an orderly way.

Roger G. Barker
Herbert F. Wright

Standing Patterns
of Behavior

◆▸◀◆▸◀◆▸◀◆▸◀◆▸◀◆▸◀◆▸◀◆▸◀◆▸◀◆▸◀◆▸◀◆▸◀◆▸◀◆▸◀◆▸◀◆

Early in our study, it became clear that data regarding designated persons were not enough, that there was something more
in Midwest of significance to us than the behavior of its individual citizens. We found, too, that the person-by-person approach
was beyond the scope of our scientific apparatus. The truth is
that we soon became overwhelmed with individual behavior. We
estimated that the 119 children of Midwest engaged in about
one hundred thousand behavior episodes daily. In our efforts to
sample this universe adequately, we found that our behavior
sample was improved if, in addition to using the usual stratifica-
tion guides—age, sex, social class, race, education, and occupa-
tion—we sampled behavior in such divergent places as the drug-

Adapted from the sections "Behavior Settings" and "Behavior Objects" in Barker and Wright (1955, pp. 7-10).

store, the Sunday School classes, the 4-H Club meeting, and the football games. Early, we made the not very startling discovery that if we collected behavior in a variety of behavior areas, the variability of our behavior sample was greatly increased. At this point, we stopped focusing exclusively on the behavior of individuals and saw for the first time a thing that is obvious to the inhabitants of Midwest; namely, that behavior comes in extra-individual wave patterns that are as visible and invariant as the pools and rapids in Slough Creek, west of town. The Presbyterian worship services, the high school basketball games, and the post office, for example, persist year after year with their unique configurations of behavior, despite constant changes in the persons involved. These persisting, extraindividual behavior phenomena we have called the *standing behavior patterns* of Midwest.

With this new sensitivity, we began to see that, for the people of Midwest, individual behavior and extraindividual pattern behavior were about equally visible and apparently about equally important. Any issue of the *Midwest Weekly,* whose job it is to report the community's behavior to the citizens, confirmed this. In the issue of August 6, 1953, for example, 393 instances of individual behavior were reported in such items as this: "Mr. and Mrs. Vernon Main and their eleven-year-old daughter, Sandra, escaped from their burning home last Friday morning with only the clothing they wore." In the same issue, 395 occurrences of extraindividual, standing behavior patterns were recorded thus: "Amateur contests again played an important part in the entertainment at the Old Settlers' Reunion at Midwest." In the former item, the behavior of three particular individuals is described; in the latter item, two patterns of behavior that are independent of particular persons are identified, namely, amateur contests and the Old Settlers' Reunion.

Standing patterns of behavior such as contests, picnics, 4-H Club meetings, choir practice, and first-grade reading are hard, empirical facts in Midwest. They are as real to Midwest citizens as the Mains' escape from their burning home. Anyone in Midwest on a Sunday at noon, can see the churches suddenly pour forth their congregations, which hurry away down streets and sidewalks. On any weekday morning at 8:30, the behavior pattern in the post office is unmistakable: efficient business against a background of the relaxed conversation of loiterers.

Standing behavior patterns are in many cases very complex configurations with many subordinate figures. Thus the Old Settlers' Reunion contains the subordinate figure, "amateur contest," and within this figure special acts are discriminated.

It is important to note that standing patterns of behavior are not qualities of behavior in general, such as tempo or prevailing mood, nor do they refer to the common content of behavior: to the ways of preparing food or of exchanging goods. Rather, they are differentiated parts of behavior, which themselves have complex qualities; they, too, are behavioral "things" such as episodes. They are units of behavior phenomena, but they are not units of individual behavior; they are units in the behavior of people en masse.

The discovery of standing behavior patterns was crucial. While important progress could be made toward describing general characteristics of the living conditions and behavior of a community by adding together the behavior characteristics and situations of representative individuals, it seemed clear that the patterned features of extraindividual behavior could not be ignored.

When the standing behavior patterns of Midwest came into focus, a number of other relationships were simultaneously seen. First, it was obvious that characteristic standing behavior patterns are attached to particular places, things, and times, that is, to parts of the nonbehavioral context of the town. The pattern of behavior in stores (buying and selling) is different from the pattern in the American Legion Hall on Saturday night (dancing); sweeping is done with brooms, stirring with spoons, and cutting with knives. There is almost never a change in these attachments: Buying and selling never occur in the American Legion Hall, and dancing does not take place in the stores; sweeping is not done with knives, nor stirring with brooms, nor cutting with spoons. We have called the place-thing-time constellation to which a standing pattern of behavior is attached the *nonpsychological milieu* or simply the *milieu*.

Second, there is often a fittingness or *synomorphism* between the patterns of behavior and the attributes of the non-psychological context to which they are anchored. It is appropriate that writing should occur in connection with a pencil rather than a shovel and that eating should occur in the cafe rather than in the library. A baseball game fits a baseball diamond, and walking and riding on streets and sidewalks conform to the directions of these routes. The total constellation of standing behavior pattern and synomorphic milieu we have called a *behavior-milieu synomorph* or, briefly, a *synomorph*.

Third, there are often abrupt changes in the behavior of a person as he leaves one of these synomorphs and enters another. Margaret Reid's hyperactivity, aggressiveness, and verbalization gave way like magic to passivity, submissiveness, and silence when she passed from the synomorph of her own yard to that of her neighbor's birthday party. The second-graders cease writing, reading, spelling, sitting, whispering, and so on with startling swiftness and unanimity when they cross the line from the school classroom to the school playground. On the basis of many observations of this kind, we were driven to the hypothesis that, in addition to being conspicuous features of the behavioral landscape of Midwest, standing patterns of behavior involve forces that in some way coerce individual behavior.

Fourth, behavior-milieu synomorphs are ubiquitous; very little behavior in Midwest occurs outside their limits.

Behavior Settings

We were now in a position to identify an extraindividual unit that stands to eco-behavioral science as the cell does to biological science, namely, the *behavior setting*. A behavior setting is a standing behavior pattern *together with* the part of the milieu to which the behavior is attached and with which it has a synomorphic relationship. Examples in Midwest are Weylen's Grocery Store, Masonic Lodge Meeting, and Beginners' Band Class. Behavior settings are behavior-milieu phenomena; the milieu is circumjacent to the standing pattern of behavior. A person is seen to enter, to be included in, to be surrounded by a store or a picnic.

Behavior Objects

Behavior objects are also extraindividual units. Like behavior settings, they are standing patterns of behavior and the part of the nonpsychological milieu to which the behavior is anchored. Examples are dolls, books, ladders, and toothbrushes. Behavior objects are differentiated from behavior settings on two grounds. First, the pattern of behavior associated with a behavior object is circumjacent to the milieu, rather than the reverse. A person does not enter and behave within the boundaries of a doll or a ladder as he does within a store and a picnic; his behavior surrounds and incorporates the synomorphic milieu of the behavior object. Second, behavior objects are, themselves, located within behavior settings. They are the furniture of behavior settings. Behavior objects are related to behavior settings as stage properties are related to the scenes of a play.

Toward Eco-Behavioral Science

Standing patterns of behavior, behavior settings, and behavior objects are all units involving extraindividual behavior. They are investigator-free units; they are not tesserae designed by investigators for their own purposes. When we discovered them and also found that data regarding individuals were not adequate for our purpose, we were launched on a course that led toward eco-behavioral science.

Roger G. Barker **4**

Behavior Settings

◆◆◆ ◆◆ ◆◆ ◆◆ ◆◆ ◆◆ ◆◆ ◆◆ ◆◆ ◆◆ ◆◆ ◆◆ ◆◆ ◆◆ ◆◆◆ ◆

There have been a number of approaches to the environment of behavior, and it may be instructive to consider them. Students of perception have been centrally concerned with this problem, and they have had some success in dealing with it. They have found it imperative to look at the environment of perception— for example, at light and sound—apart from its connections with behavior. When perception psychologists have turned from the nature of perception to the preperceptual nature of light and sound, they have discovered something very important about the ecological environment of vision and hearing: It is not random; it involves bounded manifolds of individual elements with varied and unusual patterns. The ecological environment of vision and hearing has a structure that is independent of its connections with perceptual mechanisms. All science reveals that nature is not uniform: the environments of atoms and molecules, of cells and of organs, of trees and of forests are pat-

Revision of paper entitled "Roles, Ecological Niches, and the Psychology of the Absent Organism," presented at the Conference on Role Theory, University of Missouri, 1962.

terned and structured, and this greatly facilitates their identification.

It seems to me that students of molar behavior might profitably emulate students of perception by looking at the ecological environment of the behavior with which they are concerned entirely aside from its connection with behavior. We need a science, for which we as yet have no name, that stands with respect to molar behavior as the physics of light and sound stands with respect to vision and hearing. Four different approaches to this problem are discernible in the psychological literature.

There are what Brunswik (1955) termed the *encapsulated* psychologies, including phenomenology, Lewin's life space, and the implicit theories behind most interview and questionnaire methods of defining a person's world. In these approaches, the environment is *identified* in terms of those distal phenomena outside the person's skin to which he responds, and the environment is *described* in terms of its behavioral counterparts rather than by its own preperceptual properties. The environment in the encapsulated psychologies occurs at the boundary where preperceptual phenomena are transformed into phenomena of the life space. The ecological environment does not, in fact, enter the encapsulated psychologies in a lawful way.

Another approach to the environment of behavior is found in what Floyd Allport (1955) has called the *excapsulated* psychologies, of which Brunswik's probabilistic functionalism is a prominent instance. Here, couplings between attributes of behavior and attributes of the preperceptual environment are studied directly via correlations. The environment of molar behavior in these cases is *identified* in terms of those distal phenomena with which behavior is correlated, and it is *described* in terms of its preperceptual properties. The person is excapsulated from these psychologies; he enters them only as an undifferentiated link between behavior and the environment. All life-space phenomena are bypassed by the excapsulated psychologies.

The *transactional* approach to the environment of behavior is illustrated by some data we assembled early in our work in

Midwest. In this effort to describe the everyday environment of children, we found that three children who were each observed an entire day interacted with 571, 671, and 749 different social and physical objects. These were valuable data. We were surprised by the number of objects with which behavior was transacted, and there were revealing differences between the children in the type of objects in their days and in the order and organization of the objects. Life-space phenomena, including attributes of the person, are important aspects of transactional methods.

The excapsulated and the transactional approaches to the ecological environment of behavior have similarities and differences. They differ with respect to the place they accord to life-space phenomena. They are similar with respect to their idiocentric approach: They both identify the ecological environment at its points of intersection with particular persons, and they reveal nothing about its content and pattern at points removed from its interface with behavior. Content and pattern are essential features of the environment, and methods that ignore them are inadequate.

A fourth approach to the environment of behavior is found in such studies as those by Sears, Maccoby, and Levin (1957) and by Miller and Swanson (1958). In these studies, events in the ecological environment are reported by mothers in interviews; for example, "I really spanked him for having [toilet] accidents" and "I always pick them up right away" (when babies cry). The events are rated by the investigator on various environmental scales, such as mother's responsiveness, her severity of toilet training, and her extent of using "withdrawal of love" (as a training technique), and the ratings are correlated with reports, observations, or tests of children's behavior or personality characteristics. These are neither encapsulated, excapsulated, nor transactional approaches, and they clearly involve the ecological environment; they are at least somewhat less idiocentric than the excapsulated and the transactional methods. However, the descriptions and measures of the environment that these methods provide depend on the questions asked by the investigator, and these, in turn, depend on his practical concerns, or the explicit theories he wishes to test; they also depend on the biases of the informant. These are, therefore, *hypothocentric,* or investigator- and informant-centered approaches; they reveal the ecological environment as, to some degree at least, identified and organized by the investigator and informant.

The encapsulated, excapsulated, transactional, and hypothocentric approaches to the environment of behavior are each valid for some problems, but not for identifying and describing the ecological environment of molar behavior. An analogy may help to make this clear.

If a novice, an Englishman, for example, wished to understand the environment of a first baseman in a baseball game, he might decide on a straightforward transactional approach and set about to observe the interactions of the player with his surroundings. To do this with utmost precision, the novice might view the first baseman through a tube so arranged that the player would be centered in the field of the tube, with just enough of the environment included to encompass all inputs and outputs: all balls caught, balls thrown, players tagged, and so on. Despite the commendable observational care, however, this method would never provide a novice with an understanding of "the game" that gives meaning to a first baseman's transactions with his surroundings and that in fact constitutes his environment. By observing a player in this idiocentric way, the novice would fragment the game and destroy what he was seeking.

The novice might make an encapsulated approach to the environment of a first baseman. He could do this by adding interviews to his observations and, from the two kinds of data, construct the player's life space during the game: his achievements, aspirations, successes, failures, and conflicts; his judgments of the ball's speeds, of the umpire's fairness, and of his teammates' errors. But this encapsulated description would only increase the inadequacy of the former approach to the ecological world of the first baseman. For the former fragmented picture of "the game," this method would substitute the psychological consequences of this fragment and would thus remove the novice even further from the ecological environment he sought.

If the novice were to make an hypothocentric approach and query an informant about the environment of the first baseman, the information he would receive would depend on the questions he asked and on the informant's physical geographical position, biases, and breadth of view.

Finally, the novice might study the environment of a first baseman by excapsulated methods. He could perform innumerable correlations between the first baseman's achievements (balls caught, players tagged, strikes and hits made, bases stolen, errors, and so on) and attributes of the ecological environment involved (speed of balls thrown to him, distance of throw, weight of bat, curve of balls, and so on). But he could never arrive at the rules of baseball by this means.

It would seem clear that a novice would learn more about the baseball game that is the ecological environment of a first baseman by blotting out the player and observing the game around him. This is what the student of light and sound does with elaborate instrumentation. I suggest that it is worth trying in the case of molar behavior.

It is not easy, at first, to leave the person out of the observations of the environment of molar behavior. As psychologists, our perceptual apparatus is adjusted to see persons whenever we see behavior. Long training with the idiocentric viewing tubes of individual observations, interviews, and questionnaires makes this especially difficult for us. But with some effort and experience the extraindividual assemblies of behavior episodes, objects, spaces, boundaries, and so on that surround persons can be observed and described *as* assemblies. Their nonrandom distribution and bounded character are crucial aids. Consider, for example, a particular meeting of a university lecture series. If a member of the audience were to shift his attention from the speaker and his remarks to occurrences in the auditorium, what he would see, I suggest, is an assembly of behavior episodes and behavior objects forming a unit that is the ecological environment of the individual behavior occurring there.

Let me point out some characteristics of this unit.

1. It is a natural phenomenon; it not an experiment devised by an investigator for his scientific purposes.
2. It has a space-time locus.
3. A boundary surrounds this unit.
4. The locus and boundary are selected or generated for the benefit of the meeting; they are not arbitrary fragments of the university.
5. The unit is objective in the sense that it exists independent of anyone's perception of it as a unit; it is a preperceptual ecological entity.
6. It has two classes of components: (a) humans behaving (lecturing, listening, sitting) and (b) nonpsychological objects with which behavior is transacted, such as chairs, walls, a microphone, and paper.
7. The unit, the meeting, is circumjacent to its components; they are *in* the unit.
8. The behavior and physical objects that constitute the unit are internally organized and arranged to form a pattern that is by no means random.
9. The pattern within the boundary of the unit is easily discriminated from that outside the boundary.
10. There is a synomorphic relation between the pattern of the behavior and the pattern of the nonbehavioral components, the behavior objects. For example, the chairs face the podium, and the audience faces the speaker.
11. The unity of this phenomenon is not due to the similarity of its parts; speaking occurs in one part and listening in another. Events in different parts of the unit have a greater effect on each other than do equivalent events beyond its boundary.
12. The laws that govern the functioning of the unit are different from those that govern the behavior within it, so far as we know these laws. The model of an engine seems to be more appropriate to represent what occurs than is the model of an organism or of a person. For example, this entity can be "turned off" and disassembled at the will of the operator, the chairman. He can adjourn the meeting (for a coffee break) and call it to order again. While it is dis-

assembled, some of the parts can be adjusted (a discussant replaced). Individuals have no psychological properties like these.

13. The members of this unit are to a considerable degree inter-changeable, and absent members are not greatly missed; they are replaceable. When the meeting reassembles, some former members may be absent, some new members pres-ent, and several may have changed places; but the same entity continues as serenely as an old car with new rings and the spare tire on the right front wheel.

14. The behavior of the entity, the lecture meeting, cannot, however, be greatly changed without destroying it: There must be introductions, there must be a speech, there must be listening and discussion.

15. A person has two positions; first, he is a component of the supraindividual unit, the meeting, and, second, he is an indi-vidual whose life space is partly formed within the con-straints imposed by the very entity of which he is a part.

16. There are many units of this kind within a community, and some are embedded within larger units; the lecture meeting is embedded within a superordinate unit, university, but there are many similar units that stand alone.

17. Many units of this kind have within them stable subparts. Within the meeting, there are the subparts chairman, speak-er, discussant, and audience.

The entity we have described stands out with great clar-ity; it is a common phenomenon of everyday life. When the teacher says, "Time for recess"; when a boy hurries out of the house saying, "I'm going to the ball game over at Joe's"; when a newspaper reports "Traffic was heavy on Main Street today"; when a window sign announces "Girl Scout Food Sale"—each refers to this kind of unit. We have called this a *behavior setting*. We have made extensive studies of behavior settings and found much evidence that they are the ecological environments of most molar actions (Barker and Wright, 1955; Barker, 1968; Barker and Schoggen, 1973).

Roger G. Barker   **5**

Need for an Eco-Behavioral Science

◆▬◆◆▬◆◆▬◆◆▬◆◆▬◆◆▬◆◆▬◆◆▬◆◆▬◆◆▬◆◆▬◆◆▬◆◆▬◆

Ecological problems and methods of science can be differentiated with precision from experimental problems and methods.
Ecological phenomena occur without input from the investigator; they consist of things and events unchanged by the techniques used to observe them or by conditions imposed by the
investigator; they answer the question "What goes on here?"
Experimental phenomena involve input from the investigator;
they consist of changes in things and events resulting from conditions imposed by the investigator; they answer the question
"What goes on here under these conditions that I impose?"

Ecological approaches to scientific problems are not

Revision of chapter "Wanted: An Eco-Behavioral Science," in Willems and Raush (1969, pp. 31-43).

incomplete or defective experimental approaches. On the contrary, they provide knowledge that the best experimentation cannot provide, because experimentation by arranging conditions according to the concerns of the experimenter destroys the very thing an ecological investigation seeks to determine. The importance to science of experimental methods is everywhere recognized, but it is perhaps less widely realized that the ecological side of science is also essential. From a purely scientific viewpoint, it is important to determine how nature is arranged and how it is distributed on every level without alteration of any kind, and this can only be accomplished by ecological methods. And, for the applied sciences, information about the unaltered world is necessary before applications can be made. An engineer cannot build a bridge without detailed information about the bridge site, and this information can be secured only by methods that do not destroy the site in the process of surveying it. Such knowledge is equally important for the behavioral sciences; a teacher making an assignment or a judge passing a sentence should know the psychological terrain on which the assignment or the sentence is to be placed. But this information is seldom available, because the ecological side of the behavioral sciences is poorly developed.

Questions about the effects of the environment on human behavior and development are being put with increasing frequency and urgency. What are the consequences for human behavior of poverty? of controlled climate in factories, offices, and homes? of congested cities? of transient populations? of high population density? of computer technology? of ghettos? of large schools? of "bedroom" communities? Behavior scientists often respond hopefully to these questions with the promise that, given time and resources, answers will be provided by the tried and true methods, concepts, and theories of the psychological sciences that have answered so many questions about human behavior: about perception, about learning, about intellectual processes, and about motivation. The view presented here is, on the contrary, that the methods, concepts, and theories of the psychological sciences cannot answer the new questions, that a new science is required to deal with them.

Scientific psychology knows and can know nothing about the real-life settings in which people live in ghettos and suburbs, in large and small schools, in regions of poverty and affluence. One might think that in the course of its necessary concern with stimuli, psychology would have become informed about the human environment. But this is not the case. Psychology has necessarily attended to those elements of the environment that are useful in probing its focal phenomena, namely, the behavior-relevant circuitry within the skins of its subjects, within psychology's black box. Psychology knows much about the physical properties of the environmental probes it uses: of distal objects of perception, for example, and of energy changes at receptor surfaces. But it has excised these environmental elements from the contexts in which they normally occur: from mealtimes, from offices, from airplanes, from arithmetic classes, from streets and sidewalks.

In view of psychology's concern with dismantled fragments of the environment, it is not surprising that general concepts of the environment have a minor place in the science and that they provide a distorted view of intact settings in which behavior occurs. The most common notion, which can hardly be called a *theory,* is that the nonbehavioral, the ecological environment of human beings is an unstructured, probabilistic, and largely passive arena in which humans behave according to the programming they carry about within themselves. Brunswik (1955, p. 686), for example, speaks of "the behaving organism living in a semichaotic environmental medium"; Leeper (1963, p. 388), of "the kaleidoscopically changing stimulation" organisms receive; and Lewin (1951, pp. 58-59) writes that "psychology should be interested . . . in those areas of the physical and social world which are not part of the life space . . . [but this] has to be based partly on statistical considerations about nonpsychological [events]." Although these assertions are true within the limited environmental perspective of the science of psychology, they are not true within a wider perspective. It is the universal testimony of the physical and biological sciences that the ecological environment circumjacent to human beings is organized and patterned in stable and surprising ways; it is, in fact, one task of these sciences to explore, describe, and account for the patternings.

Psychology has fallen into a self-validating roundabout here: Its prevailing methods of research shatter whatever pattern and organization may exist within the natural environment, and the conclusion is reached, on the basis of the resulting evidence, that the environment is not a source of the order and organization observed in behavior. This leads to further study of the mysterious mechanism of the black box that appears to bring order out of chaos; and this is done via ever more theory-determined and ever less setting-determined environmental variables. It is my impression that psychology fell into this error when it became, so early in its history, for whatever reason, a science of the laboratory and the clinic, when it installed psychologists as environment surrogates, and when it thereafter neglected the psychologist-free environment. For 100 years now, psychology has largely directed inputs to its subjects in accordance with theoretical games evolved from input-output relations previously observed in laboratories and clinics, and it has inevitably become more and more removed from settings that are not arranged by scientists and has become more and more impressed with the black box as the determinant of behavior.

Here is an example of what we have come to. The problem of Citizen Sam is presented in a current work. The following characterization is given of the days of Citizen Sam.

> He moves and has his being in the great activity wheel of New York City. . . . He spends his hours . . . in the badlands of the Bronx. He wakens to grab the morning's milk left at the door by an agent of a vast dairy and distributing system, whose corporate maneuvers, so vital to his health, never consciously concern him. After paying hasty respects to his landlady, he dashes into the transportation system, whose mechanical and civic mysteries he does not comprehend. At the factory, he becomes a cog for the day in a set of systems far beyond his ken. . . . though he doesn't know it, his

furious activity at his machine is regulated by the
"law of supply and demand." ... A union official
collects dues; just why he doesn't know. At noon-
time that corporate monstrosity, Horn and Hard-
art, swallows him up, much as he swallows one of
its automatic pies. After more activity in the afternoon, he seeks out a standardized daydream produced in Hollywood [Allport, 1964, p. 284].

In this account, it would appear that we are at least getting down to psychologist-free situations within an urban environment, to their nature and their consequences for behavior
and personality. The author reports that Citizen Sam is confronted by the vast, anonymous dairy; that he is incorporated
into the incomprehensible subway; that he is driven and regulated by the overwhelming factory; that he is swallowed by the
mechanical cafeteria; and that he relaxes in a ready-made movie
daydream. Citizen Sam is mightily busy, but he is not involved.
According to the author, this, unfortunately, is characteristic of
an important segment of our population, and so we are confronted with an important social question. And what is this
question? In Allport's words, it is: *"What precisely is wrong
with Sam?"* (1964, p. 284). Not "How do the city's settings
(with its vast dairy, complex subway, coercive factory, mechanical cafeteria, prefabricated movie) and Citizen Sam (with his
motives and cognitions) interact to produce the grabbing, hasty,
dashing, uncomprehending, furious, standardized, uninvolved
behavior he displays?" So far is the science of psychology removed from real-life settings.

However, writing as a psychologist, Allport is correct in
asserting that what goes on within the black box labeled Sam is
the only question psychology can answer, even though it is not
the question society is asking in this case. The black box is the
legitimate focus for psychology. It makes psychology a prospec-
tively unified science explicated by a single set of interrelated
concepts, and it makes psychology a practically important science, for the answers to many human problems (although not
the problem of cities as human habitats) are to be found in the

internal programming people carry from setting to setting. My wonder is that psychology has ever been expected to have the answer where such nonpsychological variables as poverty and wealth, segregation and nonsegregation, overpopulation and underpopulation prevail. Our only errors, as psychologists, have been to ignore the limits of our competence or to allow others to do so.

The phenomena of psychology and the environments in which it occurs are interrelated; they are interdependent. They are interdependent in the way a part of a system and a whole system are interdependent: as the electrical generator of an engine and the functioning engine, or as the bats and balls and game of baseball. Predictions from electrical generators to engines, and vice versa, and from bats and balls to ball games and vice versa, require complete accounts of the superordinate phenomenon (of the engine, the ball game) and of the place of the part system within the whole. This is true, too, for naturally occurring situations and behavior. The theory of electrical generators cannot account for the behavior of internal combustion engines, nor can engines explain generators; similarly, psychology cannot explain the functioning of taverns, school classes, or other real-life settings, and theories of settings cannot account for the behavior of the inhabitants. Generators and the environing engines within which they function and people and the settings that constitute their environments are different phenomena and require for their explanation different concepts and theories.

The distinction between the phenomena to which the urgent questions about such things as poverty, technology, and population refer and the phenomena with which psychological science deals is not a tactical one; it is basic. These are incommensurate phenomena, and they require different methodologies and facilities for their investigation.

When we do look at the environment of behavior as a phenomenon worthy of investigation for itself, not merely as an instrument for unraveling the behavior-relevant programming within persons, we find that it is *not* a passive, probabilistic arena of objects and events. This discovery was forced on us;

when we made long records of children's behavior, we were surprised to find that some attributes of behavior varied less across children within settings than within the days of children across settings (Barker and Wright, 1955; Barker, 1963a). We found that we could predict many aspects of children's behavior more adequately from knowledge of the behavior characteristics of the drugstores, arithmetic classes, and basketball games that they inhabited than from knowledge of the behavior tendencies of the particular children. Indeed, the conformity of people to the patterns of real-life settings is so great that deviations therefrom are often newsworthy or considered indicative of serious abnormality requiring social or medical attention. Such deviancies within the settings of the town of Midwest constitute an infinitesimal proportion of the opportunities for deviancy.

A simple hypothesis to account for the conformity of persons to the patterns of the settings in which their behavior occurs is that there are, after all, some interior motivational and cognitive *constancies across persons* that interact with a *single array of environmental input* from a setting, producing similar (conforming) behavior across all the inhabitants. However, work by Willems (1964) and by Gump (1964) shows that the everyday situations within which people live (restaurants, basketball games, band concerts) do not provide inhabitants with a limited and fixed array of environmental inputs; that, in fact, the inputs vary in accordance with the differing motives and cognitions of the inhabitants; and that in spite of this the characteristic behavior patterns of settings are generated. Our findings indicate that most of the environments in which people live are homeostatic systems that maintain their characteristic patterns (including the behavior of the inhabitants) within preset limits by means of control mechanisms. We all experience this: On the turnpike, when our speed deviates to the slow side, we receive recurring physical and social inputs to speed up, and if we do not do this sufficiently we are eventually ejected from the turnpike (by a rear-end crash or by a traffic officer); when our speed deviates to the fast side, we receive recurring physical and social inputs to slow down; and again if we do not do this sufficiently, we are finally ejected by a head-on crash, by missing a curve, or by a traffic officer. It is important to note that the turnpike is not concerned with the sources of the deviancy of its vehicular components. Slowness because of an overloaded and under-powered car is just as unacceptable to a turnpike as slowness because of an overly cautious driver. People and other entities are components of the environmental units they inhabit in the same way that a generator is a component of an engine and a bat of a ball game. These units are behavior settings, and the concepts and principles that explicate behavior settings are utterly alien to those that explicate their component parts, the behavior of individual persons, among others.

Here is one of many environmental differences Midwest and Yoredale provide their inhabitants. Some settings require child components; they coerce and incorporate children into their ongoing programs. This is true of 7 percent of Midwest's habitat and of 14 percent of Yoredale's habitat. Other settings do not tolerate child components; they have child-proof bound-aries, and they eject any children who manage to enter. This is true of 14 percent of Midwest's and 19 percent of Yoredale's habitat. This environmental difference between the towns makes a difference in the behavior and experiences of the chil-dren of Midwest and Yoredale, and a complete analysis of the psychology of all inhabitants of the towns would not account for it. Forces for and against children are properties of a town's settings (its school classes, its pubs, its courts, its Golden Age Club), and not of its individual citizens. Transposing the chil-dren of Midwest to Yoredale, and vice versa, would immediately transform their behavior in respect to the parts of the towns they would enter and avoid, despite their unchanged motives and cognitions. The forces of a community's settings vis-à-vis children are examples of the power of environmental units over behavior, of their superordinate position with respect to their human components, and of the need for an eco-behavioral sci-ence independent of psychology.

Facilities for an Eco-Behavioral Science

The eco-behavioral science that will answer the pressing questions society faces today requires, above all, concepts and theories appropriate to the phenomena involved. But these will not arise *de novo*; they will be grounded on empirical data concerning the patterns of events within the psychologist-free settings where people live their lives. Special facilities are required in order to obtain these data.

Archives. By definition, phenomena cannot be induced to occur by an investigator if his purpose is to study them under "natural," that is, scientist-free, conditions. Since many important phenomena occur infrequently under these conditions, it may require long periods of observation and be expensive to secure adequate instances of them. This is a fact that confronts every science in connection with its ecological investigations. The yield of data is low, for example, in studies of earthquakes, bank failures, and migrating birds. It is taxing and expensive to wait for earthquakes and bank failures and to search for banded birds. Nevertheless, geologists, economists, and biologists continue to investigate these phenomena. It is worthwhile asking how they do it.

For one thing, these scientists do not consider infrequent occurrence as unfortunate, as dross; they accept it for what it is, namely, one attribute of a phenomenon that must be recorded accurately along with its other attributes, one that must be taken into account by theory. For seismological theory, it is probably as important to know the nature and distribution of the earthquakes of the Middle West of the United States as of the more frequent earthquakes of the West Coast. Here, then, is a central operational difference between experimental and ecological science: Experiments alter phenomena of infrequent occurrence and make them frequent. In this state, they can be studied efficiently. Ecological investigations in which phenomena are studied *in situ* and "nature" is the only inducer cannot be efficient so far as frequency is concerned.

One way other sciences facilitate the study of ecological phenomena is by accumulating data as they become available over long periods of time, by preserving them, and by making them generally accessible. Archives and museums of primary data are standard research facilities of sciences with productive ecological programs. For this reason, a lone seismographer, student of banking, or ornithologist, with limited resources and but one life to live, has access to many data that he is free to study and analyze in his own way, according to his own theories. This has not been possible for psychologists; the science has been almost devoid of data archives.

Data. But even more basic is the fact that psychology has had no methods for securing archival data. It has been almost exclusively an experimental science, and the data of experiments have little value for archives. The inputs and constraints imposed by experiments are usually so uniquely tied to the intentions of the investigator—to his hypothesis, for example— that a new investigator has little freedom to ask new questions of the data. About all one can do with the data of others' experiments is to try to replicate them: an essential task but nonetheless a merely technical one. The attributes of experimental data that limit their archival value are, of course, not defects. Quite the contrary, in fact; to the degree that experiments arrange inputs and channel outputs to answer specific questions, they are good experiments. Good experimental data are problem centered and theory guided, and their significance is usually limited by the particular problem or theory that prompted and guided their generation.

The converse is true for ecological studies. Here, the task of the investigator and his apparatus is to translate phenomena without alteration into the language of data. In their most adequate form, ecological data are phenomena centered and atheoretical. It has been a heresy, in some quarters, to speak of atheoretical data. Experience has taught us, however, that even within a purely psychological context atheoretical data can be obtained and are of value. Eighteen full-day records of children's behavior and situations have been collected at the Midwest Psychological Field Station. When we made these records, we had plans, guided by theories, for analyzing them, but the plans and theories did not guide the making of the records. Our only intention was to translate the stream of behavior into a verbal record with as much completeness as possible. We made our own use of the records and made them available to others. Over the years, other studies based on these records have been made by investigators who had no part in assembling the records; most of these studies concern problems and involve theories and analytical procedures that were far from the minds of the data collectors. These specimens of individual behavior will continue to be of use in connection with problems not yet conceived. This experience has taught us that data that are dross for one investigator are gold for another.

An eco-behavioral science must have data archives. The scientists involved in this development will have much to learn about collecting, preserving, and retrieving ecological data. Undoubtedly, data suitable for archives are mouldering unknown and unused in files and storerooms; on the other hand, the new audiovisual recording techniques threaten to overwhelm a data depository with useless material. The problem of standards for atheoretical, phenomena-centered data is a difficult and important one; it deserves the best efforts of psychologists and eco-behavioral scientists.

Data Analysis. One of the purposes of experimental techniques is to arrange the data that issue from data-generating systems so they will fit prevailing machines, formulae, and concepts. So we have forced-choice tests, five-point scales, normalized distributions, equated control groups, and so on. These are not sins. They facilitate the purposes of experiments: to solve problems and test hypotheses that the investigators bring to the data. But if one's intention is to explore behavior and its environment, the phenomena themselves must dictate the choices, the scales, and the distributions. It is our experience that psychological measurement experts do not know statistical and analytical techniques for dealing with "natural" phenomena, even where they are available from other sciences. We need mathematical innovators and we need textbooks and handbooks of data-reduction methods culled from quantitative botany, demography, geography, physiology, and economics. When those who work on eco-behavioral problems do not have the analytical tools they need, they inevitably cast data in the molds of experimental psychology, molds that often destroy the essential nature of the phenomena they are investigating.

Field Stations. Ecological scientists are not a source of input to or constraint on the phenomena that they study; they do not instigate the occurrence of the phenomena with which they deal. They must, therefore, set up shop in regions where their phenomena are rich and accessible, and their shops must be manned and equipped appropriately. Field stations and observatories are regular features of the establishments of other sciences. An eco-behavioral science must have its Woods Holes and Mount Wilsons. In our experience, ecological data are more difficult to procure than experimental data. Special facilities are required, and the locating, equipping, and manning of a field station is as specialized and as expensive as establishing a clinic or an experimental laboratory.

Two different problems are involved in the collection of ecological data. One concerns specific data-generating procedures, such as observing and making records, taking photographs, making recordings, and using documents and records. The other problem relates to general policies and programs to be followed in establishing and operating a facility for gathering nonexperimental, eco-behavioral data. We shall consider the last problem briefly; we can do little more than list some of the factors we have found to be of importance.

A field station should be within a particular, bounded community or institution that encompasses the universe of phenomena to be studied. In the present state of development of eco-behavioral science, it is desirable to avoid very large and complex systems. A field station must have a sufficiently long life expectancy for the assembly of data on infrequently occurring and slowly changing phenomena. A field station is *not* a project; it is a program.

The relation of the station and its staff to the locale it investigates is of utmost importance. There must be access without interference, acceptance without reaction. The ecologist-citizen relation is not a physician-patient relation, not an experimenter-subject relation, and not counselor-client relation. It is a new relation yet to be defined, but some aspects of it are clear. The ecologist-citizen relation is a privileged relation based on trust. The field station must operate within the mores and tolerances of the community; this is a part of the essential policy of a field station of respecting and not altering its phenomena. A consequence of this is that some studies and techniques are not admissible. The ecologist-citizen relation imposes personnel requirements on a field station. It must have expert staff members whose primary job is to maintain communication between station and community, to define the functions of the field station, and especially to differentiate the field station from common conceptions of clinics and laboratories. The station must have local staff members for field work; this provides some protection against misunderstandings. Local residence is essential for many staff members, and they must participate in community affairs. Publications must be stated in objective, conceptual terms, and they must be nonevaluative. Station-community trust and mutual acceptance are the first requirements, and these must be maintained and renewed by continual effort.

Some may think these requirements very restricting. Our experience in Kansas and Yorkshire is that they impose fewer limitations than skeptics expect. This is the case, in part, because a field station has sources of support, too. Citizens are seriously concerned with the problems on which eco-behavioral field stations work, and the field station brings some status and substance to the community.

There are, then, four facility-operations problems that arise directly from the fundamental nature of eco-behavioral research: (1) an archival problem, (2) a data problem, (3) an analysis problem, and (4) a field station problem. These problems are great, but the possibility of arriving at scientifically meaningful and socially useful results are also great, and they justify the commitment of intellect, effort, and money to the task.

Part 2

Studies in Ecological Psychology

◆◆

We have defined ecological psychology as the branch of psychology that deals with the behavior and psychological situations of designated persons under natural conditions, that is, without input from the investigator. The studies in Part Two address methodological, analytical, and conceptual problems of research in ecological psychology within a field station context, and they present some findings. They exemplify the various behavior stream units described in Part One, and they show how behavior stream and behavior setting data can be complementary.

The studies demonstrate the values of a field station with its archives of atheoretical, phenomena-centered data. Four of

49

the studies analyze the same specimen records; these records were made by the field station staff without preconceptions of the problems they would be used to elucidate or the concepts and systems of analysis in terms of which they would be examined. This use of the same raw data (involving the same subjects in the same situations) by independent investigators of different problems sometimes enhances the value of findings by reference to the results of the other studies; this is discussed in connection with research reported in Chapter Eighteen.

Finally, some of the studies show how field station facilities can enrich research by providing supplementary information on such topics as the family, acquaintanceship, and social class relationships between subjects and associates that would otherwise not be available.

Roger G. Barker
Herbert F. Wright
Maxine F. Schoggen
Louise S. Barker

6

Day in the Life
of Mary Ennis

◆◆◆◆◆◆◆◆◆◆◆◆◆◆◆◆◆◆◆◆◆◆◆◆◆◆◆◆◆◆

This is an analysis of a record of what an eight-year-old girl did and of what her home and school and neighborhood and town did to her from the time she awoke one morning until she went to sleep that night. The record is objective: It describes the actions of Mary and the physical and social conditions of her life that could be seen and heard by skilled observers. The record is also interpretive: It reports what the observers inferred as to the

This chapter, up to the section titled "Hemerography," is adapted from Barker and Wright (1951, pp. 4-10); the remainder is reprinted from Burton and Harris (1955, pp. 768-808). The analysis of the record in terms of behavior structure and social variables is based on the research of Herbert F. Wright (Wright, 1967).

meanings to the girl of her behavior and of the persons, things, and events that she saw and heard and felt through the day.

This record is a specimen of the behavior and psychological habitat of a child. As with other field specimens, parts of the original have been altered, and other parts have been lost, in the process of getting and preserving it. A pressed flower in an herbarium is not the same as a flowering bloom. Nonetheless, it is useful to botanists. Similarly, this specimen of behavior is useful to social scientists; artists and laypersons who are interested in the contemporary scene also find it of value.

Making the Record

The reader will want to know how truly the record describes the behavior of Mary Ennis and the conditions of her life. Between Mary's behavior and this account of it, a number of operations have been interposed, in some of which the possibility of error was great. The steps in the preparation of the record, the possible sources of error, and the efforts that were made to avoid error all require consideration.

The Influence of the Observer. At the present time, specimen records such as this one must be made by watching behavior and reporting it in words. Questions come up therefore about the influence of the observer on the person observed. When a geologist surveys and describes an area, he does not change the geology of the region. But the presence of an observer of behavior often changes the psychological situation and hence the actions and feelings of the person observed. How can the student of psychological ecology keep the situation natural and observe naturally occurring behavior when it is not natural for an observer to be present? It is probable that the interference of an observer in field studies can seldom be reduced to zero. The problem is one of making the interference minimal, of defining it, and of holding it constant. These ends were sought in making the record.

Eight observers took turns through the day. Mary was acquainted with all but one of them. Throughout the preceding six months, they had been frequent observers in the schoolroom of the third and fourth grades where Mary was a pupil. Four were permanent residents of Midwest and were known to Mary as fellow townspeople. The seven regular observers had gone to much trouble to become accepted by the children of Midwest as friendly, nonevaluating adults with an interest in what children do—as, in truth, they were.

The observers had been trained to keep in the background by varying their behavior as the situation varied. On some occasions, inactivity and unresponsiveness make an observer stand out as a stationary figure against a moving ground. On other occasions, activity and responsiveness have the reverse effect. A good field observer is one who has mastered the technique of being present but inconspicuous.

Mary's parents had been informed of the nature and purpose of the record. Mr. and Mrs. Ennis and Mary were familiar with the making of a day record because they had seen it done with other children of Midwest. They knew that this was a part of a larger community study of children. The Ennis family, along with the other people of the town, had willingly consented to help. The evening before the record was made Mrs. Ennis told Mary that it would be their turn to have the observers the next day. She explained that the observers would be interested in seeing what an eight-year-old girl did all day long.

The observations covered fourteen consecutive hours. This allowed time for adaptation by Mary and her parents to new and uncertain elements in the situation. Also, Mary was at an age when self-consciousness and social sensitivity are not great. While it is clear that the method of direct observation used here would not be suitable for adolescent children, it seems adaptable to most children younger than nine years of age.

The observers undoubtedly had some influence on Mary's life on May 12, 1949. The record permits an estimate of the nature and extent of some of this influence. Mary's behavior when alone with an observer can be compared with her behavior when others were present as well. Comparison can also be made of Mary's responses to observers with her responses to other adults. Domination of the record by a single, unique, inter-

personal relation between Mary and a special onlooker was pre-
cluded by the use of several observers.

For a number of problems, the fact of observer influence
is not seriously disturbing. One thing to be considered here is
that any interaction of Mary with an observer is real behavior
with significance in its own right; every such interaction can be
accepted as telling something about Mary as a particular girl of
Midwest. Another thing to be considered is that particular observers were present during long periods of the day, exerting a
constant influence, so this does not need to be considered in
studying the effects of factors that varied during these periods.

What Is Recorded. The observers of Mary Ennis approached their task with the hope of seeing and recording every-
thing she did. They tried to see and record Mary's directly
observable behavior, her vocalizations and bodily movements.
Beyond that, they reported their on-the-spot impressions and
inferences of Mary's perceptions, motives, and feelings. The observers wished to recreate for others the behavior of Mary and
the situations that confronted her as they experienced them. All
who are concerned about the objectivity of this record must
face two facts. One is that behavior without motives, feelings,
and meanings is of little significance for students of personality
and social psychology. The other is that motives, feelings, and
meanings cannot be observed directly. In studying these problems, it is necessary to work with the data available, however
inadequate they may be. To those who are concerned about the
bias and completeness of the record, we can say only that, although the observers were inevitably selective in their perceptions of the rich and varied field of facts that Mary presented,
their intentions were to include as much as possible. To this it
can be added that the use of a number of observers with differing unconscious biases and perceptual bents insured the record
against any one person's idiosyncracies.

Details of Procedure. Each observational period was
about thirty minutes in length. The observer carried a writing
board with a watch attached and made brief notes. He indicated
the passage of time in intervals of approximately one minute.

The observations were dictated into a sound recorder

immediately after they had been made. The initial narrative was as spontaneous and full as the observer could make it. Each observer tried at this stage to report every fact and every impression with little regard for style or proper sequence.

A listener was present during the dictation of the report. He made notes on unclear and thin parts of the narrative. After the first dictation, the listener interrogated the observer on the points in question. His queries and the observer's replies were recorded. The final specimen record is the observer's original report as he adjusted it after the interrogation.

Hemerography

The term *hemerography* is used in this report to denote a detailed description and analysis of the life of a person during the course of one day; it is derived from the Greek words *hemero,* "day," and *graphein,* "to write."

On May 12, 1949, Mary Ennis lived in the town of Midwest, a county seat and rural trading center of 720 people in the central United States. Mary was eight years and seven months old. She was blond, blue-eyed, small-boned, and dainty. She was of normal height, but she weighed less than most Midwest girls of her age.

Mary was in the third grade. She took piano lessons, sang in the junior choir, belonged to the Brownie Scouts, and attended the Methodist Sunday School. Mary played with her school classmates and with neighborhood children. On this day the latter included Sarah Hutchings, eleven years old; Ben Hutchings, seven; Carol Lawrence, thirteen; Wally Lawrence, ten; Tommy Wechsler, four; Douglas Denham, fourteen; Geoffrey West, seven; Dutton Bland, two; and Jean Bethel, twelve. The family dog, Chico, a large white shepherd, was much beloved by Mary.

Arthur Ennis, Mary's father, was a civil engineer employed by the federal government; he was in charge of a countywide project. He had specialized college training for his work. Mr. Ennis was an Active Reserve officer, following extended service in the Army in World War II. He participated in a number of community activities: belonging to the Rotary Club, teaching an adult Sunday School class, and singing in the Methodist Church choir and in a male quartet.

Mary's mother, Penelope Ennis, beside being a good housekeeper, was active in the community. She directed the church choir, was president of the Methodist Women's Evening Guild, belonged to a woman's club, was a member of the Rotaryanns and of the American Legion Auxiliary. She was in demand as an accompanist or soloist at musical functions. Before her marriage, Mrs. Ennis had taught in a rural school following a short training course.

Timothy, the second child in the Ennis family, was a happy, healthy, seven-month-old boy.

Mary's family had lived in Midwest three years. They owned their home and had done much to make it efficient and attractive. The house was furnished entirely with antique furniture or good reproductions. The house, all on one floor, had a living room, a dining room, two bedrooms, a bath, a modern kitchen, a large screened back porch, and a basement laundry and utility room. A spinet piano added to the charm of the living room, and a new gas furnace added to the comfort of the house. The Ennis home had a relatively small yard by Midwest standards (50 X 100 feet) but it had a magnificent tree, which, with a wonderful swing, provided an attractive, shaded play place.

The Ennis family owned a 1937 Plymouth automobile that Mr. Ennis used in his work.

The morning of May 12, 1949, was bright, sunny, and cool in Midwest. When the observer arrived at the Ennis house, by prior arrangement, it was a few minutes before seven.

> I went to the back door and knocked. Mrs. Ennis opened the door and asked me in. She said that Mary had awakened about ten minutes after six, but she had put her back to bed and she thought that Mary had gone to sleep. She said, "I'll go in first and see if Mary is awake." Mrs.

Ennis did this; when she returned she said, "She is sitting up in bed, and it is OK to go ahead."

I went to Mary's room, which opened off the dining room. Timothy's crib was in the dining room opposite the door to Mary's room.

1. Greeting observer

7:00. Mary was sitting up in bed and Timothy was standing in his crib crowing and talking.

I smiled at Mary and she smiled at me.

2. Talking with brother

Mary immediately started to talk to Timothy. From her bed, she called gaily, "Hi, Timothy."

Timothy crowed in response.

This verbal play was repeated four or five times. Both children enjoyed it greatly.

3. Comforting brother

Timothy's footing was none too secure; he fell over and started to cry rather hard.

Mary immediately jumped off the bed and ran to him. I think she genuinely wanted to help.

Mrs. Ennis came in from the kitchen and said, "Well, what is the trouble, what happened?" and "You're all right, Timothy, you're all right." She was matter-of-factly reassuring, showing little concern. As she said this, she sort of pushed Mary aside. The mother picked Timothy up and told him he was all right; she looked around and said, "Where is your bottle?" She saw the bottle on the floor, put Timothy back in his crib, and took the bottle back to the kitchen for more milk.

While her mother went for the milk, Mary returned quickly and eagerly to her own room.

Before her mother got back, Mary brought a big Teddy bear, which I presume was hers, and laid it in the crib beside Timothy. She seemed to want to contribute to comforting him.

When Mrs. Ennis brought the milk, she left the Teddy bear in the crib; she pushed it over so there was room for both Timothy and the Teddy bear. Mrs. Ennis patted the Teddy bear as she settled Timothy with his bottle.

4. Putting on house clothes

7:01. Mary went again from the crib to her own room.

In a businesslike way, she opened her closet door and got out her slippers.

She put her slippers on.

She got out her bathrobe.

While she was putting on her bathrobe, she wandered out to the kitchen.

She just looked over the situation, still getting her arms into the bathrobe and tying the sash.

5. Looking at brother

She went over to the crib, took a look at Timothy, who was busy with his bottle.

6. Looking at observer

Then she turned and looked at me.

7. Stretching

As she looked at me, she yawned a great big yawn.

She put her arms up and stretched.

8. Making own bed	7:03. Mary came back to her room.

She seemed more purposeful.

She took the two pillows off her double bed.

Then she smoothed out the sheet and pulled up the covers on one side of the bed.

She walked around to the other side and smoothed out the sheet and pulled up the covers on that side.

She put the pillows on and pulled the spread over the pillows.

7:04. After Mary got it fixed, she stood back and looked at her bed critically. It didn't suit her.

She went back and pulled the spread over farther and smoothed it.

She then went around again to the other side and straightened the spread over the pillows.

The end result, from an adult point of view, was just fair. There were some wrinkles in the spread, particularly over the pillows.

Mary stopped, looked at it again critically, and was apparently satisfied.

7:05. She went into the kitchen. |
| 9. Remarking about mother's apron | Noticing her mother wearing her apron, she chuckled and said, "Oh, Mommie, a big person like you in my tiny apron."

Her mother said, "Yes, I know, but that is all I could find." |

Mary said, "Well, I have another one."

I presume she meant it was all right for her mother to wear that one because she had another one.

10. Whispering to father

7:06. Her father came out of the bathroom, which opens off Mary's room. I said, "Good morning." He said, "Good morning," and went on to his bedroom.

When Mary heard him say, "Good morning," to me, she came from the kitchen. She minced across the dining room and went into her father's room.

She said cheerily, "Hello," to him and then I heard her whisper something to him and he whispered back to her.

I couldn't hear the content.

11. Going to bathroom

Then he said in a natural voice, "You can have the bathroom now."

Mary said, "OK" very cheerfully.

She came directly back across the dining room to the bathroom and shut the door.

12. Getting dressed

The bathroom door opened.

7:08. Mary was standing in front of it.

She had taken off her bathrobe and the top of her pajamas.

She stepped into the bedroom to lay the top of her pajamas on a convenient chair.

She put on an undershirt and her bathrobe.

13. Washing hands and face

She went back to the bathroom and got a washcloth.

7:09. Mary washed her face diligently.

She continued to wash.

7:10. She scrubbed up her arms to her elbows with the washcloth.

She leaned over the washbasin as she washed her hands.

7:11. She let the water out of the washbasin.

She shook her hands, splashing the water from them onto the walls in a gay gesture.

Then she dried her hands and face with a towel.

She reached her hand back and patted the back of her hair, smoothing it.

The divisions marked 1 to 13 are the episodes into which the record has been divided. Mary's record contains 969 episodes and is approximately 100,000 words in length. For the present purpose, the remainder of the record will be synopsized by means of the titles of all episodes that carry the main action; those involving an interaction with an observer and those judged to be of minor significance for the dominant action in progress are omitted. The included episodes cover more than 90 percent of the fourteen hours and twenty-seven minutes Mary was awake on May 12, 1949; they chart the main stream of her activities. The number of each episode shows the order of its occurrence; the missing numbers designate the position of omitted episodes.

15. Getting glass (7:12)
12. Resuming getting dressed
18. Looking for socks
21. Commenting about breakfast chocolate (7:21)
22. Replying to mother's query about socks
23. Placing milk on breakfast table (7:22)
24. Eating breakfast

25. Showing off clean teeth
26. Saying the blessing
29. Bragging about early rising
32. Talking to mother about junior choir picnic
34. Talking to mother and observer about picnic
35. Correcting mother about early rising
36. Correcting father's criticism of her
37. Commenting about early rising
40. Playing with brother
41. Baby-talking to brother
24. End of eating breakfast
43. Talking to mother about mother-daughter banquet (7:38)
44. Commenting about sitting on stove
45. Telling about having made bed (7:40)
46. Informing mother she tipped over basket
47. Telling mother she wanted yellow socks
48. Talking about her room (7:42)
53. Going to bathroom (7:45)
55. Getting mother to sew button on dress
57. Enumerating own accomplishments (7:49)
59. Comparing time on clock and watch
60. Putting barrettes in hair
62. Showing perfumes to adults (7:50)
64. Looking for sweater (7:58)
65. Talking to mother about beads
66. Brushing hair
67. Playing with brother
69. Showing off circular skirt
72. Talking to mother about money (8:04)
73. Searching for new half dollar (8:05)
78. Joking with mother about bank key
79. Helping mother fold diapers (8:07)
83. Baby-talking to mother
84. Talking to mother about brother's bath (8:12)
85. Correcting mother for calling her panties *diapers*
86. Playing piano
87. Asking mother about music (8:15)
89. Warning brother to stay off furnace register
91. Playing with dog
93. Questioning mother about saying goodbye to observer (8:22)
94. Playing with baton
96. Telling adults about baton (8:23)
97. Keeping brother off furnace register
98. Taking care of brother (8:24)

101. Telling about trip baton twirlers made (8:26)
94. Resuming play with baton
105. Pulling electric plug from wall outlet to protect brother
106. Talking to mother about brother and rocking chair (8:29)
107. Watching mother fold laundry
108. Doing stunt on couch
112. Looking at own hair
113. Asking mother about riding bike to school
114. Fixing hair to suit mother
116. Going to school (8:32)
118. Picking flowers
119. Smelling flowers while walking
129. Balancing on bricks
130. Walking along wall (8:38)
116. End of going to school
131. Watching friend on merry-go-round (8:39)
132. Playing on slide
135. Picking up dropped flower (8:40)
136. Playing on merry-go-round
137. Going to classroom (8:43)
142. Talking to Shirley (8:44)
143. Putting flowers in water
145. Going to seat (8:45)
148. Looking for something in desk
150. Doing problems at the board with friends (8:46)
154. Going to wastebasket
155. Going to other classroom (8:55)
156. Working problems at the board
157. Waiting for class to start (8:58)
163. Listening to discussion about makeup work (9:02)
164. Listening to book reports (9:04)
166. Passing out reading books (9:15)
167. Reading in reader
168. Hunting for pencil (9:19)
171. Getting pencil from teacher (9:23)
172. Discovering own pencil at teacher's desk
173. Coloring traced horses' heads (9:24)
175. Trying to decide what to do next (9:28)
177. Adding to drawing (9:30)
178. Trimming drawing with scissors
180. Touching up drawing
182. Putting crayons away (9:33)
184. Waiting to go to music class (9:34)
191. Going to music room (9:43)
193. Shutting door at teacher's request
194. Listening to discussion of song

195. Listening to Shirley's answer
196. Finding page in songbook
197. Singing with classmates
198. Refusing to sing alone
199. Singing with classmates
200. Volunteering to answer question
201. Listening to class discussion
202. Asking Douglas about book
204. Volunteering to answer question
205. Reading music notes with classmates
206. Singing notes with classmates
208. Singing with classmates (9:48)
209. Singing song with classmates (9:49)
210. Talking to teacher about song
211. Accepting book from friend
212. Refusing to sing alone
213. Singing *Red and White* with classmates (9:51)
214. Singing *Bunnies in the Store* with classmates
215. Listening to discussion about next song (9:53)
216. Giving book to teacher
218. Looking on with Douglas
220. Singing *Jolly Old Miller* with classmates
221. Moving back to own seat
222. Listening to discussion about next song
223. Finding page in songbook (9:56)
224. Singing *Erie Mountain Song* with classmates
225. Returning music book to Douglas (9:58)
226. Looking at Douglas' book
227. Getting own book from teacher (9:59)
228. Returning to classroom
231. Following class recitation from reading book (10:00)
232. Reading aloud from reader
233. Reading aloud from reader (10:03)
235. Listening to teacher announce next story (10:06)
236. Following recitation
237. Reading aloud
238. Asking to read for Douglas (10:09)
239. Reading aloud (10:10)
240. Reading aloud (10:14)
241. Responding to teacher's query about end of reading lesson (10:15)
242. Collecting reading books
243. Putting things away in own desk
244. Going out for recess (10:16)

248. Sliding on slide
250. Strolling with girl friends (10:18)
251. Checking on fallen book (10:19)
255. Playing with Anna on whirligig (10:20)
256. Arguing with Anna (10:21)
258. Strolling with Betty (10:23)
259. Resting on rock
260. Playing "house" with Betty (10:25)
263. Exclaiming about worm (10:29)
264. Screaming at boys
265. Telling Betty about study
260. End of playing house (10:32)
267. Going to classroom
268. Getting drink
271. Going to restroom
274. Working in spelling workbook (10:36)
281. Watching classmates (10:45)
282. Getting cardboard out of desk (10:46)
283. Getting permission to go to board
284. Practicing problems at board
287. Working problems given by teacher at board (10:55)
290. Showing writing board to Charlotte
291. Giving unsatisfactory answer to problem
292. Giving correct answer to second problem
294. Noticing crushed chalk on floor
295. Giving answer to problem
296. Repeating answer more loudly
297. Answering teacher's question about an error
298. Telling teacher the answer was correct
287. End of working problems at board (11:12)
304. Watching Charlotte at the board
305. Watching teacher put problems on the board
306. Watching teacher scold Shirley
307. Hunting for something in desk
309. Asking permission to talk to Shirley
310. Talking to Shirley
311. Examining paper given her by Charlotte (11:15)
312. Writing arithmetic lesson
319. Taking arithmetic paper to teacher
320. Coloring on tablet back (11:23)
322. Removing paper strips from tablet back
323. Noting teacher's com-

ment regarding missed arithmetic problems

327. Drawing horses' heads (11:33)

329. Giving drawing of horse to Douglas

331. Ignoring teacher's suggestion she practice writing (11:39)

334. Putting crayons away on completion of drawing (11:52)

335. Adding signature to drawing of horses' heads

336. Glancing at teacher scolding Quentin (11:53)

337. Putting things in desk

338. Going home to lunch

340. Showing drawing of horses' heads to Anna

342. Examining fingernail polish on sidewalk

355. Showing drawing of horses' heads to mother

356. Getting chewing gum from grandmother's letter

358. Asking permission to go outdoors

359. Going out to play (12:03)

361. Swinging

365. Running along clothesline

366. Picking flowers

367. Taking flowers to mother (12:06)

368. Talking with mother about flowers

371. Going to wash hands

372. Whispering to mother

about inviting observer to lunch

373. Eating lunch (12:08)

383. Running out to watch friends in yard (12:12)

384. Telling adults about friends

387. Watching brother at the table

388. Discussing girls' names with mother

389. Discussing correct names for the colors in the iris

390. Joking about dog

391. Responding to mother's comment about feeding dog

392. Refusing to eat sandwich (12:17)

393. Feeding pet dog

400. Going out to play (12:22)

402. Smiling at mother and observer

403. Picking another iris for bouquet

405. Smelling the iris in the yard (12:23)

407. Doing acrobatics on tree branch

409. Picking radishes for mother

412. Going outdoors

414. Petting dog

417. Playing in swing

419. Resting (12:32)

420. Swinging on tree branch

421. Climbing up trailing tree branch

425. Hanging from tree branch
427. Picking dandelions (12:35)
428. Pulling down windblown dress
429. Wandering around yard
431. Picking spirea twig
434. Standing on hands
435. Playing on swing
436. Going to school
438. Picking dandelions (12:39)
450. Shaking spirea bush to make "snow"
451. Scraping fingernail polish from curb
455. Talking with girl in hall
456. Going to seat in schoolroom
458. Talking with Charlotte about a box of games
462. Talking with Anna about picnic
463. Responding to Anna's gesture about pencil
465. Responding to teacher's reprimand about attention
466. Listening to class discussion about story read aloud by teacher
467. Arranging maple leaves on desk
468. Listening to story read aloud by teacher (12:57)
469. Smoothing dress
470. Watching Anna
472. Rolling leaf

473. Rolling leaf
475. Handling leaf
468. End of reading by teacher
476. Arranging leaves in books to press (1:19)
477. Passing out corrected papers
481. Cleaning out desk
483. Following class recitation from English workbook (1:29)
491. Reading aloud when called on
492. Telling Charlotte to continue
493. Watching teacher write on board (1:40)
495. Writing spelling lesson in workbook
501. Sharpening pencil
502. Emptying shavings from pencil sharpener
495. Resuming spelling lesson
510. Writing on tablet paper (2:04)
516. Drawing on fingernails
519. Cleaning desk in response to teacher's command (2:15)
520. Singing *Birthday Song* to Stella
521. Covering eyes to await treat
522. Eating popsicles
523. Going to recess
527. Talking to girls about playing house
536. Going to classroom

538. Getting drink
539. Washing face
541. Looking around room as teacher scolds
542. Sharpening pencil (2:36)
510. Resuming writing (2:37)
548. Putting button in paint-box
562. Throwing paper at Anna
563. Rubbing eye
569. Putting writing things away (3:25)
570. Collecting papers for teacher
572. Taking belongings home from school
574. Asking teacher about picnic
579. Arguing with Jean about handwriting
581. Listening to Jean's joke
588. Painting lips with water-colors
590. Washing paint off face
591. Telling mother the paint came off
594. Asking mother's permission to go outdoors.
595. Going out to play
596. Assenting to mother's request to not pick flowers
598. Looking at roses
600. Twirling baton (3:45)
601. Swinging
602. Exclaiming about dress blowing up
603. Making "face" at Mike
604. Turning cartwheels (3:48)

607. Petting dog
608. Playing on swing
610. Climbing tree (3:50)
615. Looking at flowers (3:52)
617. Jumping to catch limb
618. Leaning on clothesline
619. Playing with iris
620. Hanging on clothesline (3:54)
621. Starting to turn cartwheel
623. Swinging
624. Getting cookie
625. Eating cookie
629. Watching adults decide about Sarah's song
630. Looking thru desk drawers (3:57)
632. Looking at brother sleeping
633. Beckoning to Sarah
634. Examining Sarah's music
635. Taking Sarah outdoors
638. Swinging with Sarah and Ben
639. Commenting about dress flying up
640. Turning cartwheels
641. Imitating Anna's poor cartwheels
642. Demonstrating own cartwheels
643. Correcting Sarah about baton
644. Pushing Sarah in swing (4:03)
645. Sitting on sidewalk
646. Reassuring Sarah about swing

647. Finding out about lesson for Sarah (4:04)
648. Giving cookie to Sarah
649. Offering cookie to Ben
650. Asking Sarah if her skirt made a complete circle
651. Telling Ben how to pump in swing (4:05)
652. Giving cookie to Ben
653. Running
654. Climbing on bike
655. Challenging Ben to catch her (4:06)
657. Doing stunts in swing for Ben
659. Swinging double with Sarah
660. Going to see about Sarah's lesson (4:14)
661. Teaching swinging stunt to Ben and Sarah
662. Rolling on grass
664. Helping Ben hunt lost pen (4:20)
665. Watching Ben swing
666. Questioning Sarah about leaving (4:21)
667. Going to tell mother
668. Pretending to break baton
669. Playing golf with baton
670. Telling Sarah goodbye
671. Watching Ben disentangle swing
672. Exclaiming to Ben about tiny bird egg
673. Explaining about swing to mother

674. Taking turns on swing with Ben (4:27)
675. Playing tree tag with Ben
676. Teasing Ben
677. Making faces at Ben
678. Playing on swing
680. Lying in grass
681. Watching Ben play with rope (4:36)
682. Swinging
683. Asking permission to ride bike (4:38)
684. Trying to think of something to do
686. Exploring
689. Playing with blocks (4:40)
693. Trying to think of something to do (4:45)
694. Getting small barrel with sand in it from garage
701. Commenting about difficulty of task (4:49)
702. Waving to dog
703. Playing in sand
705. Daydreaming
707. Moving barrel to tree
708. Hanging on tree branch
712. Making sandbox (4:55)
716. Rolling barrel
717. Kicking boards on pile
718. Picking lilacs (5:07)
720. Greeting friends
724. "Planting" lilacs in sandbox (5:10)
725. Hunting rocks for garden
726. Greeting father

727. Showing sandbox garden to father
728. Reminding father of promise of sandbox
729. Returning barrel to garage
730. Picking up blocks at father's request
725. Resuming hunting of rocks (5:16)
734. Making rock garden
743. Playing with sand and water (5:29)
752. Hanging from tree branch
753. Picking leaf
755. Pointing out observer to father (5:44)
756. Questioning Dutton
757. Commenting about dog
758. Playing on swing (5:46)
763. Picking flowers
764. Sitting on swing
770. Making dog leave observer
774. Examining flowers (5:59)
778. Riding bicycle around house (6:02)
780. Sitting in swing
782. Comforting Dutton
783. Telling Anna (Dutton's sister) about picnic
784. Discussing going to Anna's
786. Going in to supper
787. Asking to go to Anna's later
788. Going to bathroom
790. Telling mother she's ready for supper

791. Eating supper
792. Saying grace
793. Watching friends play in yard
795. Telling Tommy about sand box (6:15)
797. Watching friends in yard
801. Getting dessert (6:20)
803. Playing in wagon balanced on swing
804. Sharing in group swing play (6:22)
818. Crawling under box (6:50)
819. Going to bathroom
804. Resuming sharing in group swing play
824. Petting dog
826. Sitting in wagon (7:01)
827. Soliciting aid from Carol
828. Rejecting Tommy
829. Watching Geoffrey bring board to balance on swing
830. Helping Carol place board
831. Sharing in swing play
838. Pressing Geoffrey to swing on board
841. Reading comic book
843. Watching playmates (7:11)
844. Calling to friends
845. Going to see design made by swing
846. Placing board for watchers
849. Asking about game
850. Playing Punch-the-Icebox

with friends (7:17)

856. Sitting on swing after coming in free

874. Refusing friend's request to ride her bike

850. End of playing Punch-the-Icebox (7:43)

877. Making play house (7:41)

879. Sitting on swing (7:43)

880. Preventing boys from taking tin cans (7:45)

883. Getting Anna to join in play house

885. Running from dogs

887. Picking "berries"

889. Playing on the swing with Anna (7:51)

891. Kicking tin can with Anna

892. Playing on the swing with Anna (7:56)

893. Chanting about can (7:58)

896. Trying to get Anna to play house (8:00)

897. Pulling Anna from swing

898. Rolling on the grass by the dog

901. Hitting Wally with board

903. Playing with Anna on the swing (8:05)

904. Sitting by dog (8:07)

905. Playing with Anna on the swing (8:08)

908. Watching Anna leave

909. Fixing swing (8:14)

910. Watching Carol

911. Calling for playmates (8:15)

913. Dancing around the yard (8:16)

914. Ripping cardboard box (8:18)

915. Running around the yard

917. Resisting Mrs. Denham's (the babysitter) call to come in (8:22)

918. Watching the boys in the tree (8:23)

919. Racing around the yard with Tommy (8:24)

920. Watching the boys climb down from the tree (8:27)

921. Noting Douglas' remark that she should be in bed

922. Jumping on swing (8:28)

923. Putting on shoes

924. Running to garage (8:29)

925. Swinging from tree (8:30)

926. Going in when called by Mrs. Denham (8:31)

927. Eating cheese sandwich (8:32)

934. Commenting about the color of flowers (8:37)

938. Getting a drink (8:40)

940. Looking in refrigerator

942. Showing drawing of horses' heads to adults (8:42)

944. Playing piano (8:43)

949. Leaving living room at the request of Mrs. Denham

952. Getting undressed for bed
955. "Purring" at brother (8:54)
957. Playing with watercolors in washbowl (8:55)
960. Ignoring Mrs. Denham's suggestion that she go to bed

962. Responding to Mrs. Denham's insistence that she go to bed (9:09)
952. Resuming getting undressed for bed (9:10)
964. Getting book (9:11)
966. Going to bed (9:12)
968. Reading book (9:15)

9:25 Mary settled herself on her side, wiggling a little bit.

Her eyes were opening and closing.

She looked over once more and gave me a weak smile before she fell asleep.

This is a synopsis of Mary's day as it was seen and described by trained observers. It presents a specimen of an eight-year-old American girl's behavior in the year 1949. Mary's family and neighbors were unanimous in their testimony that she was not an unusual child; Mary's mother reported that this day was not unlike most of Mary's days.

What can a scientist do with this huge collection of behavioral raw material? When the record was made, great care was taken to see Mary with the eyes of careful, alert, pragmatical observers, rather than with the eyes of theoretically oriented scientists. An effort was made to secure a specimen of behavior that would provide as nearly as is possible for behavioral science what a collection of insects or a series of astronomical photographs provides for entomology and astronomy. There is evidence that the biases that entered into the making of this record were not those of sophisticated psychologists. For one thing, it is impossible to psychologize at a rate of more than one theory, or diagnosis, or analysis per minute, the rate at which Mary produced behavior. Neither are the biases those of a single personality with its unique perceptual selectivity and distortions. This is Mary's day as seen through eight pairs of eyes, first one and then another in random order. Few who read the complete record can identify the sections contributed by the different observers if identifying marks are deleted. Evidently all were seeing Mary Ennis.

This specimen record can be analyzed and conceptualized in many ways. We have made only a beginning at reducing it to forms that are meaningful in terms of current psychological viewpoints.

In presenting our analysis, we shall refer to Mary's position relative to some other children we have studied in Midwest and neighboring communities. For some analyses, we have comparable data on 118 children, for others on 15 children, for others on 10 children, and for still others on 2 children. In no case are the comparative data fully adequate; we shall only indicate whether Mary deviates markedly from the modal tendency of whatever data are available.

The Structure of Mary's Behavior. As with any phenomenon that occurs along a temporal continuum, Mary's behavior can be divided into an infinite number of parts. For our purposes, we have identified a unit that we call an *episode.* Episodes have been identified and illustrated in the synopsis of the record. One of their characteristics is that they coincide with the behavioral "things" laypersons see their associates and themselves doing. More important for our purposes, however, episodes have the conceptual properties of constancy of direction, high potency, and inclusion within the behavior perspective.

Differentiation of Mary's Behavior. It has already been stated that, in terms of episodes, Mary engaged in 969 molar behavior units in the 14 hours and 27 minutes of her waking day. These episodes varied in length from a few seconds, for example, "waving to friend," to 30 minutes, that is, "participating in group play on swing." Eighty-six percent of the episodes were less than 2 minutes in length; the average length was 0.89 minutes. Mary started a new action every 53 seconds on the average. When compared with similar data for 15 other children, Mary shows no evidence of deviancy with respect to the way and the extent to which the stream of her behavior was partitioned. Mary, like other children in Midwest and vicinity, kept busy.

Most of Mary's episodes did not occur in isolation; usually she engaged in two or more actions at some time during the course of an episode. We have called these *overlapping episodes*; examples have been shown in the synopsis of the record. A schematic representation of some of these characteristics of behavior is given in Figure 1. Here each bracket represents one episode.

Episodes 1 through 8, and Episodes 12 and 13 are overlapping episodes; Episodes 9, 10, and 11 are isolated episodes. Episodes 7, 8, 12, and 13 each overlap with one episode; Episodes 1, 3, 4, and 5 overlap with two episodes; and Episodes 2 and 6 overlap with three episodes. Episodes 1, 2, and 3 have two *simultaneously* overlapping episodes; the other overlapping episodes have one simultaneous overlap. In this example, the transitions between Episodes 6 and 9, between 9 and 10, and between 10 and 11 are abrupt transitions; all others are merging transitions. Episodes 1, 6, and 12 are *enclosing* episodes; Episodes 3, 7, 8, and 13 are *enclosed* episodes; and Episodes 2, 4, and 5 are *interlinking* episodes. Episode 11 is a discontinuous episode; all others are continuous. Episodes 12 and 13 are interpolated episodes. Detailed definitions of these structural features will be found in Barker and Wright (1955).

Data on the structural characteristics of Mary's behavior are summarized in Table 1.

The chief significance of these data in the present connection is that Mary's behavior was not simple in structure. It was not a series of discrete units placed end to end like a row of dominoes. It was, rather, cordlike; it usually consisted of more than one strand of behavior, and the interconnections were usually merging.

However, the complexity of Mary's behavior was sharply limited: It consisted of one or two strands most of the time and never of more than three behavior strands. Interconnected segments, that is, the behavior segments between consecutive abrupt transitions (for example, from the beginning of Episode 1 to the end of Episode 6 in Figure 1) were of limited duration.

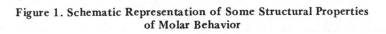

Figure 1. Schematic Representation of Some Structural Properties
of Molar Behavior

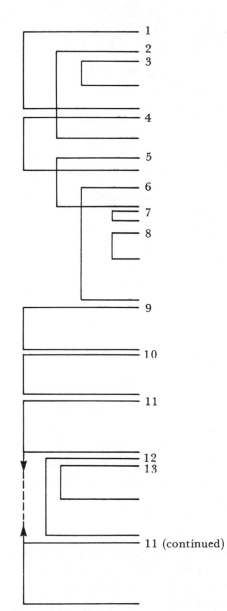

Table 1. Structural Characteristics of Mary's Behavior

	Percent of All Episodes
Overlapping episodes	76
Isolated episodes	24
Episodes with merging transitions	62
Episodes with abrupt transitions	38
Discontinuous episodes	2
Interpolated episodes	8

	Percent of Overlapping Episodes
One overlapping episode	82
Two overlapping episodes	9
Three overlapping episodes	2
More than three overlapping episodes	6
One simultaneously overlapping episode	91
Two simultaneously overlapping episodes	9
Enclosing episodes	17
Enclosed episodes	78
Interlinking episodes	1

In Mary's record, their average duration was 3.1 minutes; the average number of episodes in them was 3.4. These figures exclude all isolated episodes.

Some Dynamic Aspects of Behavior Structure. In 90 percent of Mary's episodes it was possible to judge whether the episode was psychologically completed, that is, was continued until its goal was gained. Eighty-three percent of Mary's episodes were completed in this sense. This includes 8 percent of all episodes that ended in clear-cut success, gratification, or attainment, that is, had "good" endings. Six percent of Mary's episodes were incomplete; this included no instances of frustration, only one episode that ended in failure, and two that ended in nonattainment, that is, had "bad" endings. In comparison with fifteen other records on which data are available, Mary's episodes showed a high degree of completeness and "good" endings; only one other child exceeded her in these. She was low in incomplete episodes and in episodes with "bad" endings. Mary's day was, in general, serene and satisfying.

There was considerable spontaneity to Mary's behavior, as indicated by episode initiation and termination. Forty-five percent of the episodes were initiated in response to some perceptible outside instigator, as when, in answer to Mrs. Ennis' query, "Did you do this, kiddo?" (referring to a basket of clean clothes spilled on the floor) Mary answered, "Yeah, I tipped it over trying to find my stockings." On the other hand, 53 percent of Mary's episodes had no perceptible instigator; they appeared to be spontaneous. The terminations were even more predominantly spontaneous, being so judged in 66 percent of the episodes.

Behavior Objects in Mary's Day. Mary used 571 different objects as essential supports for her behavior during the day, and with these objects she transacted behavior 1,882 times. Any occurrence of a behavior object in an episode has been counted as a separate transaction; verbal transactions with objects not physically present are included in this total. This means that Mary used 39 different behavior objects each hour, had 130 transactions with behavior objects each hour, and had 3.3 transactions with each different behavior object, on the average. Things were important in Mary's life; they flowed through her psychological habitat at the rate of a different object every 1.6 minutes, and of a behavior transaction with a new or an old object every 28 seconds. The rate of behavior transactions per minute for consecutive behavior settings in Mary's day is shown in Figure 2. This suggests a general decline in rate of object transactions throughout the day, with the peak in the middle of the day. These data are not out of line with those for the two other subjects for whom comparative data are available.

We have classified the behavior objects Mary used into broad categories or kinds and into narrower categories or varieties. The kinds and varieties of behavior objects used by Mary are listed as follows. The kinds are presented in order of frequency of Mary's transactions with them, and the varieties are

Figure 2. Rate of Object Transactions in Consecutive Behavior Settings
During the Day for Mary

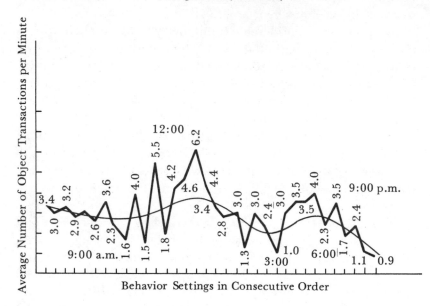

listed alphabetically under the appropriate kinds. The *percent* of Mary's object transactions carried out with each kind of behavior object and the *number* of different objects falling in each variety classification are indicated. The data on people do not include the observers as behavior objects. Mary had behavior transactions with two male and six female observers during the day; her transactions with them constituted 13.4 percent of all her object transactions.

People: 33 percent of all object transactions

Varieties and number of different individuals

Boys	28	Women	11
Girls	40	Unspecified persons	14
Men	4	Total number	
		of people	97

Reading, Writing, School Supplies and Equipment: 11 percent of all object transactions

Varieties and number of individual objects

Blackboard	1	Paper, arithmetic	
Books, general	8	lesson	6
Books, text	10	Paper, writing and con-	
Books, school work-		struction	10
books	2	Pens	2
Books, music	6	Pencils	3
Books, comic	1	Pencil sharpeners	4
Book cover	1	Pictures, own and	
Chalk pieces	3	printed	5
Chalk crushed	1	Poem	1
Crayons and box	5	Problems, arithmetic	17
Eraser, blackboard	3	Ruler	1
Inkwell	1	Scissors	1
Letter (correspon-		Seating chart	1
dence)	1	Songs	7
Magazine	1	Total number	
Newspaper	1	of objects	103

Furniture, Household and Office Equipment, and Parts of Buildings: 10 percent of all object transactions

Varieties and number of individual objects

Banister of stairs	1	Chests of drawers	2
Basket	1	Cleansing powder	1
Beds	2	Clocks and watches	2
Bed linen (spread,		Cup	1
sheets, pillows)	4	Desks (home, school,	
Blinds (window shades)	3	office)	5
Boxes, wood and card-		Doors (cupboard and	
board	6	room)	8
Cans, empty	4	Drinking fountain	1
Can opener	1	Faucet	1
Chairs	8	Floor	1

Fork	1	Sink (bathroom,	
Furnace	1	kitchen)	1
Furniture (unspecified)	1	Sink stopper	1
Glasses, water	2	Sofa	1
Hammer	1	Spoon	1
Key	1	Steps	2
Knife	1	Stove	1
Lamp (light)	1	Table	1
Meter (housing of		Table cloth	1
gas meter)	1	Toilet	2
Nail	1	Towels (cloth, paper)	2
Pan	1	Typewriter	1
Piano	1	Wall plugs	2
Piano bench	1	Wash cloth	1
Pitcher (water)	1	Washing machine	1
Porch	1	Wastebaskets	2
Radiator	1	Window	1
Refrigerator	1	Wires (electric)	2
Screens	2	Total number	
Sewing machine	1	of objects	96

Plants: 6 percent of all object transactions

Varieties and number of individual objects

Bushes	9	Trees (branches,	
Flowers (seeds, petals,		twigs)	19
stems, weeds)	23	Vegetable	1
Grass	1	Total number	
Leaves	6	of objects	60
Mushroom	1		

Clothing and Articles of Adornment: 5 percent of all object transactions

Varieties and number of individual objects
(Collective objects refer to transactions in which Mary used as a single unit a number of objects of the same variety.)

Aprons	4	Bathrobe	1
Barrettes	2	Buttons	3

Diapers (collective)	1	Shoes (slippers)	6
Dresses (skirt, sweater)	7	Socks	2
Fingernail polish	1	Toothbrush	1
Hairbrush	1	Toothpaste (powder)	1
Handkerchiefs	2	Underclothing (pants,	
Jewelry	3	shirt, slip)	4
Pajamas	3	Total number	
Perfume	3	of objects	46
Ribbon	1		

Playthings: 5 percent of all object transactions

Varieties and number of individual objects

Blocks (collective)	1	Playing cards	1
Bicycle	1	Rules of game	1
Designs in dirt or sand	2	Slide	1
Dolls	3	Swing	1
Doll dress	1	Toy animals	1
May baskets	2	Wagon	1
Merry-go-round	1	Whirligig	1
Paints	4	Total number	
Paint brush	1	of objects	23

Physique: 2 percent of all object transactions

Varieties and number of individual objects

Arms	2	Leg	1
Eye	1	Lip	1
Face (chin)	1	Mouth	1
Foot	1	Nose	1
Fingers	2	Teeth (collective)	1
Fingernail	1	Thumb	1
Hair	1	Total number	
Hands	2	of objects	18
Knee	1		

Foods: 2 percent of all object transactions

Varieties and number of individual objects

Bacon	1	Beans	1

Bread (including rolls)	2	Radishes	2
Butter	1	Salad	1
Chewing gum	1	Sandwiches	3
Chocolate, hot	1	Scraps	1
Cookies	3	Soup	1
Dessert	1	Steak	1
Dog food	3	Toast	1
Egg	1	Tomato juice	1
Lettuce	1	Vegetables	1
Milk	3	Total number	
Popsicle	1	of objects	33
Pudding	1		

Animals: 2 percent of all object transactions

Varieties and number of individual objects

Bees	2	Worm	1
Bird	1	Total number	
Bug (insects, moths)	1	of objects	7
Dogs	2		

Outdoor Equipment: 2 percent of all object transactions

Varieties and number of individual objects

Barrels	3	Trash pile	1
Boards (sticks, poles)	10	Walls, retaining	2
Clothesline	1	Total number	
Pump, water	1	of objects	19
Sidewalk, part of	1		

Earth Materials: 2 percent of all object transactions

Varieties and number of individual objects

Earth (dirt, ground, mud; collective)	3	Sand (collective)	5
Pebbles (collective)	5	Total number	
Rocks (large)	2	of objects	15

Vehicles: 0.2 percent of all object transactions

Varieties and number of individual objects

Automobiles	2	Wagon	1
Truck	1	Total number of objects	4

Money: 0.2 percent of all object transactions

Varieties and number of individual objects

Half dollars	2	Money (collective)	1
		Total number of objects	3

Miscellaneous: 4 percent of all object transactions

Varieties and number of individual objects

Bag, for blocks	1	Pasteboard	1
Bank (coin)	1	Pencil shavings	1
Batons	3	Rope	1
Bell (school)	1	Spectacle case	1
Belongings (unspecified)	1	String	1
Birds' egg	1	Sun	1
Blessing	1	Ticket, bus token	1
Camera	1	Violin	1
Cane	1	Water	2
Castle	1	Writing board	1
Cobweb	1	Total number of objects	26
Fish skeleton	1		
Paper (wrapping, Kleenex, cellophane)	1		

The fifteen varieties of behavior objects most frequently used by Mary and the percent of all transactions with them are:

Women	12.3%	Boys	8.6%
Girls	9.6%	Books	3.4%

Trees	2.4%	Boxes	1.4%
Flowers	2.2%	Men	1.2%
Swings	2.0%	Arithmetic problems	1.1%
Dogs	2.0%	Pencils	1.0%
Desks	1.9%	Batons	0.9%
Dresses	1.8%		

The fifteen individual behavior objects with which Mary had most frequent transactions and the percent of all object transactions with them are:

Mother	6.5%	School desk	1.6%
Regular teacher	3.1%	Music teacher	1.4%
Anna Bland, neighbor	2.1%	Timothy, baby	
Swing	2.0%	brother	1.4%
Ben Hutchings, neigh-		Dress, own	1.1%
bor	1.9%	Tommy Wechsler,	
Charlotte, classmate	1.4%	neighbor	1.1%
Sarah Hutchings,		Douglas Crawford,	
neighbor	1.3%	classmate	1.0%
Chico, pet dog	1.8%	Father	1.0%

From these data, it is clear that Mary was highly selective as to the kinds, the varieties, and the individual behavior objects she used. The results show that 54 percent of her transactions were with 3 of the 13 kinds, 52 percent were with 15 of the 211 varieties, and 29 percent were with 15 of the 571 individual behavior objects.

Some of Mary's preferences are clear: (1) People constituted the kind of behavior objects that Mary most preferred, with women, girls, and boys being the three most prominent varieties and with men falling twelfth in the rank order. Among prominent individuals, Mary's mother came first, followed by her classroom teacher, neighbor children and classmates, her music teacher, her brother, and her father, who was fifteenth in rank order of prominent individuals in Mary's day. (2) Reading, writing, and school materials were Mary's next preference as to kind of behavior objects, with books, desks, arithmetic problems, and pencils being prominent varieties. Mary's school desk was a prominent individual object. (3) Furniture and household equipment constituted Mary's third preference in kinds of behavior objects. No single variety or individual object of this kind was prominent. (4) Plants were fourth in the rank order of kinds of objects with which Mary chose to transact behavior, and here trees and flowers were preferred varieties. No single plant fell among the fifteen most-used individual objects. (5) Clothing and articles of adornment were next in order of kinds of behavior objects frequently used by Mary. Dresses, in particular the dress she wore on the day of the observation, were prominent. (6) Among playthings, swings were a preferred variety, and her home swing was a particular behavior object Mary frequently used.

In comparison with the two subjects for whom similar data are available, Mary stood high in her preference for plants as a kind of behavior object. Among varieties, she was high with respect to flowers, swings, arithmetic problems, and batons. With respect to individual behavior objects, Mary was lower than the other subjects in her transactions with her father.

Most of these "preferences" were, in fact, forced on Mary. Midwest surrounded her with a family and with neighbors; it decreed that she have many transactions with teachers, that she live in a house with much furniture and equipment to be dealt with, that she wear clothing. The kinds of preferred objects that appeared to be primarily of Mary's own choice were plants, playthings, and animals. The varieties of these that Mary actively selected were trees, flowers, swings, dogs, and batons. No one pressured Mary to pick flowers, to swing, to play with Chico, or to twirl her baton.

Some attributes of Mary's behavior objects are presented in Table 2, together with data on their frequency of occurrence and on Mary's transactions with them. In the case of some attributes, there was an ambiguous category that is not reported.

From these data, it appears that Mary used four times as many nonsocial as social objects; however, her transactions with the social objects were so much more frequent that social and nonsocial objects entered into Mary's behavior almost equally.

Table 2. Attributes of Behavior Objects Used by Mary

	Percent of Behavior Objects[a]	Percent of Object Transactions[a]
Social objects	17.3	37.9
Pets	0.4	2.3
Nonsocial objects	82.4	59.9

	Percent of Social Behavior Objects[a]	Percent of Transactions with Social Objects[a]
Family members	6.1	27.6
Nonfamily	93.7	72.4

	Percent of Nonsocial Behavior Objects	Percent of Transactions with Nonsocial Objects
Natural objects	24.9	22.8
Man-made objects	75.1	77.2
Objects with esthetic significance[b]	10.0	10.1
Objects with educational significance[b]	14.1	17.2
Objects with hygienic significance[b]	3.9	3.4
Objects with nutritional significance[b]	6.5	5.2
Objects with recreational significance[b]	5.4	10.7
Objects with religious significance[b]	0.2	0.3
Objects belonging to Mary	22.7	39.0
Objects belonging to Mary's family	32.2	25.9
Objects belonging to other persons	5.0	4.3
Objects in the public domain	9.3	12.0

[a]Observers are not included in these computations.

[b]This item refers to the general significance of the object in the local culture irrespective of Mary's use of it.

At eight years of age Mary's social contacts were with persons outside her family four times as frequently as they were with family members. Mary lived in a man-made world so far as the things that she used were concerned; three and one half times as many transactions were with manufactured articles as with articles in their natural state. In terms of their meaning within the local culture, Mary's behavior transactions were most frequently with things of educational significance; next in order were recreational, esthetic, nutritional, hygienic, and religious objects. On May 12, 1949, Mary's day was heavily loaded with things that her associates saw as having educational, recreational, and esthetic values.

Mary's Social Situation and Behavior. Each episode of Mary's record has been analyzed for its social characteristics. The data to be presented are based on 48 percent of all the episodes. These are the episodes in which Mary interacted with a single person other than an observer. Episodes in which Mary did not interact with any person, those in which she interacted with more than one person, and those in which she interacted with the observers are not included. The episodes to be considered are called *regular, standard episodes.*

Mary's Associates. Pertinent data on Mary's associates are given in Table 3. These data show that Mary's social world, as sampled by the regular, standard episodes

- Was about equally divided between adults and children (including adolescents).
- Included both younger and older children (Mary's child associates ranged from seven months to fourteen years of age).
- Was predominantly female (although males were not negligible, constituting one quarter of her associates).
- Was predominantly of her own middle social class (but included contacts that covered the whole social class range in Midwest).
- Was centered about her mother, with her teachers forming the second focus (her father was on the periphery so far as frequency of contacts was concerned).

Mary's day was varied with respect to the age, social class, and sex of her associates. This takes on more significance in the context of the fact that her social interactions were all free, spontaneous ones not governed by institutionalized codes. Mary had to make her own way in a world with considerable social

Table 3. Percent of Regular, Standard Episodes in Which
Mary Had Various Classes of Associates

Adult associates		48
Adolescent associates		7
Child associates		40
Younger than Mary	15	
Same age as Mary	16	
Older than Mary	9	
Male associates		24
Female associates		73
Mother an associate		25
Father an associate		3
Teachers associates		16
Animal associates		3
Social Class I[a]		24
Social Class II[a]		58
Social Class III[a]		8

[a]These correspond to the upper middle (I), lower middle (II), and upper lower classes (III), as identified by Warner, Meeker, and Eells (1949).

diversity. In this respect, her day was not unlike the days of other children we have studied in Midwest.

Modes of Social Interaction. Mary's social interactions with her associates were rated on both Mary's side and her associates' side for the degree of dominance, aggression, resistance, avoidance, submission, appeal, and nurturance displayed.

Brief definitions of these modes of behavior follow.

- *Domination:* the exerting of social pressure in an arbitrary way.
- *Nurturance:* the meeting of a need of another person; may be spontaneous or may follow appeal from the other person.
- *Appeal:* the indication to another person of the presence of a need; a request for help, support, protection, or consolation.
- *Submission:* the giving in to actions of any kind that are coercive; can immediately follow pressure or may follow a period of resistance.
- *Resistance:* the withstanding of actions of any kind that are coercive.
- *Aggression:* the attacking of another person by attempts to

injure the person physically (as causing pain) or in other ways (as causing embarrassment or frustration).
• *Avoidance:* the withdrawing from another person.

The frequencies with which each of these modes occurred are shown in Figure 3. It should be noted that one episode sometimes received a rating on more than one interaction mode. Data are given for all associates together, and separately, for adults, for Mary's mother, for Mary's regular teacher, and for her child associates.

We shall first consider Mary's relations with all of her associates en masse. Pertinent data are represented by the top bar of each panel of Figure 3. It will be noted that the most frequent mode of social interaction with Mary by her associates was domination, which occurred in 30 percent of all regular, standard episodes. Following in order of frequency come nurturance (26 percent), resistance (16 percent), appeal (16 percent), submission (14 percent), aggression (8 percent), and avoidance (2 percent). The total occurrence of authoritative interactions (domination, resistance, and aggression) by Mary's associates was 54 percent, and it almost exactly equaled the occurrence of their subordinate interactions (nurturance, appeal, submission, and avoidance), which totaled 58 percent.

On Mary's side, too, domination (24 percent) and nurturance (23 percent) were most frequent, although slightly less so than in the case of her associates. Mary exhibited resistance (19 percent), appeal (20 percent), and submission (20 percent) almost equally frequently, and she did so somewhat more often than her associates did with her. Aggression (7 percent) and avoidance (3 percent) were almost exactly what she received from her associates. The total occurrence of authoritative interactions by Mary was smaller (50 percent) than the total occurrence of subordinate interactions (66 percent). This is one indication of the power Mary's associates had over her. Considering the fact that more of her interactions were with adults and adolescents than with children, this is not surprising. On the other hand, it is clear that Mary was by no means downtrodden: In almost one fourth of her interactions with her associates, she

Figure 3. Frequency of Modes of Interaction

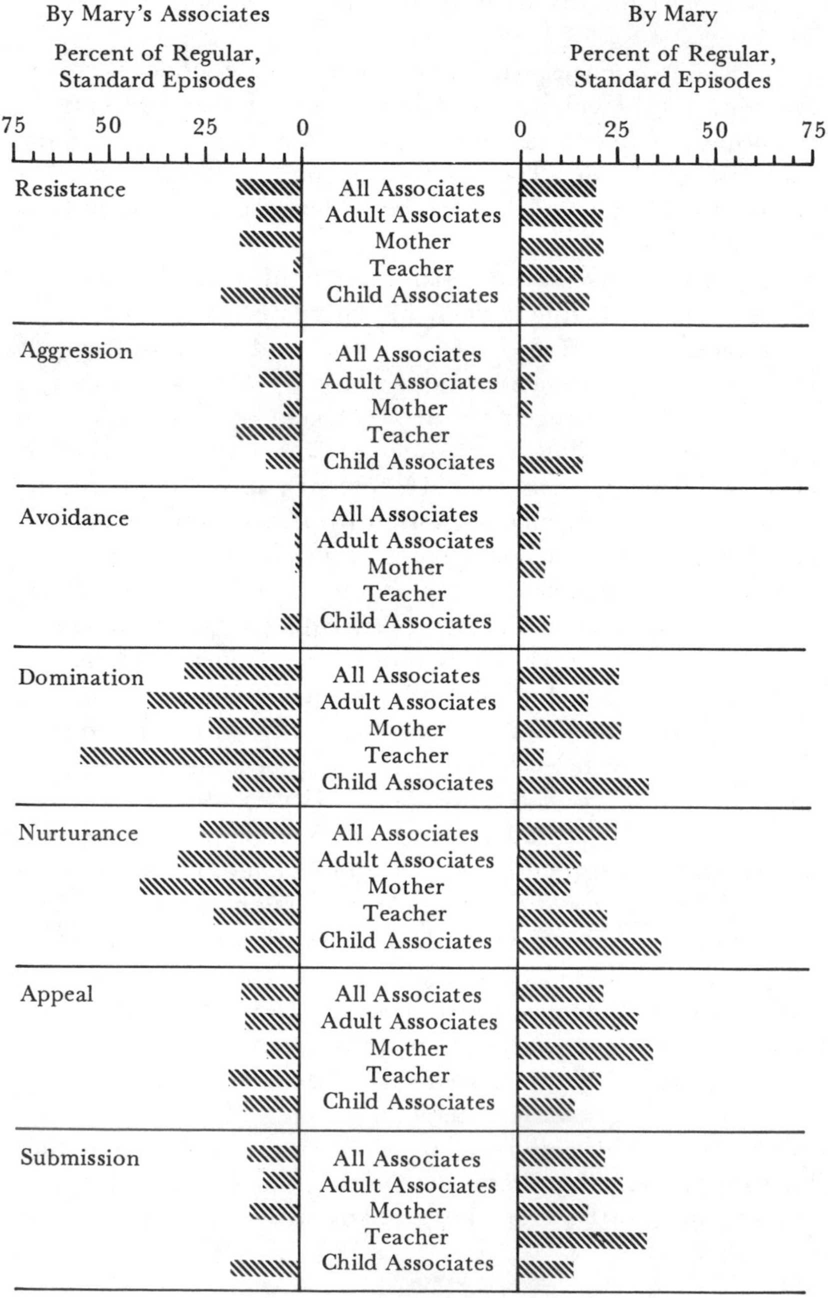

By Mary's Associates			By Mary		
Percent of Regular, Standard Episodes			Percent of Regular, Standard Episodes		

75   50   25   0   0   25   50   75

Resistance
- All Associates
- Adult Associates
- Mother
- Teacher
- Child Associates

Aggression
- All Associates
- Adult Associates
- Mother
- Teacher
- Child Associates

Avoidance
- All Associates
- Adult Associates
- Mother
- Teacher
- Child Associates

Domination
- All Associates
- Adult Associates
- Mother
- Teacher
- Child Associates

Nurturance
- All Associates
- Adult Associates
- Mother
- Teacher
- Child Associates

Appeal
- All Associates
- Adult Associates
- Mother
- Teacher
- Child Associates

Submission
- All Associates
- Adult Associates
- Mother
- Teacher
- Child Associates

showed domination, and in one fifth of them she showed resistance. Furthermore, it should be recalled that Mary spontaneously initiated episodes as frequently as she responded to
the instigation of others.

When we turn to Mary's adult associates (second bar of
each panel), we find their modes of interaction to be in essentially the same order as those of her associates en masse. Again
authoritative and subordinate modes are about equal *in toto,*
but here both domination (38 percent) and nurturance (31 percent) are higher in frequency than in the former case. In her
interactions with adults, Mary's most frequent action was
appeal (28 percent), with submission (26 percent) and resistance (21 percent) next in order. Mary exhibited less than half as
much domination and nurturance and one quarter as much
aggression to her adult associates as they did toward her; she
exhibited about twice as much appeal, submission, and resistance as they did. The total of her authoritative interaction
modes was much less (39 percent) than the total of her subordinate modes (71 percent). It is clear that Mary was under the
control of her adult associates; still it was not a tight control
that allowed only submission and appeal. Mary exhibited domination with adults in 16 percent of the episodes and resistance
in 21 percent of them.

An examination of data for the two chief individual adult
associates, namely, Mary's mother and her classroom teacher,
reveals that one source of much of the domination and aggression Mary received from adults was her teacher. This is depicted
more clearly in Table 4, which gives the rank order of inter-

Table 4. Rank Order of Interaction Modes

Mother	Vis-à-Vis	Mary	Teacher	Vis-à-Vis	Mary
Nur (41)		Apl (32)	Dom (57)		Sub (30)
Dom (24)		Dom (24)	Nur (23)		Nur (21)
Res (16)		Res (21)	Apl (19)		Apl (19)
Sub (13)		Sub (16)	Agg (17)		Res (15)
Apl (9)		Nur (11)	Res (2)		Dom (4)
Agg (4)		Avd (4)	Avd (0)		Agg (0)
Avd (1)		Agg (1)	Sub (0)		Avd (0)

action modes for Mary vis-à-vis her mother and her teacher. The percent of each mode is also given.

Mary's relationship with her mother has an interesting pattern of interaction modes in which the only appreciable difference is a reversal of nurturance and appeal. Nurturance (41 percent) and appeal (9 percent) are first and fifth respectively in the mother's rank order of interaction modes, and they are fifth (11 percent) and first (32 percent) in Mary's. To us, this looks like a dependent relation in which the nurturance of the mother instigated and supported the appeal by Mary, and vice versa. But it was a dependence that was held within bounds by a sizable component of dominance, resistance, and submission of almost equal strength on both sides. Both Mrs. Ennis and Mary exhibited fewer authoritative than subordinate interaction modes, and the proportions of each were almost exactly the same for Mary and her mother, that is, 46 percent and 44 percent authoritative and 63 percent and 64 percent subordinate, respectively.

Domination is first (57 percent) and submission last (0 percent) in the rank order of the teacher's interaction modes with Mary; for Mary, domination is fifth (4 percent) and submission is first (30 percent). Another pair of reversals is aggression and resistance; aggression occurred in 17 percent of the teacher's episodes and was not exhibited by Mary vis-à-vis her teacher. Resistance occurred in 15 percent of Mary's episodes and in only 2 percent of the teacher's episodes.

On the teacher's side, the relationship with Mary appears to have been a rather dictatorial-hostile one, although the relatively high nurturance and appeal have to be kept in mind. These may be indicative of a benevolent autocracy; but the record suggests that they are often signs of ambivalence on the part of the teacher. Undoubtedly the school situation itself coerced a certain amount of nurturance and appeal by the teacher.

The relatively high place of nurturance and appeal in Mary's behavior is surprising. A study of the record suggests to us that these were about the only ways left for Mary to approach this dictatorial teacher. Avoidance, aggression, and domination she found to be virtually impossible to engage in or entirely uncongenial to her. Mary's relations with her mother and with her child associates make it clear that she wanted to be an outgoing, socially effective person. When confronted with a tyrant, nurturance and appeal may have been the only social mode that was in any way acceptable to Mary.

In her relations with her child associates, Mary exhibited some aspects of her mother's pattern of interaction with her. Mary most often showed nurturance, dominance, and resistance, too. She differed in showing considerable aggression. This may have been misplaced aggression that could not be directed against the teacher, her mother, or other adults. Mary's child associates reciprocated with relatively high resistance, domination, and submission.

In comparison with ten other children on whom similar data are available, Mary did not receive unusual patterns of interaction modes from her associates. She was, however, more nurturant of her child associates, and she showed a tendency toward greater domination of and less submission to adult associates.

Attributes of Social Interaction. Episodes were rated for Mary's and for her associates' liking for each other, for their happiness in the association, and for their evaluation of each other. Eleven-point rating scales ranged from negative to positive affection, mood, and evaluation. On each of these three dimensions of social interaction, Mary's associates were positive toward her; they liked her, they were happy with her, and they approved of her and her behavior. On all scales Mary was rated positively in more than three quarters of the episodes. She reciprocated these positive feelings and attitudes of her associates.

Power Relations. Although she associated frequently with adults and older children who were more powerful than she, Mary exerted pressure on associates to change their behavior at least as frequently as she was pressured by them to change her behavior; in fact, Mary exerted pressure on her associates in 41 percent of the social episodes, and pressure was exerted on her in 38 percent of them.

The Behavior Settings of Mary's Day. On May 12, 1949, the town of Midwest presented Mary with approximately 200 behavior settings, in addition to those within her home, in which to live her life. Behavior settings are independent behavior areas of a community where characteristic patterns of behavior are observed to occur; they are the parts of the town that are generally recognized by the citizens. The behavior settings of Midwest presented Mary with a wide range of behavior opportunities; however, she entered only eight, or 4 percent, of them on the day the record was made. This was less than Midwest school children entered on an average day. The settings where Mary lived her life are given in Table 5, together with the

Table 5. Behavior Settings Mary Entered

	Percent of Episodes	Percent of Time
Behavior Settings Outside Mary's Home		
School playground	4.5	3.7
School halls and coatroom	2.3	1.7
School classroom, before and after school	3.3	2.8
School academic activities	19.5	31.0
Girls' basement (toilet)	0.4	0.2
Grade school music	3.7	1.7
Recreation period	0.3	0.3
Streets and sidewalks	5.0	3.2
Total outside home	39.0	44.6
Behavior Settings Within Home		
Indoors	18.8	15.0
Bathroom	1.8	3.7
Meals	4.9	3.7
Outdoors	35.0	33.0
Total within home	60.5	55.4

percent of the day she spent in each and the percent of all episodes that occurred in each. It will be noted that at eight years of age, Mary was dividing her time almost equally between situations within and without her home. She was spending most time outdoors at home, with school academic activities following closely, and with home activities indoors next in order.

Ratings were made of the social weather Mary encountered

in all the behavior settings she entered. Judgments were made for each variable on a five-point scale, which ranged from negative expression of the variables at the low end of the scale through neutral to positive expression of the variables at the high end of the scale. When these ratings were pooled, we obtained the following modal descriptions of Mary's living areas in terms of nine social weather variables. These global ratings were made independently of the episode analysis that has already been reported. They indicate that

- With a few exceptions, Mary received expressions of affection from her associates.
- She was generally accepted by them into the emotional warmth of intimacy, but sometimes with reservations and with occasional exclusions.
- Associates' evaluation of Mary's behavior ranged from balanced approval as merited to favorable bias in which disapproval was sugar coated.
- Mary's associates made some efforts at adaptation of their own behavior to her needs when her wants were obvious.
- They were fairly permissive with her; restrictions on her behavior were determined by practical considerations.
- Their sharing of knowledge, ideas, and feelings with Mary usually fell between dutiful, polite communication and efforts to promote and maintain communication.
- Mary's associates provided assistance for her when she needed it, but not when she could get along alone.
- Mary had freedom of choice between alternatives, which were, however, rather closely restricted by her associates.
- The attention focused on Mary by her associates was unstable and divided; she was not the center of their concern, but was not ignored by them.

In general, Mary's behavior settings provided her with greater affection, acceptance, approval, permissiveness, and adaptation than they did attention, choice, assistance, or communication. In some behavior settings, the social weather Mary encountered varied from these modal characteristics. The school academic setting was below the general mode on all scales except attention; school playground was above the mode on all scales except communication; and meals (particularly supper) were above the mode on all scales. School music was above the modal value on all scales except privilege and choice; in the latter respects the school music period was sharply limiting.

Mary's Day: A Résumé

This hemerography of Mary Ennis shows that on May 12, 1949, when she was in her ninth year, Mary's behavior situation continuum was observed to consist of many molar units (slightly more than one per minute on the average), with two of them often, and three of them sometimes, overlapping and interweaving in complex ways. About half of these episodes were spontaneously initiated by Mary, and more than half of them were spontaneously terminated by her, usually with the completion of an action, and with success, gratification, or achievement being much more frequent endings than failure, frustration, or nonachievement.

Pari passu with the high degree of differentiation of Mary's stream of behavior and psychological habitat, there was a great proliferation of objects with which Mary transacted behavior. A different behavior object entered her psychological habitat about every one and one half minutes, on the average, and an object transaction occurred approximately each half-minute. Mary was highly selective in her uses of behavior objects. About half of her transactions were with 23 percent of the kinds of objects and with 7 percent of the varieties of objects; 29 percent of Mary's transactions were with 3 percent of the individual behavior objects. Kinds of behavior objects that Mary preferred were people; reading, writing, school supplies, and equipment; and plants. Preferred varieties of behavior objects were women, girls, boys, books, trees, and flowers. Individual objects with which transactions were frequent were Mary's mother, her classroom teacher, Anna Bland, her swing, Ben Hutchings, and Chico, the dog. Transactions with social behavior objects were about as frequent as with nonsocial ones.

Among the social behavior objects, behavior transactions with children and adolescents were of about the same frequency as transactions with adults. Females and associates of Social Class II were the objects of Mary's transactions more frequently than male or Class I or Class II associates (see Table 3, footnote). Mary had transactions with members of her family about one third as frequently as with nonfamily members. Among non-social behavior objects, those with educational, recreational, and esthetic significance within the local culture most frequently entered Mary's psychological habitat. Man-made behavior objects were three times as frequent as objects in their natural state.

Mary's associates exhibited domination toward her in almost one third of the social episodes and nurturance in one fourth of them; resistance, appeal, submission, aggression, and avoidance followed in rank order. In return, Mary showed domination in about one fourth of the episodes and nurturance in almost the same number; resistance, appeal, and submission were more frequent on the part of Mary than on the part of her associates.

Adults were both more dominant and more nurturant in their relations with Mary than were her associates at large, and she was more submissive and exhibited more appeal than the generality of her associates. Mary's mother was the most frequently nurturant of her associates, and Mary appealed most frequently to her mother. This pattern of dependency was counteracted by domination in one fourth of their interactions on the part of both Mary and her mother and by appreciable and almost equal amounts of resistance and submission by both of them. Mary's classroom teacher was a domineering person in whose interactions with Mary domination, aggression, and resistance were almost twice as frequent as nurturance and appeal (there was no submission or avoidance by this teacher). Mary reacted with one fourth as frequent domination, aggression, and resistance as nurturance, appeal, submission, and avoidance. With her peers, Mary interacted most frequently with nurturance, domination, and resistance, and she received in return resistance, domination, and submission.

In general, Mary's associates showed a medium degree of affection for her, of approval of her, and of happiness with her. They made some efforts to adapt their own behavior to her needs, they were fairly permissive with her, they were usually polite and communicative, they provided her with assistance when she needed it, she was given limited choices, and she was not ignored nor yet made the center of her associates' concern.

Although comparative data are not adequate, what there are suggest that this picture of Mary's behavior and psychological situation is not very different from that existing for most other children in Midwest. However, there were some indications that Mary's day had fewer incomplete episodes; that failure, frustration, and nonattainment were less frequent for Mary than they were for most children; and that she was less submissive and showed more domination toward adults and more nurturance toward children.

Despite a somewhat restricted contact with the behavior settings of the town on this day, Mary met in free, spontaneous interaction a wide range of the age, sex, and social class differences existing in Midwest, and she met and adjusted to some of the hard things of life, notably those exhibited by her teacher, as well as the pleasant.

It will be obvious to all that only a beginning has been made in analyzing and conceptualizing psychological data of this sort, and that hemerographical studies will be more meaningful when they are available for a variety of persons.

Social Actions of American and English Children and Adults

◆-◆◆-◆◆-◆◆-◆◆-◆◆-◆◆-◆◆-◆◆-◆◆-◆◆-◆◆-◆◆-◆◆-◆◆-◆◆-◆◆-◆◆-◆

This research explores differences in the interactions of children with adults and of children with children in America and England. A common way of carrying out this kind of research is to observe or question a representative sample of the inhabitants of each country. However, if one is interested in obtaining data on interactions within representative environments as well as by representative subjects, as we were, this greatly increases the problem. It means that data must be obtained for each sub-

Revised and abbreviated version of chapter entitled "Social Actions in the Behavior Streams of American and English Children" in Barker (1963b, pp. 127-168).

ject within the particular streets, schools, stores, playgrounds, and so forth, that constitute that subject's particular habitat. The number of data sources, therefore, becomes greater than the number of subjects by factors of ten, twenty, or more. This is an imposing task for a research project that deals with even a few subjects; 50 subjects, then, multiply to 500 or more locales from which data must be obtained. Practicality suggests, therefore, that the investigation be limited to one town, with its streets, schools, stores, playgrounds, and so on, rather than extended to fifty towns and ten or more settings within each. So one is on the horns of a dilemma: representativeness versus practicality. If one goes the practical route, this requires, first, selecting a representative town in each nation and, second, determining via independent evidence how far the findings for the towns are in fact general for the country.

In this study, we have gone the practical route: We have attempted to satisfy the first requirement by carefully selecting an American town and an English town that are, at least, not atypical of other towns of America and England, and we have attempted to determine the generality of findings for America and England by methods reported in the second part of the chapter.

Social Actions in Midwest and Yoredale

In 1957, when the data were collected, both towns were nonindustrial, rural, trading, and local government centers; Midwest (MW) was a county seat and Yoredale (YD) the seat of a rural district council. Both were within a similar size range: MW had a population of 830, and YD had 1,300 citizens. The towns were similarly situated with respect to cities; MW was twenty, thirty-five, and forty-five miles, respectively, from cities of 20,000, 10,000 and 800,000 population, and YD was seventeen, thirty, and forty-five miles from cities of 15,000, 100,000 and 700,000 population. Both were inland towns located almost equidistant from each country's borders. The people of both MW and YD were overwhelmingly from family lines whose historical roots were in northern Europe; in MW there are thirty-seven blacks. Both towns were naturally bounded regions separated from the surrounding farming areas by greater population density. Neither town was isolated in a cultural backwater; both had open channels of communication with the larger culture via roads, telephones, radio, television, newspapers, and mail. Neither MW nor YD was obviously atypical within its culture; both are vigorous, thriving communities.

General Method

The data consist of measures of the occurrence of designated social actions (attribute units) within the behavior streams of children in fifty-one MW and fifty-one YD behavior settings. Examples of the actions are "child *helps* child," "adult *dominates* child," and "child *complies with* adult." And examples of the behavior setting environments that were explored are school academic classes, school lunchrooms, and religious services.

Here is an example of the social action "adult values child" in the behavior stream of Clare within the behavior setting arithmetic class: Miss Graves (the teacher) asked, "Does anyone have twenty right?" Clare raised her hand, and Miss Graves said, "Well done, Clare." Then she asked, "How many missed only one?" Heather and another child held up hands. She asked, "How many missed two?" Gregory raised his hand; Miss Graves said, "Very good, Gregory." She said, "Gregory is in the fourth group; that's very good for him."

The methods of the study are widely used in biological ecology. They consist, there, of recording the presence and absence of specified organisms within sampling areas without regard for their frequency within the areas. The basic results are expressed in terms of the number of areas in which species are present. Thus Beals and Cottam (1960) reported that *Quercus borealis* occurred in twenty-seven of seventy-five stands of forest on the Apostle Islands of Lake Superior; while *Pinus strobus* was present in fourteen of the same stands. The percents (36 and 19), called *presence indices* (PI), express the chances that the species will be encountered when stands are inspected at random. They are measures of the dispersion of the two species of trees across the forest stands of the Apostle Islands.

The adequacy of this method depends (1) on the degree to which the areas studied (for example, forest stands) represent the total region they are intended to represent and (2) on the adequacy with which the areas are inspected for the presence and absence of the designated organisms. This inspection usually requires two steps, namely; (1) systematically inspecting the areas (the primary sampling units) via secondary units, for example, points or quadrats, and (2) making complete inventories of the designated species within the secondary sampling units.

In the present research, we followed with fidelity the main lines of this standard ecological technique; the corresponding phases of the present study and of Beals and Cottam's investigation (1960) of forest vegetation are tabulated as follows (Table 1):

Table 1. Comparison of Phases in Two Ecological Studies

	Forest Study	Present Study
Region studied	Apostle Islands	MW, YD
Primary sampling units	Seventy-five different forest stands	Fifty-one behavior settings in each town
Secondary sampling units	Points and quadrats located at equal intervals along compass lines through each forest stand	A child's behavior stream within each behavior setting
Inventory data	Record of (1) nearest tree to each point; (2) all herbs, shrubs, and saplings within each quadrat	Record of specified social actions in behavior stream of child

Details of Method

BEHAVIOR SETTINGS INSPECTED

We inspected behavior within fifty-one pairs of equivalent behavior settings of the towns: arithmetic class versus arithmetic class, playground versus playground, and so forth. These types of settings included music classes, physical education classes, academic subject classes, school lunchrooms, playgrounds, athletic contests, religious services, and social and cultural meetings. The selected settings do not adequately represent all types within the two towns; they are almost all public settings, and among the public settings those that are school related are overrepresented. However, approximately two thirds of the time the children of MW and YD inhabit the towns' public behavior settings is spent in these settings-these settings therefore sample a large part of the public environments of the towns' children.

SAMPLING SOCIAL ACTIONS WITHIN SETTINGS

Within the paired settings, we used the behavior streams of pairs of children 6:2 to 11:10 years old equated for age, sex, and social class as "compass lines" along which to identify social actions. Specimen records of the behavior of these children provide the primary social action data; this includes (1) *the behavior of the compass-line children,* themselves, and (2) *the behavior of other children and adults with reference to the compass-line children* in the records. Other children were present in all settings and ranged in age from one-year-old infants to fifteen-year-old adolescents; adults other than the observer were present in forty-three of the MW settings and in forty-six of the YD settings.

By these means, behavior of children of equivalent age, sex, and social class, and of others vis-à-vis them, varies without restriction within equivalent ecological regions of the towns.

VARIETIES OF SOCIAL ACTION

The research deals with the forty varieties of social action. These are identified and defined as follows in alphabetical order. X stands for the actor (child or adult) and Y for the object of the action (child or adult).

1. *X accommodates* his behavior *to Y. X* adjusts his behavior, including his thinking, to Y; he tries to behave by Y's standards.
2. *X* is *affectionate to Y. X* shows by explicit behavior

that he loves *Y*; he kisses *Y*, hugs *Y*, tells *Y*, "I love you."

3. *X* is *antagonistic to Y*. *X* tries to inflict maximal injury of which he is capable on *Y* (not as punishment); he tries to hurt *Y*.

4. *X* is *baffled by Y*. *X* does not show insight into *Y*'s behavior; he is confused by *Y*.

5. *X comforts Y*. *X* consoles *Y* when *Y* is sad or hurt; he feels for *Y*, soothes *Y*.

6. *X competes with Y*. *X* tries to win over *Y*; he promotes own behavior to detriment of *Y*.

7. *X complies with Y*. *X* accepts *Y*'s authority realistically; he accepts *Y*'s supervision without enthusiasm.

8. *X accepts Y's control*. *X* willingly accepts *Y*'s influence; he identifies with *Y*, says, in effect, "You are right."

9. *X cooperates with Y*. *X* joins with *Y* in common task; he is a partner of *Y*.

10. *X defends Y*. *X* is protective of *Y*; he shields *Y*, stands up for *Y*.

11. *X deprives Y*. *X* withholds or withdraws something of value from *Y*; he neglects *Y*, dispossesses *Y*.

12. *X devalues Y*. *X* makes specific negative evaluation of *Y*; he criticizes *Y*, compares *Y* unfavorably with others.

13. *X disagrees with Y*. *X* engages in verbal opposition to *Y*; he delays compliance while he disputes with *Y*.

14. *X disciplines Y*. *X* determines *Y*'s behavior by his authority plus threat of physical action; he rebukes, admonishes *Y*.

15. *X* is *distant from Y*. *X* appears indifferent to *Y*; he disregards *Y*, is inattentive to *Y*.

16. *X* is *distressed by Y*. *X* is grieved by *Y*'s behavior; he is saddened by *Y*.

17. *X dominates Y*. *X* applies maximal personal pressure on *Y*; he dictates to *Y*, bosses *Y*, decides issues for *Y*.

18. *X enjoys Y*. *X* shows by specific expressive action that he is pleased to interact with *Y*; he has fun with *Y*, is entertained by *Y*.

19. *X exploits Y*. *X* uses his power over *Y* to benefit himself; he makes *Y* work for him, wait on him.

20. *X asks favor of Y.* X makes own need explicit to Y; he appeals to Y for gifts, attention, help, love.
21. *X forgives Y.* X overlooks faults or misdemeanors of Y; he excuses Y, makes allowances for Y.
22. *X is friendly with Y.* X shows medium affection for Y; he is glad to see Y, welcomes Y.
23. *X gratifies Y.* X gives to Y without request or effort on Y's part; he indulges Y, waits on Y.
24. *X hates Y.* X expresses maximal negative emotion toward Y; he can't stand Y, loathes Y.
25. *X helps Y.* X adds his power to Y's efforts; he assists, lends a hand to Y.
26. *X hinders Y.* X tries to prevent Y from reaching Y's goal; he delays Y, restrains Y.
27. *X is impatient with Y.* X inflicts medium injury on Y; he assaults Y verbally.
28. *X influences Y.* X applies routine personal pressure to Y; he makes requests and gives advice to Y.
29. *X manages Y.* X applies medium personal pressure on Y; he supervises, teaches, regulates, leads Y; he takes charge of Y.
30. *X provides opportunity for Y.* X increases positive valence or removes obstacle for Y.
31. *X plays with Y.* X enters into game with Y, not as a supervisor or official, but as a player.
32. *X is polite to Y.* X shows proper forms of conduct with Y; he is courteous to Y, well-behaved with Y.
33. *X punishes Y.* X determines Y's behavior by his authority plus actual punishment; he deprives Y of something of value; he shakes, strikes Y.
34. *X resists Y.* X does not comply with Y's efforts at domination; he refuses, defies Y.
35. *X surrenders to Y.* X complies under Y's duress; he accepts Y's order reluctantly.
36. *X teases Y.* X inflicts minimum injury on Y; he pesters Y, bothers Y.
37. *X understands Y.* X expresses insight into reasons for Y's behavior; he analyzes Y's problem, seeks Y's motives.

38. *X* is *unfriendly to Y*. *X* expresses medium negative emotion toward *Y*; he is unkind to *Y*, rebuffs *Y*.
39. *X values Y*. *X* makes specific positive evaluation of *Y*; he rewards *Y*, praises *Y*, compares *Y* favorably with others.
40. *X works with Y*. *X* engages in serious activity with *Y*.

Direction of Social Actions. Each of the forty varieties of social action can occur in three directions: (1) adult acts toward child (*A-C*), for example, adult helps child; (2) child acts toward adult (*C-A*), for example, child helps adult; (3) child acts toward child (*C-C*), for example, child helps child. We, therefore, searched the specimen records for the occurrence of social actions with 120 different variety-direction attributes. To check the accuracy with which the attributes were identified, two analysts independently inventoried forty-three records with respect to their presence and absence. There was agreement on every decision in the case of three records and on 82 percent of the decisions in the case of the record where the analyst's ratings were most discrepant; the mean agreement was 95 percent.

DIVERSITY OF SOCIAL ACTIONS

The number of varieties of social action occurring in a town is a measure of their diversity within it.

DISPERSION OF SOCIAL ACTIONS

Measures of the dispersion of a social action of a designated variety and direction are (1) the *number* of behavior settings in which it is present one or more times—this is its *presence value* (PV) and (2) the *percent* of the behavior settings inspected in which it is present one or more times—this is its *presence index* (PI). For the social action adult values child, for example, PV is 23 and 13 and PI is 50 and 30, for YD and MW, respectively; actions by adults that make specific positive evaluations of children are more widely dispersed among the behavior settings of YD than among those of MW.

POWER OF SOCIAL ACTIONS

We have been especially concerned with the power relations between the persons involved in social actions. Therefore, two categories of social action have been identified, as follows:

Application of social power. In some social actions, X exerts power on Y to behave in accordance with the desires of X. Seven of the 40 varieties of social action involve the application of power. In four of them, X brings *indirect* or *moderate* pressure to bear on Y; namely, X provides opportunity for Y, asks favor of Y, influences Y, manages Y; and three social actions involve the application of *strong power—X* dominates Y, disciplines Y, punishes Y.

Reaction to social power. In five varieties of social action, X acts with reference to the social power of Y. In three of these, X *yields* to Y's power, namely, X accepts control by Y, complies with Y, surrenders to Y; and in two X *does not yield* to Y's power—X disagrees with Y, resists Y.

HARMONY OF SOCIAL ACTIONS

Twenty-two varieties of social action clearly have implications for the interpersonal harmony of X and Y. In eleven of these *harmony is initiated, maintained, or increased* by the action; namely, X gratifies Y, is affectionate to Y, comforts Y, defends Y, is friendly to Y, enjoys Y, helps Y, is polite to Y, values Y, cooperates with Y, plays with Y, accommodates his behavior to Y. In ten of the varieties, *disharmony is fostered*; namely, X hates Y, is antagonistic to Y, is unfriendly to Y, is impatient to Y, teases Y, is distressed by Y, devalues Y, hinders Y, deprives Y, competes with Y.

RESULTS REPORTED

In this abbreviated report, only sufficient data are given to indicate the trends of the complete analyses. The PIs are shown in the parentheses following the actions thus: A manages C (93) means that the action is present in 93 percent of the town's behavior settings. In connection with the dispersion of social actions, we report only those actions that are "widely dispersed" in each town and those that are "more widely dispersed" in one town than the other. The former social actions have PIs of twenty or more in the designated town, and the latter have PIs that *differ* by ten or more in the towns.

Actions of Adults Toward Children (A-C) in Midwest

Diversity. In their actions toward children, the adults of MW display twenty-one of the forty varieties of social action.

Dispersion. Widely dispersed *A-C* actions in MW are *A* manages *C* (93), influences *C* (51), dominates *C* (33), values *C* (30), is friendly with *C* (28), helps *C* (21).

Power. MW adults are in charge of children in almost all settings; their control is implemented more generally by moderate or indirect than by strong pressures. *A-C* actions with moderate or indirect power are *A* manages *C* (93), influences *C* (51), provides opportunity for *C* (14), and asks favor of *C* (2); those with strong power are *A* dominates *C* (33) and disciplines *C* (7); punishment does not occur. MW adults react to children's power in only a single setting: *A* disagrees with *C* (2).

Harmony. Actions of adults that foster harmony with children are greater in number and more widely distributed than those that foster disharmony. Harmonious *A-C* actions are *A* values *C* (30), is friendly to *C* (28), helps *C* (21), comforts *C* (9), defends *C* (9), enjoys *C* (5), plays with *C* (5), accommodates to *C* (5), and cooperates with *C* (2); *A-C* actions that foster disharmony are *A* devalues *C* (14), is impatient with *C* (14), and is unfriendly to *C* (2).

Actions of Adults Toward Children (A-C) in Yoredale

Diversity. The adults of YD engage in twenty-four varieties of social actions with the children of the town.

Dispersion. *A-C* actions that are widely dispersed among YD's settings are: *A* dominates *C* (93), manages *C* (80), devalues *C* (63), values *C* (50), disciplines *C* (48), is impatient with *C* (37), influences *C* (26), and provides opportunity for *C* (26).

Power. Adult power is pervasive in YD, and it is more generally strong than moderate or indirect. Strong *A-C* actions are, *A* dominates *C* (93), disciplines *C* (48), and punishes *C* (13); moderate and indirect actions are *A* manages *C* (80), influences *C* (26), provides opportunity for *C* (26), and asks favor of *C* (2). YD adults react to children's power as follows: *A* complies with *C* (9), surrenders to *C* (2), and resists *C* (2).

Harmony. *A-C* actions that foster disharmony are more widely dispersed than those that foster harmony. Disharmonious actions are, *A* devalues *C* (63), is impatient with *C* (37), is distressed by *C* (4), and teases *C* (2); harmonious *A-C* actions are, *A* values *C* (50), helps *C* (17), is friendly with *C* (13), enjoys *C* (4), and defends *C* (2).

MIDWEST VERSUS YOREDALE

Actions of adults toward children are more diverse, more widely dispersed, more powerful, and less harmonious in YD than in MW. With respect to diversity, there are twenty-four varieties of *A-C* action in YD and twenty-one in MW. Data on dispersion, power, and harmony are reported in Table 2. Seven

Table 2. *A-C* Actions More Widely Dispersed
in One Town Than in the Other

	A-C Actions	Difference in Dispersion $(MW_{PI} - YD_{PI})$
Actions more widely dispersed in MW	*A* influences *C*	+25
	A friendly with *C*	+15
	A manages *C*	+13
Actions more widely dispersed in YD	*A* provides opportunity for *C*	−12
	A punishes *C*	−13
	A values *C*	−20
	A impatient with *C*	−23
	A disciplines *C*	−41
	A devalues *C*	−40
	A dominates *C*	−60

A-C actions are more widely dispersed in YD than in MW and three of these (dominates, devalues, disciplines) are more widely dispersed by greater margins than any of the three *A-C* actions that are more widely dispersed in MW (influences, friendly, manages). Three powerful *A-C* actions (dominates, disciplines, punishes) and one moderate action (provides opportunity) are more widespread in YD than in MW, whereas two moderate *A-C* actions (manages and influences) are more widely dispersed in MW. Two disharmonious actions (devalues, impatient) and one harmonious action (values) are more widely dispersed in YD, whereas one harmonious action (friendly) is more widely disseminated across MW.

Actions of Children Toward Adults (C-A) in Midwest

Diversity. The children of MW engage in fifteen of the forty varieties of *C-A* actions.

Dispersion. Widely dispersed *C-A* actions are *C* complies with *A* (91), accepts control of *A* (56), and influences *A* (51).

Power. The power of MW's children vis-à-vis adults is very limited. Only *C-A* actions of moderate power occur, namely, *C* influences *A* (51), and asks favor of *A* (16); children react to adult power by yielding more generally than by resisting, thus: *C* complies with *A* (91), accepts control of *A* (56), resists *A* (9), disagrees with *A* (7).

Harmony. Actions of MW children fostering harmony with adults are not widespread, but they are present: *C* friendly with *A* (14), enjoys *A* (7); no disharmonious *C-A* actions are present.

Actions of Children Toward Adults (C-A) in Yoredale

Diversity. The children of YD display eleven varieties of action toward adults.

Dispersion. The *C-A* actions that are widely dispersed are *C* complies with *A* (87), accepts control of *A* (50), is polite to *A* (35), influences *A* (33), and resists *A* (22).

Power. YD children bring only a single moderately strong action to bear on adults, namely, *C* influences *A* (33); they react to adult power by yielding more generally than by opposing: *C* complies with *A* (87), accepts control of *A* (50), *C* resists *A* (22), and disagrees with *A* (9).

Harmony. YD children engage in three harmonious actions toward adults: *C* polite to *A* (35), helps *A* (15), enjoys *A* (15), and is friendly with *A* (11); there are no disharmonious *C-A* actions, but *C* polite to *A* (35) and *C* distant from *A* (4) may indicate latent disharmony and uncertainty.

MIDWEST VERSUS YOREDALE

$C\text{-}A$ actions are more diverse in MW than in YD (fifteen varieties versus eleven varieties). The data on dispersion presented in Table 3 show that the children of the towns differ

Table 3. $C\text{-}A$ Actions More Widely Dispersed
in One Town Than in the Other

	$C\text{-}A$ Actions	Difference in Dispersion $(MW_{PI} - YD_{PI})$
Actions more widely dispersed in MW	C influences A	+18
Actions more widely dispersed in YD	C helps A C resists A C polite to A	-13 -13 -23

little in the dispersion of their actions toward adults. However, $C\text{-}A$ actions that apply moderate direct pressure on adults are more widespread in MW (influences), actions strongly resisting adult power are more pervasive in YD (resists), and actions fostering harmony with adults are more widely distributed in YD (helps, polite to).

Actions of Children Toward Children (C-C) in Midwest

Diversity. The children of MW engage in twenty-seven of the forty varieties of $C\text{-}C$ actions.

Dispersion. Widely dispersed $C\text{-}C$ actions are C friendly to C (78), provides opportunity to C (73), enjoys C (69), plays with C (41), influences C (35), cooperates with C (29), helps C (25), manages C (23), disagrees with C (23), competes with C (23), accepts control of C (22), gratifies C (20).

Power. The most widely distributed actions of child to child in MW are those exerting indirect and moderate pressure, namely, C provides opportunity for C (73), influences C (35), and manages C (23); strong pressure occurs in only a single setting, C dominates C. Opposing and yielding to other children are almost equally pervasive in MW, namely, C disagrees with C (23), accepts control of C (22), and C resists C (8), complies with C (14).

Harmony. C-C actions that foster harmony between children are more pervasive than those that foster disharmony. The former are C friendly to C (78), enjoys C (69), plays with C (41), cooperates with C (29), helps C (25), gratifies C (20), values C (16), accommodates to C (4), defends C (4), comforts C (2); the latter are C competes with C (23), teases C (14), is impatient with C (12), devalues C (12), deprives C (8), is unfriendly with C (4), distressed by C (4).

Actions of Children Toward Children (C-C) in Yoredale

Diversity. The children of YD engage in twenty-nine of the forty varieties of social actions.

Dispersion. Widely dispersed C-C actions are C provides opportunity for C (67), is friendly with C (61), enjoys C (61), accepts control of C (57), helps C (35), cooperates with C (35), plays with C (31), complies with C (29), competes with C (29), manages C (27).

Power. Indirect and moderately strong power are widely distributed, namely, C provides opportunity for C (67), manages C (27), and influences C (18); however, strong C-C pressure is not missing: C dominates C (14). YD children reacted to the power of their child associates by accepting control (57) and complying (29) more widely than by resisting (18) and disagreeing (10).

Harmony. C-C actions that foster harmony are more pervasive than those that foster disharmony. The harmonious actions are: C friendly with C (61), enjoys C (61), helps C (35), cooperates with C (35), plays with C (31), values C (20), accommodates to C (8), gratifies C (6), defends C (2). The disharmonious C-C actions are: C competes with C (29), devalues C (20), is impatient with C (16), teases C (14), hinders C (14), unfriendly with C (10), antagonistic to C (10), deprives C (6), distressed by C (2).

MIDWEST VERSUS YOREDALE

Actions of children toward children are somewhat more diverse in YD than in MW, and a greater number of C-C actions are more widely dispersed in YD, particularly those that are powerful and disharmonious. There are twenty-nine varieties of C-C actions in YD and twenty-seven in MW. The data on dispersion reported in Table 4 show that eight C-C actions are more

Table 4. C-C Actions More Widely Dispersed
in One Town Than in the Other

	C-C Actions	Difference in Dispersion $(MW_{PI} - YD_{PI})$
Actions more widely dispersed in MW	friendly	+18
	influences	+18
	gratifies	+14
	disagrees	+14
	plays	+10
Actions more widely dispersed in YD	helps	−10
	resists	−10
	exploits	−10
	antagonistic	−10
	dominates	−12
	hinders	−14
	complies	−16
	accepts control	−35

widespread in YD and five in MW. Strong power between children is more pervasive in YD (dominates, resists) and moderate power in MW (influences, disagrees). Yielding between child and child is also more widely dispersed in YD (accepts control, complies). C-C actions that foster disharmony are more pervasive in YD (hinders, antagonistic) and harmonious actions are more widely distributed in MW (friendly, gratifies, plays).

Social Actions in American and English Fiction

Having discovered differences in the social actions occurring in the towns, we were confronted with the questions "How general are the differences? Are they limited to Midwest and Yoredale, or do they hold generally throughout America and England?" So we sought other, more general evidence of the social behavior of children and adults in America and England. Our familiarity with fiction for children in the two countries led us to look there. It was our impression that some classes of stories written by American and English authors for and about American and English children, respectively, make an effort to present child-adult and child-child relations realistically. By using samples of these classes of fiction, we would, in effect, let authors choose behavior settings and describe the behavior of the child and adult inhabitants. These data would have plus and minus features relative to the Midwest and Yoredale data: They would be less restricted and more general as to place, time, and characteristics of subjects and settings and the observations and records would not be subject to possible bias by the field station staff; but the universe they represent would be less well defined, the methods of the "observers" (the authors) would be unknown and impossible to duplicate, and the behavior settings within the American and English samples would not be matched for equivalence.

It appeared that a comparison of culture differences as revealed by the analysis of scientific and artistic observations and reports would be of value. The occurrence of similar differences in the two sets of data would show, on the one hand, that the Midwest-Yoredale differences were not peculiar to those towns and, on the other hand, that the American-English book differences were not divorced from the reality observed in the towns.

The following guides governed the selection of the sample of fictional narratives.

1. Books of fiction written by American authors, about American children, for American children, and books written by

English authors, about English children, for English children were inspected.

2. Only stories about "real-life" situations and experiences were retained; fairy stories, science fiction, animal stories were eliminated.
3. Historical books and books about children of other lands were excluded. The year 1930 was selected as the earliest publishing date to be included.
4. Stories written for particular, didactic purposes were eliminated; religious and political tracts, and books about vocations and limited social problems were rejected.
5. Only books whose "authenticity" had been demonstrated by a fair degree of popularity were included.
6. Books whose main characters ranged in age from seven to sixteen years were retained.
7. In order to avoid the biases of the investigators, nominations of books suitable for our purposes were secured from American and English library associations.

From the lists submitted to us by the librarians, a number were eliminated by applying the selection principles more uniformly and stringently than the librarians had been able to apply them; others were eliminated in order to secure roughly similar age distributions of the main characters. After these eliminations, we had eighteen American books by seven authors and eighteen English books by fourteen authors.

Behavior settings within the books were selected for analysis as follows: The total number of pages (X) in a book was divided into six equal parts. At the beginning of the second part, page $X/6$, we began reading until the principal character, or characters, entered a new behavior setting; this was marked as the origin of a segment of a "fictional specimen record." The place in the text where the locus of the behavior changed to another setting was marked as the termination of the unit. The same procedure was repeated beginning with page $2X/6$ and it was continued, similarly, to page $5X/6$. Five behavior settings were thus selected from every book, making ninety American and ninety English behavior settings.

The text of the story within each selected setting provided the specimen record that was inventoried for the 120 social actions in the same way that a MW or a YD record was inventoried. Here is an example of a record that reports the occurrence of the social action: *A affectionate with C* in the behavior setting school program. "Now there was no question of what Dot must do. She must recite the speech so well that the audience would remember her words long after they had forgotten what a failure she had almost been. She straightened her shoulders, stood her very tallest, and turned to face the audience. Her eyes looked straight into Mommy's, and Mommy nodded lovingly" (Friedman, 1967, p. 68).

A comparison of the dispersion of social actions across the behavior settings of MW and YD with their dispersion across the behavior settings of the American and English books revealed a marked similarity between the towns and the books. For example: A *influences* C has a PI of 51 in MW and 59 in the American books, A *disciplines* C has a PI of 7 in MW and 8 in the books. A *influences* C has a PI of 26 in YD and 32 in the English books, A *disciplines* C has a PI of 49 in YD and 40 in the books. Precise evidence of the extent of this agreement is provided by the product-moment correlations between the PIs from the towns and the books; these are, for the American and English data, respectively, .51 and .66 for *A-C* actions, .63 and .76 for *C-A* actions, and .66 and .81 for *C-C* actions. These are all statistically significant correlations and their magnitudes indicate that the dispersion of social action tends to be similar across the very differently selected samples of the behavior settings of America and England. In view of this, we have computed a single American and a single English general presence index (GPI) by treating the settings of the towns and the books as one sample. This index, obtained from the 141 American and the 141 English behavior settings, weighs the data of the towns less than the data of the books, inasmuch as the towns contribute 36 percent (51 settings) of the total samples and the books contribute 64 percent (90 settings) of the samples.

Social Actions in America and England

The five most widely dispersed varieties of *A-C, C-A,* and *C-C* action in America and England as indicated by the GPI are reported as follows:

ADULT-CHILD ACTIONS

In America, *A* influences *C* (56), manages *C* (53), friendly with *C* (41), dominates *C* (41), provides opportunity for *C* (39).

In England, *A* dominates *C* (79), devalues *C* (51), manages *C* (43), disciplines *C* (43), provides opportunity for *C* (41).

CHILD-ADULT ACTIONS

In America, *C* accepts control of *A* (70), complies with *A* (55), influences *A* (43), friendly to *A* (30), accommodates to *A* (26).

In England, *C* complies with *A* (66), accepts control of *A* (61), influences *A* (34), friendly to *A* (28), asks favor of *A* (26).

CHILD-CHILD ACTIONS

In America, *C* provides opportunity for *C* (71), friendly to *C* (62), accepts control of *C* (56), enjoys *C* (50), influences *C* (40).

In England, *C* provides opportunity for *C* (70), accepts control of *C* (69), friendly to *C* (52), cooperates with *C* (47), enjoys *C* (39).

America Versus England

We report below the social actions that are more widely dispersed in one country than in the other to an extent indicated by a GPI difference of 10 or more. The nature of each difference is explained in terms of the definition of the social action, and its extent is given in terms of the ratio of its American and English presence values.

ADULT-CHILD ACTIONS

American adults, in comparison with English adults, exercise routine personal influence over children—making requests, asking advice, giving suggestions—in 1.9 times as many settings (*A* influences *C*); they try to gain insight into the motives and circumstances of children's behavior—analyzing, probing, explaining—in 1.7 times as many settings (*A* understands *C*); they respond willingly to routine personal influences from children—answering requests, accepting advice, considering suggestions—in 1.4 times as many settings (*A* accepts control of *C*); they express liking for children in explicit ways—hugging, kissing, expressing devotion—in 1.3 times as many settings (*A* affectionate with *C*); and they use the authority that attaches to adult roles and greater competence—teaching, supervising, regulating, guiding—in 1.2 times as many settings (*A* manages *C*).

English adults, in comparison with American adults, exercise authority over children—scolding, admonishing, threatening physical action—in 12 times as many settings (*A* disciplines *C*); they are indifferent to children—unconcerned, inattentive, unaware—in 11 times as many settings (*A* distant to *C*); they make negative evaluations of children—deprecating, disapproving, belittling—in four times as many settings (*A* devalues *C*); they do not understand children—confused, without insight, uncomprehending—in three times as many settings (*A* baffled by *C*); and they use maximal pressure on children without threat of punishment—bossing, commanding, giving orders, making decisions—in 1.9 times as many settings (*A* dominates *C*).

CHILD-ADULT ACTIONS

American children, in comparison with English children, exhibit liking for adults—kissing, hugging, expressing devotion—in 3 times as many settings (*A* affectionate with *C*); they adjust their behavior to adults—trying to behave by the adult's standards—in 2.4 times as many settings (*C* accommodates to *A*); and they engage in verbal opposition to adults (disputing, arguing) in 2 times as many settings (*C* disagrees with *A*).

English children, in comparison with American children, are indifferent to adults—unconcerned, unaware, inattentive—in

7.5 times as many settings (C distant to A); they make negative evaluations of adults—deprecating, disapproving, belittling—in 4 times as many settings (C devalues A); they show proper forms of conduct to adults—courteous, well behaved—in 3 times as many settings (C polite to A); and they accept adult authority realistically—without enthusiasm—in 1.2 times as many settings (C complies with A).

CHILD-CHILD ACTIONS

American children, in comparison with English children, express liking for children—hugging, kissing, voicing devotion—in 7 times as many settings (C affectionate with C); try to understand the motives of children—analyzing, probing, explaining—in 2.5 times as many settings (C understands C); exercise routine personal influence over other children—making requests, asking advice, giving suggestions—in 1.6 as many settings (C influences C); are pleased to be with other children—laughing, being merry—in 1.3 times as many settings (C enjoys C); and they are congenial with children—welcoming, befriending—in 1.2 times as many settings (C friendly with C).

English children, in comparison with American children, dominated other children—bossing, demanding, giving orders—in 2.4 times as many settings (C dominates C); engage in joint actions—sharing responsibilities and rewards—in 1.6 times as many settings (C cooperates with C); obey other children willingly in 1.6 times as many settings (C accepts C's control); and accept the authority of other children realistically in 1.2 times as many settings (C complies with C).

Implications of the Study

This research bears on a number of methodological issues. First, it demonstrates the utility of specimen records in cross-national studies and the value of behavior settings as behavior sampling areas. Second, it provides empirical evidence of the value of fiction as a source of some behavior data.

The research raises the question of whether random samples of subjects are necessary for some studies of national behavior characteristics. It shows that within geographically and temporally circumscribed Midwest and Yoredale (with their limited varieties of people and environments) some attributes of the inhabitants' behavior are similar in relative pervasiveness to their pervasiveness among the much more varied inhabitants of the more widely dispersed and varied environments described in the American and English books. It appears that some currents of national culture that affect behavior flow strongly through even the smallest communities. One is reminded that for some diagnoses a physician only requires a single small specimen of tissue or fluid, and it appears that some properties of national behavior can be discovered in a single, small town.

There is evidence, some of which is reported in Chapters Seven and Eighteen and more in Barker and Schoggen (1973) that the American-English differences discovered in this research are deeply imbedded in the behavior setting structures of the towns. The greater pervasiveness in England of authoritarian A-C actions and submissive C-A actions appears basically to be a product of the English and American environments rather than of English and American personalities. In any case, we find that relations between children and adults in the two countries are congruent with the behavior setting arrangements that have other consequences, such as more leadership responsibilities for the old people of Midwest, greater security of tenure for the leaders of Yoredale, and greater busyness by residents of Midwest in the public settings of the town. These and other findings point to the view that the social actions of American and English children, adults, old people, leaders, and so forth are all manifestations of the different, dynamic habitat systems within which American and English people are essential components with prescribed positions and functions.

Maxine F. Schoggen
Louise S. Barker
Roger G. Barker

8

Behavior Episodes
of American
and English Children

In this study, we have sought to determine if there are differences in the *structural-dynamic* units of the behavior streams of the Midwest and Yoredale children that Barker and Barker investigated and found to differ with respect to *content* units (Chapter Seven). The same pairs of specimen records provided the data of the investigation, with these exceptions: For statistical reasons, it was necessary to eliminate (1) records in which

Abbreviated version of chapter entitled "Structure of the Behavior of American and English Children" in Barker (1963b, pp. 160-168).

there were fewer than ten behavior episodes in either one of a pair of records and (2) records in which the target children were identical with those in another pair. There remained thirty-nine pairs of specimen records, nineteen for girls and twenty for boys in each community. The records varied in length from 3 to 63 minutes; the average length was 29 minutes. There were 853 minutes of observation in Midwest involving 1131 episodes and 903 minutes of observation in Yoredale involving 771 episodes.

Spontaneity of Episodes

All episodes were judged in three categories with respect to their initiation, as follows:

1. *Spontaneous episode.* The action of the episode begins in the absence of any observed and reported environmental change; the action is initiated without evident dependence on active behavior objects.
2. *Instigated episode.* The action is seen to occur in response to some observable event or change in the situation, provided only that the event or change does not constitute pressure, as defined in Item 3.
3. *Pressured episode.* The action appears to begin as a result of external influence that is opposed to the child's momentary direction of behavior. In almost every instance the pressure comes from another child or an adult associate.

The percents of all episodes that received these ratings are, for Midwest and Yoredale respectively: spontaneous 55 and 38, instigated 43 and 55, and pressured 2 and 7. Midwest children produced relatively more episodes that were spontaneously initiated, and Yoredale children produced more with instigated or pressured initiations.

Termination of episodes was judged in the same way as their initiation. These are the results of the analysis for Midwest and Yoredale: spontaneous 83 and 75, instigated 16 and 20, and pressured 1 and 5. Again Midwest children produced relatively more episodes with spontaneous endings, and Yoredale produced more with terminations instigated or pressured by the environment.

The episodes of the Midwest and Yoredale children were partitioned into (1) those with spontaneous initiation and spontaneous termination (S/S); (2) those with spontaneous initiation and instigated or pressured termination, that is, with termination influenced by the environment (S/E); (3) those episodes with environmentally influenced initiation and spontaneous termination (E/S); and (4) episodes with environmentally influenced initiation and termination (E/E). The results, stated in terms of percents, are given in Table 1.

Table 1. Percent of Episodes with Certain Kinds of
Initiation and Termination Combinations for
Midwest and Yoredale Children

Subjects	N	Kinds of Initiation and Termination				
		S/S	S/E	E/S	E/E	CNJ
Midwest	1,131	48	6	29	14	3
Yoredale	777	34	7	30	27	2

A chi-square test indicates that the chance that the two distributions came from the same population with respect to initiation and termination combinations is remote; the probability is less than one in a thousand. The differences between the communities accrues almost entirely from the relatively greater frequency of completely spontaneous episodes (S/S) among the episodes of the Midwest children and from the greater frequency of completely nonspontaneous episodes (E/E) among those of the Yoredale children.

Episode Output

Midwest children produced 1.33 episodes per minute, Yoredale children 0.86 episodes per minute. The mean durations of the episodes were 0.75 minutes for Midwest children and 1.16 minutes for Yoredale children. Episode output was 55 percent greater in Midwest and episode length 55 percent greater in Yoredale. These differences are highly significant statistically.

Discussion

According to this study, certain structural and dynamic properties of the episodes within the behavior streams of Midwest and Yoredale differ, and they differ in ways that are in accord with the social content differences reported in Chapter Seven. In that research, it was discovered that strong social actions toward children are more pervasive in Yoredale than in Midwest. In the present study, where we turned our attention from actions toward children to the internal arrangements of the children's behavior streams, we find that external pressures (associates' social actions) are involved in the beginning and ending of more of Yoredale's than of Midwest's episodes. It may be that the greater incidence of external constraints produced the lower output and greater length of behavior episodes in Yoredale.

Phil Schoggen **9**

Environmental Forces on Physically Disabled Children

This is a study of similarities and differences in the social-psychological environments of children with and without physical disabilities in ordinary, everyday life situations. We wanted to know whether—and if so, in what respects—there are differences between children with and without physical impairments in the ways they are treated by parents, siblings, teachers, and friends in natural, real-life situations.

It is sometimes assumed that physical disability almost necessarily produces marked differences in the behavior of others toward the person with a disability. Children with disabilities especially are thought to receive treatment that differs in important ways from the treatment they would receive if they had no disability. Overprotection by adults and social rejection by children are frequently suggested as prominent features of the social-psychological environments of children with physical disabilities. But we do not know to what extent this is true. Autobiographical testimony of articulate persons with disabilities, certain theoretical arguments, and some clinical evidence support such a generalization. But scientifically adequate evidence is both extremely limited and inconsistent. Studies at the Midwest Field Station involving direct observation of children with and without physical disabilities in ordinary everyday life failed to support the common expectations (Barker and Wright, 1955). The behavior and environmental conditions of the children studied appeared not to vary systematically with the presence or absence of physical disability except on a few selected variables. And even these few differences had to be offered in a tentative way, because the number of cases was extremely small and because the children with disabilities were not well matched with nondisabled children. It was this marked discrepancy between the expected results and the actual findings that called so urgently for new and better data.

This study is based primarily on the field theoretical approach of Kurt Lewin as applied to the psychology of disability by Barker and others (1953). Disability is viewed as a phenotypical phenomenon that has no simple, direct relation to behavior and personality but that does have potential for modifying behavior in two important ways. First, disability can modify the instrumental value of physique—can change the adequacy of the person's physique for carrying out important activities leading to significant goals. We saw an example of this in our study when Patrick, a fourth-grader whose right foot was carried in a sling as a result of Perthes disease, asked a teammate to stand by while Patrick was at bat in order to run for him to first base in case he got a hit—which, incidentally, he often did. Although Patrick could play ball, he could not gather up his crutches after batting and make it to first base ahead of the throw except on unusually long hits, so he asked for help because his physique was inadequate as an instrument for achieving a goal important to him.

Secondly, disability can modify dramatically the social stimulus value of physique—can change the way in which the person is seen by others and by the person himself. Patrick's teammate was happy to do this small favor for him, but only because he knew of Patrick's physical limitation. Because of his disability, Patrick was seen as deserving special treatment. One can readily imagine the dispatch with which such a request would be rejected were it to come from a nondisabled child. Changed social meaning stemming from physical disability was apparent also in the case of Danny, who, although his age and disability were the same as Patrick's, was seen by his teacher as too severely disabled to play regular ball. She kept him standing on the sidelines watching or at best permitted him to catch or to serve as umpire. In such instances, it is clear that the child's social-psychological situation is markedly influenced by the meaning that his physique carries for others.

The present study extends this conception of the psychological significance of physique and disability to the investigation of the nature of the socialization process of disabled and nondisabled children. The fundamental question is whether the social-psychological living conditions of children with physical disabilities differ in systematic ways from those of comparable nondisabled children. The answer to this question appears to have value in improving our understanding of (1) the social-psychological significance of physical disability, (2) the socialization process more generally, and (3) the ways in which behavior and naturally occurring environmental factors are interrelated.

Methodology

Basic data for this study are specimen records of fourteen children in the six- to ten-year age range, seven of whom had clearly visible peripheral motor impairments. These children were located through the assistance of public school nurses, principals, and teachers. Of the five boys, three used crutches because one leg was immobilized in a sling due to Perthes disease, one showed a slight limp due to residual paralysis from polio, and one had the right leg amputated below the knee, requiring crutches or a prosthesis. One of the two girls was confined to a wheel chair by muscular dystrophy, and the other wore a partial prosthesis to correct for residual foot and leg damage from accidental injury. All the conditions had been stable for one year or more, and the children had no other complicating conditions such as sensory impairment or central nervous system involvement. The children were of average intelligence, were regular students in public schools, grades 1 through 4. Each child lived with his natural parents and siblings in a normal home. The fathers were all regularly employed as semiskilled wage earners, small business managers, or salesmen.

We have used a matched-pairs design in which each of the seven children with a disability was matched with another child as much like him as possible in all other respects except that the matching child had no disability. In every case, the matching nondisabled child was in the same classroom in school and was of the same sex. With the help of the classroom teacher in each case, we matched the children as closely as possible on other variables of known importance, such as age, intelligence, socioeconomic status of the family, and family structure.

Our procedure included initial talks with each family, the child himself, and the classroom teacher. Here we discussed openly the aims, purposes, and methods of the research and gave a demonstration of our observational equipment. A similar demonstration was given in each of the seven classrooms before any observations were made, but here the child subjects were not identified nor did we specify our interest in children with disabilities. Then followed two or three—sometimes more— "adaptation observations" in the home or classroom to enable the observers to become familiar with the situation and the persons in it, as well as to give these persons a chance to get used to having an observer present before observations were made for the permanent record. While we are not so naive as to think that the behavior we observed in these homes and schools was unaffected by the presence of the observer, we are reassured by the rapid disappearance of "company manners" and the ease with which these children, their classmates, teachers, and families, came to accept the observer in his role as an interested but nonparticipating bystander who wanted nothing more than to be ignored.

Because we wanted data that would be reasonably representative of the ordinary social-psychological living conditions to which the children were exposed, our design called for making observations on each child in relatively free and more structured behavior settings both at home and at school. At home, the observations were scheduled for free play activities, usually in the late afternoon or early evening or at mealtimes when there would be a good chance that the entire family would be present. At school, we aimed to make observations in free-time activities, and in academic periods such as reading recitation or English workbook exercises. In selecting these situations, our hope was to obtain a good sampling of the social action directed toward our subjects by parents, teachers, and friends. Each observer made matching observations. For example, after making an observation of one child of a pair in "reading recitation" on one day, the same observer would try to make an observation of the other member of the pair in the same activity within the next few days. The observations lasted on the average about twenty-five minutes each, and two, and in some cases, three, observations were made on each child in each situation. (See Table 1 for data on number of observations.)

Previously developed procedures for the identification of the child's behavior episodes were adapted to the task of utilizing environmental action with respect to the child. A method for unitizing environmental action was devised that is analogous to the behavior episode methodology, and the resulting units are called *environmental force units* (EFU). Each unit is labeled with a brief descriptive title, the first word of which identifies the environmental agent, usually a person, who is the source of the action. A reading of the consecutive EFU titles from a record gives an impression of the kinds of action that the child's environment took with reference to him during the period covered. Here, for example, are the titles of the first few environmental force units in the record of a four-year-old girl (S means *subject*):

1. Mother: Getting S to Bible School on time (8:00 a.m.).
2. Mother: Questioning S about cold.
3. Mother: Getting S dressed.

Table 1. Number of Observations, Total Time, and Number of EFUs in Home and School Settings

Pair	Name	Home Settings				School Settings			
		Number of Observations	Total Time Hours-Minutes	Total Number of EFU	Rate: EFU/Minute	Number of Observations	Total Time Hours-Minutes	Total Number of EFU	Rate: EFU/Minute
1	Nick	5	1 - 59	225	1.89	6	2 - 18	188	1.36
	Steve	6	2 - 26	207	1.42	6	2 - 39	165	1.04
2	Patrick	6	2 - 36	199	1.28	6	2 - 16	117	0.86
	Ed	6	2 - 18	303	2.20	6	2 - 19	175	1.26
3	Dan	6	2 - 9	271	2.10	6	2 - 51	140	0.82
	Sammy	6	2 - 9	223	1.73	6	3 - 2	160	0.88
4	Harry	4	2 - 0	279	2.33	4	1 - 14	140	1.89
	Ernie	4	1 - 35	149	1.57	4	1 - 37	113	1.16
5	Robert	4	2 - 7	245	1.93	4	1 - 41	125	1.24
	Stanley	4	1 - 43	185	1.80	4	2 - 12	104	0.79
6	Libby	4	2 - 16	148	1.09	4	1 - 58	78	0.66
	Marge	4	1 - 44	188	1.81	4	1 - 31	72	0.79
7	Loreen	4	1 - 15	137	1.83	4	2 - 3	179	1.45
	Doreen	4	2 - 28	191	2.17	4	1 - 56	221	1.90

4. Mother: Chatting with S about hair curls.
5. Mother: Teasing S affectionately.
6. Observer: Commenting on S's hair curls.
7. Mother: Answering S's question about observer.
8. Mother: Feeding S breakfast.
9. Mother: Cautioning S to sneeze courteously.
10. Mother: Asking S to turn down radio.
11. Observer: Responding to S's comment.
12. Mother: Asking S to cover mouth when coughing (8:25 a.m.).

An environmental force unit is defined as *an action by an environmental agent* that (1) occurs vis-à-vis the child, (2) is directed by the agent toward a recognizable end state with respect to the child, and (3) is recognized as such by the child.

From this definition, it is clear that this study is concerned only with *units of environmental action.* We include only the observable and successful attempts made by the agents of the environment to penetrate the child's psychological world. Inactive parts of the environment, environmental action that is not directed to the child, and unsuccessful attempts to "contact" the child are not included.

Not all actions of agents that are directed toward the child occur vis-à-vis the child. Often an agent will do something for the child, something directed to the child but not in the child's immediate presence; for example, a mother bakes cookies for the child to have when he comes in after school. On the basis of both practical and theoretical considerations, we elected to eliminate all such action from the present study and to focus only on those actions that occurred vis-à-vis the subject.

It is obvious that a great deal of what goes on around the subject, much of the environmental action reported in the record, is not directed toward the subject. Such action is not included in the present study. Unless the agent is trying at least to communicate with the child, either individually or as one of a group, we are not here concerned with his action. Thus, for example, a conversation between two parents would not be marked as an environmental force unit, provided that neither parent directs action to the child.

The third part of the definition of an environmental force unit states that the action of the agent that is directed toward the child must also be recognized as such by the child. Unless the agent is successful in penetrating the child's psychological world—getting his attention at least long enough to communicate his intention—his action is not included as an environmental force unit. No matter how vigorous the attempt by the agent, it is not marked as a unit unless there is some evidence that it registers on the child. We did not wish to include influence attempts of which the child was not aware. Rather, we have hoped to focus our analytical efforts on and to include *all* of the active environmental forces in the immediate situation of the child that are directed toward the child and that are successful at least to the extent of being recognized by the child.

The second step of our analytical process involves classifying or categorizing each EFU on a number of descriptive variables intended to measure qualitative aspects of the active social environment of the child. For this study, a special rater's guide was developed that included a careful definition and a set of examples for each of the eighteen descriptive variables included in the analysis. Studies of agreement between independent analysts yielded median agreement percents ranging upward from 83 percent.

A detailed report on the results of describing each of the EFUs in terms of all of these eighteen variables is presented elsewhere (Schoggen, 1964). Here we limit ourselves to a brief summary of some of the most interesting findings.

Like most studies in the behavioral sciences at the present time, the variables in which we are interested in this study can be measured in only relatively crude, primitive ways. The variables were necessarily rated only in terms of qualitative classifications or at best in terms of scales that indicate only greater-than or less-than measurements corresponding respectively to nominal scales and ordinal scales. With such weak levels of measurement, only nonparametric statistics are appropriate. For many of the comparisons of children with and without physical disabilities on the variables used in this study, the Wilcoxon matched-pairs, signed-ranks test is especially well suited. This test, which utilizes information about both the direction and the magnitude of the differences within pairs, is the most powerful test that is appropriate for use with our data.

Results

Turning now to the results of the analysis of these specimen records, Table 1 presents results of the EFU unitization process in terms of the number and rate of occurrence of EFUs identified in the records of each subject in home settings and in school settings. The table also shows the number of observations and the total behavior time observed and reported in the specimen records.

Frequency of EFUs. Three findings of significance are apparent in the figures on rate of EFU occurrence. First, the intrapair differences between children with and without physical disabilities are neither consistently large nor in one direction. This is true both at home and at school. Admittedly, simple rate of EFU occurrence is a gross measure incapable of showing possible differences of a qualitative sort or differences among types of associates such as teachers, classmates, parents, and siblings. Still, it seems significant that in general the social environment of these children with visible physical impairments appears to be neither more nor less stimulating and responsive to the child than that of the nondisabled matching children. The data in this table provide no support for the proposition that the social environment of children with physical disabilities tends in general to be either oversolicitous or rejecting and indifferent.

Second, it is clear that the rate of EFU occurrence is consistently lower at school than at home. This is true for both members of every pair—the median is about one EFU per minute at school and nearly twice that rate at home. We assume that this difference reflects the effectiveness of the restrictions on social behavior common to most of the school settings. Nevertheless, it is impressive to have evidence that, even in the relatively restrictive environment provided by the school settings, someone directed a purposive action to the child subject on the average once every minute.

This clear difference between the home and school situations on a rate of EFU occurrence gives added significance to the lack of difference between members of each pair on this measure; that is, a method that is capable of detecting the difference in situations can be expected also to detect differences associated with disability. Taken together, then, these two findings suggest that the analytical method used is sensitive to real differences and that rate of EFU occurrence is associated with the situation in which the behavior occurs but that it is not associated with physical disability of the child who is the object of the agent's directed social action in the EFU.

A third finding may be mentioned. In every case, save one in which the difference is negligible, the direction of the difference between members of a pair is the same for both home and school situations; that is, if the rate is higher for the child with a disability than for his nondisabled match in the one situation, it is also higher for him in the other. These consistencies provide evidence that the method of EFU analysis is sensitive to differences in the social environments at the level of individual subjects.

Selected Agents as Sources of EFUs. Going beyond these gross comparisons, we present in Table 2 data on the percent of EFUs in home and school settings with selected agents and classes of agents of special interest. In the home settings, data are shown in separate columns for mother, father, siblings, all adults, and all children. Inspection of these columns for consistent intrapair differences reveals only a trend toward higher percents with siblings for the children with disabilities, but this trend does not reach statistical significance. Even so, these data suggest that these children with disabilities, as compared with the nondisabled subjects, were not ignored or isolated and rejected by their siblings or, for that matter, by all children as a class in the home situation. The data on adults similarly show no consistent intrapair differences, suggesting that mothers, fathers, and all adults as a class in the home settings are neither more nor less stimulating and responsive to children with dis-

Table 2. Percent of EFUs in Home and School Settings with Selected Agents

Pair	Name	Home Settings						School Settings		
		N	Mother	Father	Sibs	All Adults	All Children	N	Teacher	Children
1	Nick	225	31	32	36	63	36	188	46	54
	Steve	207	49	20	8	77	17	165	56	43
2	Patrick	199	30	16	24	46	52	117	26	74
	Ed	303	30	15	16	45	55	175	15	85
3	Dan	271	45	8	26	53	47	140	21	77
	Sammy	223	17	4	30	21	78	160	11	89
4	Harry	279	28	10	61	38	61	140	27	73
	Ernie	149	20	10	68	30	68	113	44	55
5	Robert	245	42	6	51	48	51	125	70	30
	Stanley	185	55	10	34	65	34	104	61	39
6	Libby	148	35	11	25	53	44	78	29	71
	Marge	188	62	15	22	78	22	72	39	61
7	Loreen	137	46	7	36	60	37	179	38	60
	Doreen	191	28	5	33	34	67	221	37	63

abilities than to nondisabled children. Here again we find no evidence of oversolicitousness by adults in relation to children with disabilities.

Mother-Child EFUs. Because of the unique importance of the mother and the great interest in current research on the mother-child relationship, we have examined more closely our data on the rate of occurrence of EFUs in which the mother was the agent. For this purpose, an analyst examined each specimen record and counted the number of minutes in each that the mother was actually near enough to the child subject to permit any sort of social transaction between them. These figures totaled across all the records on any one child in the home settings and divided by the total time observed in these settings is a measure of how much time the mother made herself available to the child during the observational periods. For example, Nick's mother was available to him—in the same room or near enough to talk with him—for 90 of the 119 minutes of observed behavior in the home settings. Thus she was a potential EFU agent 76 percent of the time.

The first finding from this study was that there was no difference between the mothers of children with disabilities and the mothers of nondisabled children in the proportion of total time observed in which the mother was available to the child. There was a trend toward higher proportions for mothers of children with disabilities, but it did not approach statistical significance.

The second finding from this special analysis concerns the rate of occurrence of EFUs with the mother, using only the time the mother actually was available to the child rather than the total time observed. It is a somewhat more refined measure of the extent to which the mother reached out or responded to the child during the observations. These data reveal no consistent intrapair differences. In four of the seven pairs, the rate is actually higher for the mother of the nondisabled child. Here, then, is one important aspect of the social-psychological environment that is not related to physical disability in our data: Mothers, and probably all adults at home, direct social actions neither more nor less frequently to children with disabilities than to nondisabled children.

Teacher-Child EFUs. In the school settings, the data for teachers show no consistent intrapair differences, suggesting that the number of EFUs directed toward a child by the child's classroom teacher is a function of a number of factors peculiar to his individual situation and is not associated consistently across children with the presence of visible physical impairment in the subjects of this study.

As a further test of the data on teachers, rates of EFU occurrence were computed for teachers following the procedure described for mothers, that is, using as a base the total time the teacher actually was available to the child during the observational periods. The results showed no consistent intrapair differences on either the amount of time the teachers were available or on the rate of EFU occurrence. We conclude, therefore, that in our records teachers, like the mothers, did not direct social actions toward children with disabilities either more or less frequently than to nondisabled children. There is nothing in these data on number of EFUs and rate of EFU occurrence to indicate that these mothers and teachers encouraged dependent behavior in the children with disabilities.

Overprotection of Children with Disabilities by Adults. Although little is known about the kinds of treatment children with disabilities actually receive from adults in ordinary, everyday life, there are indications that overprotectiveness, oversolicitousness, "pampering," and the encouragement of dependency on adults are thought to be more common in the behavior of parents and teachers of children with disabilities than is the case with nondisabled children.

Several of the measures used in the present analysis provide evidence relevant to this question, and the bulk of this evidence points to the conclusion that these children with disabilities received no more "overprotective" behavior from adults than did their nondisabled counterparts.

Number and Rate of Adult Contacts. We would expect that overprotectiveness by adults and the encouragement of dependency of a child on adults would be reflected in the number and frequency of adult contacts with the child; that is, adults would tend to be relatively more prominent features of the child's world as a result of the adult's wish to supervise, manage, and direct the child's activities. In our data (Tables 1 and 2), however, we find no intrapair differences of this sort that are consistent across the seven pairs. The result is the same whether the measure used is percent of all EFUs that are with adults, rate of EFU occurrence with adults, amount of time in which the mother or the classroom teacher makes herself available to the child, or rate of EFU occurrence with the mother or the teacher in relation to the available time: Differences between children with and without disabilities on these measures, in our data, are essentially random. To us, this is very strong evidence indeed that these children with disabilities were not subject to strong overprotective behavior by the adults that count most in their lives, particularly mothers and teachers.

Beyond these findings on the quantity and frequency of adult contacts with children, the same conclusions are generally supported by other data (Schoggen, 1964) derived from describing a number of qualitative aspects of the social actions directed to the children by mothers and teachers, who were the most frequent associates of the children in nearly every case.

Individual Attention by Adults. Overprotectiveness virtually requires the singling out of the child for special, individual attention to the child alone. Mothers of children with disabilities showed only a weak tendency in this direction, and teachers showed none at all.

Adult Intrusion. A common picture of the overprotective mother is one in which the mother frequently "butts in" on what the child is doing, either to redirect the child's behavior or to give the child "help" that he may or may not need. Mothers and teachers of children with disabilities in our data showed weak tendencies in this direction, but the intrapair differences were not statistically significant.

Adult Devotion. Another characteristic of overprotective adult behavior is the conviction on the part of the adult that he is acting in the interest of the child, either to make him happier at the time or to benefit him in the long run. The overprotective parent, in his own view, is the model of selfless interest in the welfare of the child. Our data on mothers and teachers of children with disabilities again show weak trends toward more frequent behavior of this type, but they are not statistically significant.

Preferential Treatment by Adults. Along with the propensity for giving the child help that he may not need, our prototypical overprotective adult is likely to spare the child some of the demands made on other children to take responsibility for a share of the routines of everyday living, such as helping with household chores. Special exemption may also be given from participation in activities that other children accept as a matter of course. Preferential treatment may take the form of fewer requirements being placed on the child to carry out some specific action. Our findings on this measure, however, show that mothers of children with disabilities tended to place such demands on their children more—not less—frequently than do other mothers, but this difference is not statistically significant, nor do teachers differ in this respect. Again, therefore, we find evidence that does not support the notion that children with disabilities are overprotected.

These, then, are the several measures in the present analysis of the social-psychological environments of children with and without physical disabilities that appear to be most closely related to the question of overprotectiveness in the behavior of adults. On most of these measures, there are no consistent intrapair differences, and the few weak trends toward differences that were found are not statistically significant.

Isolation and Rejection of Disabled Children by Other Children. It is widely assumed and there is some, largely indirect, evidence that social isolation and rejection are common in the experience of many children with disabilities. We have been keenly interested, therefore, in determining the extent to which this assumption would be supported in our data. Several measures in the present analysis appear to bear on this question, and in general they reveal no significant support for the contention that social isolation or rejection was common to the subjects with disabilities.

Other Children as Sources of EFUs. In our judgment, one of the best of our measures is found in the percentages of EFUs that occurred with siblings and other child associates. Over an extended period of time, social isolation almost necessarily includes avoidance of the person by those who reject him and a resulting reduction in the number of social actions directed to him. Therefore, if our subjects with disabilities are social isolates, we should find lower percents of EFUs in which other children are the environmental agents. But this is not the case. Considering siblings alone as EFU agents, the trend actually is toward higher percents for children with disabilities. While this trend is not strong enough to be statistically significant, it does suggest at least that siblings of these children with disabilities do not ignore and avoid them. The data for all child agents (siblings and friends) at home and classmates at school reveal no trends toward consistent intrapair differences. On this measure, therefore, the evidence is quite clear: There is no suggestion of isolation or rejection of children with disabilities by siblings or child friends.

Distribution of EFUs Across Other Children. We have been interested also in analyzing our data on identity of primary agent for information on how the EFUs with the subject's child friends at school were distributed. Even though the subjects with disabilities had about as many EFUs with children at school as did the nondisabled subjects, there could still be consistent differences in the patterns of distribution. For example, if the children with disabilities were less well accepted by their schoolmates, their social transactions might tend to be concentrated on one or two special friends in contrast to the nondisabled subjects, for whom a more even distribution of EFUs over several good friends would presumably be typical.

But we have been unable to find any support for this possibility. The children with disabilities did not have fewer child associates, and there was no tendency for the EFUs of children with disabilities to be concentrated in a few child friends whether one looks at the data on all child agents or on only the child agents with the highest percents of the EFUs of the subject. There is no discernible difference in the distribution of EFUs for the children with disabilities as compared with their nondisabled counterparts.

Individual Attention by Other Children. Another measure

of interest in relation to this question is the frequency with which children singled out the subject for special, individual attention. If such singling out occurs with disproportionate frequency, it may mean, coming from children, that the target child is not considered one of the group, that he requires special consideration. The results show no significant intrapair differences but do show a trend toward fewer instances of such singling out of children with disabilities at home and more at school. If our interpretation is correct, this suggests that these children with disabilities were accepted less well at school than at home by other children. Much more corroborative evidence would be needed, however, before such a conclusion would be warranted.

Benefits from Other Children. Rejection of the subject should also be apparent in the results on the intended beneficiary of the agent's directed social action in the EFUs with child agents. We would expect lower percents of EFUs intended by the agent for the benefit of the subject when the subject is someone the agent does not like. But we find no consistent intrapair differences of any kind in the data on this variable.

Conflicts with Other Children. Concerning the frequency of conflict between the subject and the child agents in the EFUs, cogent arguments could be put forward for expecting either higher or lower percentages of conflict EFUs in the case of children with disabilities. But nothing is to be gained by doing so, because the data show no consistent intrapair differences in either direction.

Extensive Participation by Other Children. Another measure, however, which we consider to be crucial to the question of isolation and rejection of children with disabilities, is the frequency with which child agents engage in extensive participation during the course of the EFU with the subject. EFUs placed in this subcategory, when the agent was another child, most frequently involved a joint activity that extended over some appreciable time, such as playing a game or working on a joint project in school. If such sharing in mutually enjoyable activity can be regarded as a sign that the subject is "accepted" by the agent, then we can expect the number of such EFUs to be relatively low for subjects who are social isolates. If this is reasonable, then we must conclude that our data on this variable provide no support for the contention that these subjects were not well accepted among their friends—there are no consistent intrapair differences on this variable either at home or at school.

Other variables could be discussed, but none can be used to support the notion that these children with disabilities were rejected by their child friends at home and at school, because no significant intrapair differences were obtained on any of them. We are left, then, with virtually no evidence from this analysis suggesting that our subjects with disabilities were any less well accepted socially than their nondisabled counterparts.

Differences Between Situations. In contrast to the largely negative findings on the two questions of special interest just discussed, our data show a number of clear differences between different situations in the characteristics of the social-psychological environments of the subjects. We will now summarize the main differences found in comparing the results of analysis of EFUs in three situations: home mealtime, home free time, and school.

The rate of occurrence of EFUs was consistently higher at home than at school: On the average, EFUs occurred nearly twice as fast at home. This same difference, only slightly less clear, was apparent in the comparison of the rates of EFU occurrence for mothers and teachers. Social actions were directed to the subject alone more frequently at home than at school, reflecting a greater amount of individual attention given to the children at home, and, as one would expect, mothers did give children more individual attention than did teachers.

Environmental agents intervened in the subject's ongoing activity more frequently in both home settings than at school. Conflict between the subject and the EFU agent was more frequent at home than at school. Extensive demands were made on the subjects much more frequently in the school settings, which probably reflects the work of the teachers in making assignments and directing class activities. Negative feelings expressed by the EFU agent to the subject and by the subject to the agent were more frequent at home than at school. Finally, EFU agents were more frequently unsuccessful in achieving their goals in EFUs in the home settings than in school settings.

Each of these differences is statistically significant at the 1 percent level of confidence. It seems to us that they are important for two reasons. First, in view of the failure of this analysis to identify consistent intrapair differences in the ways children with and without disabilities are treated in ordinary, everyday life situations, it is reassuring to find that the same analysis does reveal marked differences in predictable directions in the ways children are treated in the different situations, because this demonstrates that the method of analysis is sensitive to real differences. Therefore, we may have more confidence in the negative findings on intrapair differences than would otherwise be the case.

These intersetting differences also seem important; however, they are so in a more substantive sense, because they point to the need to measure in more precise terms situational determinants of differences in the child's social-psychological environment and behavior. Everyone knows, of course, that the school and home situations are quite different, but little is known in psychologically meaningful terms about the dimensions on which these differences would appear nor about how extensive they in fact are. The findings of the present study join those of a number of other investigations (for example, see Barker, 1968; Barker and Gump, 1964; Barker and Schoggen, 1973; Gump, Schoggen, and Redl, 1957) in pointing to the importance of situational factors. Our findings suggest that situational factors are more important than the presence of physical disability of the child in determining how he is treated by his child and adult associates.

Conclusion

We cannot generalize from these seven children to all children with disabilities. Had it been possible to double the number of pairs studied, we could have a great deal more confidence in the trends apparent in the data. However, children with disabilities cannot be produced as in an experiment. The data we have been able to secure have been placed in archives at the University of Kansas and are available to be added to other data when the latter are collected. It is one of the characteristics of ecological data of all sorts that nature provides them, often in limited amounts and at a particular place and time.

There are reasons for having considerable confidence that the impressively consistent failure of these data to reveal any important differences in the ways children with and without physical disabilities are treated by their everyday associates is a true reflection of reality. Our personal experience based on extensive direct contact with the subjects is that disability was not a particularly potent determinant of the quality of social action directed to these children. It appeared to be, rather, only one aspect of the relatively complex social stimuli provided by the child to his associates. The behavior of others toward these children appeared to be determined by the total complex of personal attributes, of which physical disability was only one small part. The child friends and adults who interacted with one of these children appeared to be responding to the whole child as a person, and the fact of physical disability seemed to be virtually disregarded or at most to play a very minor role. This one characteristic of disability seemed to the associates of these children to be embedded in the larger context of all the child's personal qualities. They were not responding to a "crippled child" but rather to Nick and Patrick or Libby, as persons who, almost incidentally, had a physical disability.

If this interpretation seems hard to accept, let us remind you that we were observing children with disabilities in ordinary, everyday situations at home and at school where they were intimately or at least well known to nearly all other persons with whom they came into contact. Moreover, in every case the disability was a stable characteristic of some duration—everyone who knew the child was familiar with his physical limitations. There was nothing novel about Robert's prosthesis, Libby's wheelchair, or Danny's sling and crutches. They were scarcely more noticeable than Ed's bright blue eyes and blonde hair, Margaret's freckles, or Sammy's horn-rimmed glasses.

Under these circumstances, the focus of an associate's attention shifts from the superficial characteristics of physical appearance to deeper, more important traits of personality and behavior. It is possible that observational studies have a nearly unique advantage in being able to tap really natural behavior of others toward persons with disabilities. Perhaps interviews, questionnaires, and attitude tests can hardly avoid giving an inaccurate picture, because they almost necessarily isolate disability as an abstraction or focus attention artificially on disability as the characteristic of special interest or importance. Even sociometric studies, which may be free from this type of distortion, often measure only hypothetical choices that may be quite different from the actual behavior of the respondent.

Our findings agree with other lines of evidence that there is no necessary relation between the simple fact of physical impairment and important characteristics of the social-psychological environment of the person, and we believe they create an obligation to examine very closely indeed the basis on which claims are made that parents and teachers of children with disabilities "resort to unusual, ill-defined procedures" (Jordan, 1962) in raising handicapped children.

The dramatic differences in our results between different situations in the characteristics of social actions directed to the subjects also urgently call for further study. From these data, it appears that the number and the qualitative aspects of environmental forces impinging on the child are clearly related to the situation in which they occur. Obviously, therefore, it is a matter of primary importance, both theoretically and in terms of practical implications, to explore these relations much more extensively. More precise definition and measurement of situations together with better assessment of intersituation differences in important variables of social behavior hold the promise of eventually making possible the prescription of particular types of situations to meet the needs and capacities of children with or without disabilities for exposure to particular kinds of social-psychological environment.

Clifford L. Fawl **10**

Disturbances Children Experience in Their Natural Habitats

◆◆◆◆◆◆◆◆◆◆◆◆◆◆◆◆◆◆◆◆◆◆◆◆◆◆◆◆◆◆◆◆◆◆◆◆◆◆

This is a study of incidents experienced as disturbing by children in their natural habitats. We have aimed to discover how common, how intense, and how long these disturbing incidents are. Since some disturbances obviously are socially evoked, we have attempted to evaluate the role of other people as causal factors in the disturbance of children, distinguishing between adult and child associates, and in some analyses, between mothers and fathers. In addition, we have hoped to gain at least a rudimentary notion of the various psychological determinants of disturbance.

The background for the present investigation was a study

Reprint, with some omissions, of chapter by the same name in Barker (1963b, pp. 99-126).

of the frustrations occurring in the natural habitat of children. "Goal blockage" was employed as the working definition of frustration. The results of the study were surprising in two respects. First, even with a liberal interpretation of blockage, fewer blocked goals were detected than we expected (mean, 16.5 per child for an entire waking day). Second, frustration defined as goal blockage usually failed to produce an apparent state of disturbance on the part of the child. Meaningful relationships could not be found between blockage, analyzed in several respects, and consequent behaviors, such as aggression, regression, sublimation, disturbance, and other theoretically relevant behavioral manifestations. The data indicated, moreover, that many incidents that were experientially disturbing had been omitted by the goal-blockage approach. Therefore, since blockage evidently was neither a sufficient nor necessary condition for producing a state of disturbance, we decided to restructure our orientation to focus on experientially disturbing incidents per se.

The Concept of Disturbance

In keeping with the reorientation of the research, disturbance was conceptualized as an unpleasant disruption in the ongoing feeling tone of immediate awareness, evoked by, and in reference to, a discernible event or situation.

Following is an incident taken from one of the records employed in this investigation, which illustrates disturbance as here defined: As Roy was standing in line at the drinking fountain, Geoffrey came up from behind him and with considerable vigor swatted Roy on the back with the palm of his hand. Roy turned around, faced his assailant. He looked somewhat hurt and angry. Certainly Roy had done nothing to Geoffrey. As soon as Geoffrey saw Roy's expression, he dashed into the toilet room. Roy gave immediate chase.

The source of data for this study were twelve day-long specimen records of Midwest children.

Instructions for identifying disturbances provided descriptive evidence that raters were to consider as indicative and as not indicative of disturbance. We emphasized in these instructions that disturbance was to be regarded as a *behaviorally inferred* construct of experiencing. Criteria were provided for identifying disturbances, their duration, and their intensity.

Frequency of Disturbance

As indicated earlier, one of our principal aims was to gain some perspective as to how commonly disturbance occurs in the everyday lives of children. Children can be expected to differ considerably in this respect as a function of both situational and personality variables, and so the twelve subjects of this investigation cannot be considered representative of the universe of children. But to know the number of disturbances experienced by even a few children represents a step forward from the almost total ignorance now existing.

The data for the Midwest children are presented in Table 1

Table 1. Frequency of Disturbances Occurring in the Days of Midwest Children (Subjects Arranged in Order of Increasing Age)

Subjects	Total Number of Disturbances in Day	Average Number of Disturbances per Hour
Preschool subjects		
Mary C.	143	11.39
Jimmy	30	2.68
Lewis	119	10.60
Dutton	94	7.32
Margaret	86	5.97
Maud	90	7.52
Preschool mean	93.67	7.58
School-age subjects		
Roy	75	5.58
Ray	58	4.28
Ben	32	2.56
Mary E.	57	3.94
Douglas	27	1.90
Claire	18	1.26
School mean	44.50	3.25
Midwest mean	69.08	5.42

Note: Disturbances for which the observer was primarily responsible have not been included in the frequencies. Seventy-nine disturbances, or 6 percent of the grand total of 1,330, were excluded on this basis.

and Figure 1. They show that these children experienced a daily average of 69 disturbances, at the rate of 5.4 disturbances per

Figure 1. Frequency of Disturbance in Days of Midwest Children with Respect to Age, Sex, Social Class of Family, and Number of Siblings

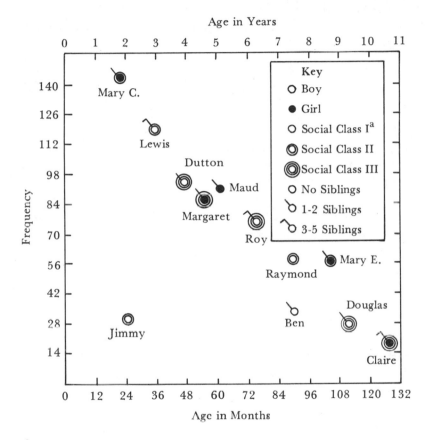

[a]See footnote for Table 3, Chapter Six.

hour. The data show, too, that the children varied considerably in number of disturbances. The range of daily totals was from 18 to 143, and the standard deviation of the individual totals was 39.2.

Much of the variability among subjects in Midwest was related to the age of the child. Preschool children had an average of 93.67 disturbances, compared to 44.50 for the school children. The nonparametric Mann-Whitney statistic for independent samples indicates that this difference between age groups is statistically significant at the .026 level of probability. (Since this is not a theory-oriented study with specific predictions, two-sided statistical tests have been employed throughout.) Expressed in terms of a rank-order correlation coefficient (Spearman's rho), the age of the child was correlated $-.73$ with the number of disturbances occurring during the day ($p = .01$). Age and frequency per hour of disturbance were correlated approximately the same: rho $= -.76$.

One explanation for the drop in frequency of disturbance with age is that only the older subjects were within the protective and restrictive setting of the formal classroom a large proportion of the day. Two findings indicate that something other than the classroom setting must be operative, however. In the first place, if we analyze for disturbance only those portions of the day in which each child was at home, we still find a negative correlation between age and frequency of disturbance; rho $= -.70$. Secondly, as Figure 1 suggests, there was a tendency for the frequency of disturbance to fall with age when comparing subjects within each age group as well as between age groups.

Frequency of disturbance was not related to the sex of subject, to the number of siblings present on the day of the observation, or to the social class of the child's family. This fact is apparent from inspection of Figure 1 where each subject is identified with respect to the variables mentioned.

Intensity of Disturbance

Each incident of disturbance was judged as either mild, moderate, or strong in intensity. For some analyses, disturbances judged to be mild in intensity were assigned a weight of 1; moderate disturbances, 2; and strong disturbances, 3.

By and large, the disturbances experienced by Midwest subjects were mild in intensity. Of all 829 Midwest disturbances, 61.7 percent were rated mild, 35.1 percent moderate, and only 3.2 percent strong. The mean of the average intensity rating for the Midwest children was 1.37.

The mean frequency rates of disturbances of each degree of intensity are presented in Table 2. The rate of occurrence

Table 2. Rate of Occurrence of Disturbances of Different Degrees of Intensity: Mean Number of Disturbances per Hour for Midwest Children

Subjects	Intensity Rating		
	Mild	Moderate	Strong
Preschool subjects	4.50	2.82	0.26
School-age subjects	2.15	1.01	0.10
All Midwest subjects	3.32	1.91	0.18

was lower for the older subjects at each intensity level. The difference between age groups in the rate of mild disturbances was significant at the .02 level of confidence; in terms of rank-order correlation, the hourly rate of mild disturbances was inversely related to age: rho = $-.74$ (p = .01). The frequency rate of disturbances of moderate intensity was less definitely higher for the preschool subjects than for school-age subjects (p = .064); the correlation with age was $-.57$ (.576 required for significance at the .05 level of confidence).

There were few disturbances of strong intensity, and their frequency was not clearly related to age of subject. If we combine as one figure those disturbances that were greater than mild in intensity, the correlation with age was $-.57$.

The average disturbance intensity per child was not related to his age; the means were 1.38 for the preschool children and 1.35 for the school-age group. The rank-order correlation between age and mean intensity rating was $-.37$; this falls well short of statistical significance.

Duration of Disturbance

Duration judgments were trichotomized as brief (less than one minute), medium (one to three minutes), and long (greater than three minutes). The duration refers to the span of time over which the subject was judged to be actually disturbed; it does not refer to the duration of his concern regarding the evoking referent of disturbance.

Weights of 1, 2, and 3 were assigned to disturbances that were brief, medium, and long, respectively, and the average weighted duration of the disturbances was determined for each subject.

The vast majority of Midwest children's disturbances (88.1 percent) were less than one minute in duration. A few (10.9 percent) were between one and three minutes, and very few (1.0 percent) were longer. The mean duration rating per disturbance per child was 1.14.

The data of Table 3 show that the frequency of each range of duration was greater for preschool than for the older subjects.

Table 3. Rate of Occurrence of Disturbances of Different
Durations: Mean Number of Disturbances per Hour
for Midwest Children

	Duration Rating		
Subjects	Less than One Minute	1-3 Minutes	Longer than Three Minutes
Preschool subjects	6.85	0.68	0.07
School-age subjects	2.75	0.48	0.04
All Midwest subjects	4.80	0.58	0.05

Only with respect to the brief disturbances, however, was the difference statistically significant ($p = .016$). The rank-order correlation between age and frequency rate of brief disturbances was $-.76$ ($p = .01$). When the frequencies of all disturbances greater than one minute in duration are combined, we find that age and the frequency rate of these longer disturbances were correlated $-.52$; this is slightly short of the .576 required for significance at the .05 level of confidence.

Social Determinants of Disturbance

Here we turn to those disturbances in whose evocation another person clearly had a role—was the "causal source," if you will. In these cases, another person was the referent of the child's disturbance or was in some way identified with the referent. An example of a disturbance of the latter type would be a boring, unpleasant lesson that was required by the teacher. Excluded from this section are disturbances in which we judged that the referent of the disturbance was the child himself, a physical object, or physical conditions (for example, the prospect of rain when a picnic was being planned), or an animal.

Obviously, the frequency of socially evoked disturbances for a particular child is in part a function of the frequency of his social interaction: The more often the child is in contact with other people, the more opportunity there is for socially evoked disturbances. To take this factor into account, we have employed a rather rough measure we call the "D/EFU index." Following Schoggen (1963), we have used the frequency of environmental force units (EFU) as a measure of the child's degree of social interaction. The D/EFU index is the ratio of the frequency of disturbances to the frequency of environmental force units. One can think of the index as the *number of disturbances per social interaction.* The index is employed to reflect in one figure the relation between disturbance frequency and social interaction frequency for a subject.

Most disturbances were evoked by another person; for 72.4 percent of all disturbances another person was the referent or was closely implicated with the referent. Socially evoked disturbances outnumbered nonsocially evoked disturbances in the case of every Midwest subject. This unanimity far exceeds chance expectation ($p < .01$, by sign test). The proportion of a child's disturbances that were socially evoked was independent of his age, but the mean rate per hour was related to age; the older the child, the lower the rate of socially evoked disturbances, rho = $-.72$ ($p < .01$). Schoggen's discovery (1963) that the number of EFUs decreases with the age of the Midwest subjects suggests a declining opportunity for socially evoked disturbances to take place. Nevertheless, when we take the interaction frequency into consideration by means of the D/EFU index, we find that the older the child, the lower the frequency of disturbances per social interaction, rho = $-.578$ ($p < .05$). This amplifies the earlier findings that the age of the child was negatively related to the frequency of his disturbances.

Social disturbances were more intense than nonsocial disturbances; the means of the average intensity ratings were 1.39 for social disturbances and 1.29 for the nonsocial disturbances. This difference, although not great, is significant at the 5 percent level of confidence as determined by Wilcoxon's matched-pairs signed-ranks test. Social disturbances were more intense for five of the six preschool children and for three of the six school children.

The average duration of social disturbances was greater than the duration of nonsocial disturbances for nine of the twelve subjects, but the differences tended to be very small. Wilcoxon's test does not reveal a significant difference.

Adult and child associates of our subjects differed in the roles they played as evokers of disturbances. The data of Table 4 show that adults evoked a far greater percent of the distur-

Table 4. Percent of Disturbances Evoked by Adults, by Children, and by Both Adults and Children (Midwest Children)

	Evokers of Disturbance		
Subjects	Adults	Children	Adults and Children
Preschool subjects	55.2	18.3	73.5
School-age subjects	32.8	37.4	70.2
All Midwest subjects	47.8	24.6	72.4

bances of preschool children than did child associates but that by school age adult and child associates were essentially equivalent in the extent to which each was the source of disturbance. Percent frequency of adult-evoked disturbances declined with age, rho = $-.77$ ($p < .01$), and percent of child-evoked disturbances increased with age, rho = $+.77$ ($p < .01$). The data of Table 5 show that the findings with respect to hourly rate of disturbance differ from the results just given in only one respect: The rate of child-evoked disturbances did not increase with age of child. That the percent of child-evoked disturbances was higher for school-age subjects than for preschool subjects,

Table 5. Rate of Occurrence of Disturbances Evoked by Adults
and by Children: Mean Number of Disturbances per Hour for
Midwest Children

Subjects	Evokers of Disturbance		
	Adults	Children	Adults and Children
Preschool subjects	4.10	1.37	5.53
School-age subjects	1.04	1.21	2.25
All Midwest subjects	2.57	1.29	3.89

even though the absolute number of child-evoked disturbances
was lower, is, of course, due to the fact that the number of disturbances in general for school-age children was very low.

The fact that adult-evoked disturbances were especially
common among preschool subjects is related to the fact that the
preschool children had more social interactions with adults than
with other children. Schoggen's EFU analysis (1963) revealed
that 73 percent of the EFUs of the preschool children were
with adults and only 23 percent with children. For the school-
age children, 50 percent of the EFUs were with adults and 50
percent with children. When we use the D/EFU index, the resulting picture as given in Table 6 is revealing: The D/EFU

Table 6. Number of Disturbances per Social Interaction
(D/EFU Index) with Child Associates and with Adult Associates
(Midwest Children)

Subjects	Evokers of Disturbance		
	Adults	Children	Adults and Children
Preschool subjects	.123	.184	.135
School-age subjects	.085	.099	.093
All Midwest subjects	.104	.142	.114

index was significantly higher for EFUs involving child associates than for EFUs involving adult associates ($p < .05$). In
other words, the Midwest children had more disturbances per
social interaction with children than with adults. This was especially true at the preschool level; in this case the D/EFU index

was higher for all six of the children. With both child and adult associates, the D/EFU index tended to drop with the age of the child, although only for child associates was the correlation significant, rho = $-.62$ ($p < .05$). Thus, the older the subject, the fewer were the disturbances per interaction with other children.

Disturbances evoked by children differed little in intensity from those evoked by adults, and with neither associate was intensity of disturbance related to the age of the subject.

Disturbances evoked by adults tended to be slightly longer than those evoked by children; the mean duration ratings were 1.18 and 1.07, respectively. This difference barely misses significance at the .05 level of confidence. There was some tendency for adult-evoked disturbances to be longer for the school-age children than for preschool children; the difference in the mean ratings was 1.24 and 1.12 ($p < .08$). The correlation between mean duration of adult-evoked disturbances and age of child was $+.66$ ($p = .02$). No age relationship was found for duration of child-evoked disturbances.

The mother evoked more disturbances than the father in every case where both parents were present on the day the record was made; this difference is significant beyond the .01 level of confidence by Wilcoxon's matched-pairs, signed-ranks test. Mothers evoked, on the average, 3.37 disturbances per hour of preschool children, and 0.54 per hour of school children; the mean hourly rate of father-evoked disturbances was 0.43 for preschool children, and 0.15 for school children. However, the D/EFU index revealed no significant difference between mothers and fathers in disturbances per unit of social interaction, and none of the analyses contrasting the D/EFU index for parents of the same sex with parents of the opposite sex produced significant differences.

Father-evoked disturbances were more intense than those evoked by the mothers for ten of the eleven subjects whose parents were both present ($p < .01$); however, the intensity differences were not great, the mean ratings being 1.65 and 1.33 for father- and mother-evoked disturbances, respectively. On the other hand, the duration of disturbances evoked by mothers and fathers did not differ, and there were no differences in the frequency, intensity, or duration of disturbances evoked by parents of the same sex in contrast with those evoked by parents of the opposite sex.

Psychological Determinants of Disturbance

One of the purposes of the study was to determine the causes of disturbance, the "causal types" as they will be called. Causal types of disturbance occur at different levels of explanation, and we have attempted to deal with a single level, namely with the *contemporaneous* causes of disturbance on a *psychological* level.

Goodenough (1931) recognized the importance, and also the difficulty, of specifying the "immediate causes" of anger outbursts in young children. We would consider her classification of immediate causes to be "nonpsychological." For instance, one of her classes was "routine physical habits," which included "going to toilet," "washing face, bathing, combing hair, brushing teeth, dressing," and "objection to specific kinds of foods." Inselberg (1958), on the other hand, mixed nonpsychological with psychological or quasi-psychological categories; for example, "medical and dental care" along with "conflict with children." The different orientation of our effort to type causes of disturbance should be evident in the presentation below.

Various causal types of disturbance were empirically identified before they were given conceptual formulation. The conceptualizations of Lewin (1935) and of Heider (1958) influenced these formulations, although the types were not derived from them. From Lewin, emphasis on goal-directed behavior, and the concept of force in particular, were found to be useful. Force, being a key concept in the formulation of several causal types, requires formal definition. Leeper (1943, p. 208) has succinctly summarized Lewin's concept of force as "a hypothesized variable, or construct, conceived as the immediate determinant of the locomotions [actions] of a person." Every force has a direction, which is an important consideration in the present analysis. A force serves to move the subject toward or away from something specific. Force also has magnitude and point of application. In our classification, we have spoken of force only when the point of application was the child or something pertinent to the child's specific goal (the path to the goal and the goal itself in Lewin's life space analysis).

The technique for symbolically describing a subject's perception of a situation is borrowed from Heider (1958). Application of Heider's concise statements often enables one more easily to get at the essentials of a description. The notations used and their meanings are:

    ch . . . child
    C . . . causes
    not C . . . does not cause
    W . . . wants
    WC . . . wants to cause
    TrC . . . tries to cause
    S . . . suffers, experiences, undergoes
    x, y . . . specific entities, things, situations
    (+) (−) . . . positive (pleasant) negative (unpleasant)

A colon (:) is to be translated as the conjunction *that*. See Heider (1958, pp. 299-300) for further clarification.

Imposition is another key term we have employed that requires comment. By imposition, we have reference to something that is thrust on the child or that confronts the child not by choice of the child. This something can be an act of another person or simply physical conditions not produced by the child. Baldwin (1955, p. 142) defines impositions as those events that are "the results of the actions of someone else or of natural processes." Functionally, we have used the term when the child has attributed the cause of his disturbance to foreign factors.

Seven causal types of disturbance were identified in the records. These were interference, failure, imposed driving force, choice conflict, offending imposition, own act, and psychological loss. The types are presented below in the form employed in the analysis of each of the 1,251 disturbances of the seventeen subjects.

Interference. Either (1) an imposed force operates in a direction diametrically opposed to the one in which the subject is striving; or (2) an imposed incident or situation, not necessarily operating as a force, serves to impede, or hinder, the subject's ongoing goal-directed behavior. Neither the absolute magnitude of the interference, its magnitude relative to the subject's own force, nor its duration enter into the determination of this type.

$$\text{Symbolically:} \quad \text{ch WC } x, \text{ but}$$
$$\text{imposition C: ch not C } x.$$

(This statement may be read: "The child wants to cause something or do something, but some foreign factor [person or thing] causes that the child *not* do or cause the desired act.")

Examples: (1) Margaret wanted to enter the house, but the door was locked; (2) Verne had to wait until the girls had left the bathroom before he could enter; (3) Dutton wanted to continue playing with his sister, but she wanted to stop; and (4) A conversation taking place in the classroom interfered with Roy's recitation.

Failure. Failure to attain or maintain to the subject's satisfaction a goal accepted by the subject is attributed by him to his own inadequacies. The failure need not be complete or permanent.

$$\text{Symbolically:} \quad \text{ch WC } x, \text{ but}$$
$$\text{ch C: ch not C } x.$$

Examples: (1) Wally O. wanted to climb a certain tree, but he failed to reach the first branch even though his little brother had been successful; (2) Douglas shot an arrow that fell short of the mark; and (3) Claire had great difficulty getting the correct answer to an arithmetic problem.

Imposed Driving Force. A force is applied to move the subject *toward* a specific region (activity) by someone or something other than the subject himself. Whether or not the subject yields to the force is of no consequence. Also, it is of no consequence for the identification of this disturbance type whether the disturbance is in reaction to the application of the force or to the anticipated negative valence of the region toward which the child is being forced. (When an imposed force *toward* a specific region also operated as a restraining force opposing the subject's own force, the imposed driving force rating took precedence [see Example 3]. In one sense, if we assume continuous purposivism, *all* imposed driving forces are interferences; that is, every imposed driving force interferes with something already going on, yet we consider it to be important to distinguish between those incidents where the foreign agent is perceived as driving subject *toward* or *away* from a region.)

Symbolically: imposition C: ch C x, or
imposition TrC: ch C x.

Examples: (1) Maud was told to pick up her toys; (2) Douglas was assigned a lesson that was very boring to him; and (3) Mary E. was having a good time playing outside and did not want to stop when her mother called her to supper.

Choice Conflict. Mutually exclusive forces acting on the subject present a situation in which a movement in any direction has negative consequences, either directly by leading the subject toward an activity of negative valence, or indirectly by leading the subject away from an activity of positive valence.

Symbolically: ch WC x, but also
ch not WC x; or

ch WC x, but also
ch WC y; or

ch not WC x, but also
ch not WC y (forced choice).

In each of the above cases, x and y are assumed to have different directions in the Lewinian sense of direction.

Examples: (1) Douglas was momentarily confused when he started in the direction of the boys' restroom and remembered that the observer was a woman; (2) Mary C. became disorganized when she could not decide what to play.

Offending Imposition. This refers to actions or conditions or situations, impinging on the subject or on a personal belong-

ing, that are not determined by the subject and that are disturbing in their own right rather than as a result of the effect that
they might have on the subject's ongoing goal-directed behavior.
The marking of this causal type is not dependent on the hostile
intention of the offender or on the subject being the intended
target of the offending action (see Example 4 below).

Symbolically: imposition C: ch S −x.

Examples: (1) Roy was annoyed by a slap on the back he
received while standing in line at the drinking fountain; (2)
Wally W. was chagrined by his cousin's criticism of a remark
Wally made; (3) Lewis was both disgusted and embarrassed by
the presence of cow dung in the adjoining field; and (4) Raymond was disturbed by the way another boy treated a dog.

Own Act. The subject performs an act that he himself
negatively evaluates; or the subject attributes the cause of his
disturbance to an impact with the environment brought about
as a consequence of his own, not necessarily intended, act. The
impact is disturbing in its own right rather than as it relates to
the subject's ongoing goal-directed behavior. If there is evidence
that the subject places the blame on the environment, then the
incident is judged as "offending imposition" rather than "own
act."

Symbolically: ch C −x, or
ch C: ch S −x.

Examples: (1) Margaret regretted that she had been hostile toward her little brother; (2) Lewis rolled off the davenport
and hurt himself slightly; and (3) Jimmy accidentally stuck himself with a pin.

Psychological Loss. Something valued by the subject no
longer exists, or if it still exists there has been a sharp drop in its
value. Emphasis is on the lost or damaged object itself rather
than on who or what might be responsible.

Symbolically: +x followed by
no +x.

Examples: (1) Lewis entered the room to find that his toy gun had fallen apart; (2) Roy had hoped to listen to his favorite radio program, but it was already over when he arrived home; and (3) Maud was quite anxious when she thought that her mother was going to leave the house.

The number and percent of each type of disturbance are given for Midwest children in Table 7; data are given for all chil-

Table 7. Distribution of the Disturbances of Midwest Children
among Causal Types of Disturbance

	Causal Types							
Subjects	Inter-ference	Fail-ure	Imposed Driving Force	Choice Con-flict	Offend-ing Imposi-tion	Own Act	Psycho-logical Loss	Can-not Judge
Number of Disturbances								
All sub-jects	281	64	153	2	191	57	39	22
Percent of Judged Disturbances								
Preschool sub-jects	41.3	5.7	19.8	0.2	18.5	8.4	6.1	
School-age sub-jects	24.4	13.0	18.7	0.4	35.9	4.9	2.7	
All sub-jects	35.7	8.1	19.4	0.3	24.3	7.2	5.0	

dren and for the younger and the older children separately. These data show that there were a substantial number of each causal type except choice conflict. We were unable to analyze, for a variety of reasons, about 3 percent of the disturbance units.

Three causal types predominate: interference, offending imposition, and imposed driving force. Together they account for roughly three quarters of all disturbances. A greater percent of the older than of the younger children's disturbances were offending imposition and failure types (the rho correlations with age are +.68 and +.65, respectively); the reverse was true of interference, psychological loss, and own act (the rho correlations with age are $-.82$, $-.78$, $-.70$, respectively). Imposed driving force was unrelated to age.

Table 8 provides data regarding the mean hourly rate of each causal type for all subjects, and for the two age levels. The

**Table 8. Rates of Occurrence of Causal Types of Disturbance:
Mean Number of Disturbances Per Hour for Midwest Children**

Subjects	Inter-ference	Fail-ure	Imposed Driving Force	Choice Con-flict	Offend-ing Imposi-tion	Own Act	Psycho-logical Loss
Preschool subjects	3.01	0.42	1.47	0.01	1.36	0.62	0.45
School-age subjects	0.79	0.41	0.59	0.01	1.15	0.16	0.09
All subjects	1.90	0.42	1.03	0.01	1.26	0.39	0.27

rates for interference, offending imposition, and imposed driving force were higher than for the other types and are therefore in accord with the data of Table 7. Furthermore, the mean hourly rate of occurrence of interference, psychological loss, and own act declined significantly with age (rho correlations with age are $-.77$, and $-.80$, and $-.80$, respectively). The rate of imposed driving force decreased also, but not significantly; whereas failure, choice conflict, and offending imposition showed virtually no tendency to decrease in rate with age.

The tendency and duration of interference, failure, imposed driving force, and offending imposition were analyzed for all subjects. The other disturbance types did not occur with sufficient frequency for an overall analysis. A Friedman two-way analysis of variance of ranks revealed that neither intensity nor duration varied significantly among the four types. And no sizable differences in intensity or duration were found between the two age groups with respect to the four causal types.

Discussion

The most characteristic disturbance of Midwest preschool children was mild in intensity, lasting only a few seconds; it

164

resulted from an interference by the mother. For the school-age children, the most characteristic disturbance was an offending imposition imposed by a child associate; it was mild in intensity and of less than a minute in duration. It is of some significance, we think, that so substantial a number of disturbances was not connected in any way with ongoing, goal-connected behavior. All subjects considered, offending imposition was the second most common causal type, and for school-age children it was the most common type. In identifying this particular type, we have done nothing more than indicate that certain events or situations can be intrinsically disturbing. We have not spelled out the perceptual conditions under which the event or situation is found disturbing. However, our findings indicate that the occurrence of nongoal-related disturbances is sufficiently common to justify intensive investigation of their conditions. Since so many of this type of disturbance involve other people, Heider's analysis of commonsense interpersonal perception appears to be useful (Heider, 1958, p. 17). Undoubtedly the perception of intentionality, for example, is important. If someone steps on your foot, your reaction, and especially the likelihood that you will be disturbed, is influenced by whether you perceive that he intended to do so. Informal study of this problem has revealed that intentionality is but one variable among many, however, and that it is neither a sufficient nor necessary condition for a disturbance reaction. Commonsense variables seem to us to be a profitable aid to further inquiry.

Adult associates evoked more disturbances than child associates. Adults in our society, especially mothers, are the responsible environmental agents for directing the behavior of children, and this is a consuming job, especially in the case of preschool children. It is our impression that this role accounts for both the high frequency of interactions with children and the high number of adult-evoked disturbances. However, child associates evoked more disturbances per interaction. This may mean that child associates provided a more antagonistic social environment than adult associates. We use the word *antagonistic* rather than *hostile,* since child-evoked disturbances were not more intense than adult-evoked disturbances. A truly more hos-

tile environment would be the source of more intense disturbances as well as more frequent disturbances per interaction.

By virtue of her much greater contact with the child, the
mother was in the position of accounting for more of the child's
disturbances than was the father. However, the father, when in
interaction with the child, was almost as likely as the mother to
evoke a disturbance. But there was this difference: When the
father was responsible for a disturbance, it tended to be more
intense. In fact, it was so in fourteen of the fifteen cases analyzed. Why this should be is not clear. It did not seem to matter, so far as the evocation of disturbances was concerned,
whether the parent was of the same or the opposite sex as the
child. All in all, differences between mothers and fathers as they
related to the child were not as great as we had anticipated.

That a relationship between age and emotional behavior
exists seems fairly certain on the basis of several other observational studies of children as well as this one. Goodenough
(1931) and Ricketts (1934) each report that the frequency of
anger incidents decreases with age; Blatz, Chant, and Salter
(1937) and Inselberg (1958) report a drop with age in the
occurrence of "emotional episodes." These findings raise an
interesting theoretical question, namely, does the relationship
between age and frequency of disturbance represent a developmental change in the psychological characteristics of the child,
or does it reflect a change in the role of the environment as the
child matures, or both?

Probably all theories of child development allow for
changes occurring within the child *and* for changes in the role of
the environment impinging on the child as he grows older. In
1963, it was a truism to state that the child is a component in a
social system and that changes in the child affect changes in the
child's social environment, and vice versa. So, when we oppose
person-centered and environment-centered explanations of the
age-disturbance relationship, we do not imply that one can
argue one position to the exclusion of the other. Rather, we
wish to point to differences in the emphases of the person-
centered and environment-centered orientations. The positions
considered represent divergent ones that *can* be taken; they

are not necessarily positions that *have* been taken by theo-reticians.

From the person-centered point of view, the child be-comes less vulnerable to disturbing experiences as he grows older; he becomes less sensitive to, or more tolerant of, negative incidents. Changes occur within the child in a personality sense as well as physically and intellectually. These changes can be thought of as changes in the dynamic structure of the child's personality.

Lewin's (1935) theory of the inner personal development of the child can be used to illustrate the person-centered orien-tation, keeping in mind that Lewin also recognized the impor-tance of social factors for psychological understanding. Follow-ing Lewin, we can think of the person as a system of needs represented by topological regions. Briefly, development can be characterized in part as involving the following changes within this system: an increasing differentiation of needs (more re-gions), an increasingly definite demarcation between the self and nonself (a more rigid boundary for the system as a whole), and increasingly greater articulation among needs (boundaries separating regions less permeable, more rigid). These changes are illustrated topologically in Figure 2 where the younger and older child are compared.

One of the consequences of the process outlined is the

Figure 2. A Topological Representation of the Need System of a Younger Child and an Older Child (after Lewin, 1935)

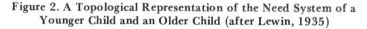
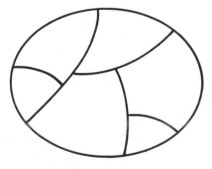

Younger Child   Older Child

distinction between central and peripheral needs or regions. Impinging stimuli can be thought of as having less access to the central regions of the older child due to the presence of intervening regions and to the lesser permeability of all boundaries. Assuming that an experience of disturbance is directly related to the involvement of the central needs (regions) of the person, it follows that the older child is better buttressed against disturbing stimuli. Disturbances would be expected to be not only less frequent for the older child (as was found) but also less intense (as was detected to only a slight degree). An additional expectation would be that the disturbances of the older child would be longer in duration (as was found), since the greater impermeability of boundaries would make it more difficult for tension to dissipate.

The fact that so many of the disturbances were evoked by other people urges us to consider the merits of an environment-centered orientation. Here we think in terms of the social psychology of disturbance. It is assumed that the child undergoes change with age from this point of view also. As he matures physically, he requires less guidance from other people. As a creature capable of learning, he comes to realize what is encouraged and what is discouraged by his culture. In short, he becomes socialized. We do not need to assume, following this orientation, that the dynamic structure of the child's personality undergoes change. Rather, the decrease in frequency of disturbance can be seen as a function of the older child being more in tune with his environment: He is disturbed less often because he has fewer conflicts with the environment. Especially appropriate from this point of view is the finding that interference and imposed driving force disturbances decrease sharply with age, since each implies conflict with the culture. Again, however, not all findings are so clearly in line with the environment-centered contention. The longer duration of disturbance in the case of the older child is not as easily explained here as by the person-centered theory, for instance.

Speculation regarding the relative merits of the two orientations is profitable only up to a point. The data necessary for further consideration of the issue are not available. We need a better basis on which to calculate the role actually played by the environment in life situations. We need to know, for example, how often children *do* encounter interference by their environment. Knowing this, we would be much closer to answering the important question "Does the older child have fewer interference disturbances than the younger child because he is *more tolerant of interference* or because he is *interfered with less often* by his environment?" If the older child truly is more tolerant of interference, then we should expect that the percentage of environmental interferences resulting in disturbance would be lower for him than the younger child. If, on the other hand, it is not a question of tolerance level but rather a case of less environmental interference for the older child, then the percentage of interferences resulting in disturbance should not be substantially different for the older and younger child: The one third as many interference disturbances that we observed for the school-age child would be based on one third as many interferences by the environment.

We have not succeeded in covering all facets of the problem we have outlined. Clearly, though, there seems to be a need for further ecological investigation. An important theoretical issue is at stake, namely, the conceptualization of child development itself. The relationship of ecology to theory has not always been stressed, but it nevertheless exists. Not only is the field situation a fruitful source for the origin of hypotheses, but, as exemplified in the theoretical question raised in the present study, it also is occasionally preferable to the laboratory as the vehicle for evaluating them.

Edwin P. Willems
Lauro S. Halstead

11

An Eco-Behavioral Approach to Health Status and Health Care

The purpose of this chapter is to describe the application of some of the principles and techniques of ecological psychology to the real-world problem of rehabilitation for persons with spinal cord injuries. In our program of research and demonstration, the development of new clinical tools goes hand in hand with our attempts to understand eco-behavioral relationships. Thus, we are involved in applied ecological psychology, and we wish to share our conviction that it has direct bearing on problems of health status and health care. After giving some background on spinal cord injury and rehabilitation, we will describe some of our procedures and present some illustrative data. For the interested reader, more detail is presented elsewhere (Halstead, 1976; Willems, 1976a; Willems and Campbell, 1975; Willems and Halstead, in press).

The Problem of Spinal Cord Injury

During each day and within the life span of the individual, various processes of adaptation lead to the development of a repertoire of behavioral performances in the everyday environment. This repertoire is part of the substance of everyday life and is critical to survival, but it is usually overlooked by the healthy person because it is taken for granted. Onset of a severe physical disability, such as spinal cord injury, eliminates or alters this repertoire, and the person's major means of coming to terms with his everyday environment is impaired, often drastically.

Just as the everyday repertoire of performances is taken for granted by the healthy person, so does he take for granted many features of his environment. With the onset of a severe physical disability, the person's environment suddenly becomes formidable, intimidating, and in some cases, insurmountable. Thus the central problems of rehabilitation cluster around performance and environment. Rehabilitation comprises programmatic arrangements designed to restore or substitute as much as possible in a person's lost or altered repertoire, to teach him new forms of performance and new kinds of relations to the environment, and to alter environments in appropriate ways. The goals of rehabilitation are usually stated in terms of performance or behavior; for example, "to help the person become maximally independent." Independence is a behavioral issue because it points to performances that the person can carry out in his usual environment with a minimum of intervention and support from others. In these terms, rehabilitation means intensive and goal-oriented addition, rearrangement, and substitution in the client's repertoire of behavior and behavior-environment relations.

In addition to being heavily oriented toward functional performance, the perspective and focus of rehabilitation must also be longitudinal. The evolution of the disabled person's repertoire of performance often occurs gradually over time, but the transition to resettlement in the world outside the hospital is not one event—it is also a gradual process and sometimes a lengthy one. Much of the person's time and effort is devoted to carrying out functions and procedures he has been taught, and his well-being depends on his ability to apply and practice what he has been taught. Thus, the rehabilitation process is a very long one, extending for months or years. Given the importance of what the disabled person does and uses in his everyday environment over a long period of time, it follows that assessment of his status at any given time and his progress or regression over time should focus on his actual performance.

While in the hospital, the patient's behavior is like a continuous stream that sometimes damps down to a minimal level and sometimes quickens to a very brisk pace, sometimes widens or even splits into several simultaneous occurrences and sometimes narrows to one, sometimes intertwines with the behavior of others and sometimes moves in isolation, sometimes changes form or direction at the patient's initiative and sometimes at the instigation of others. Each of the discrete events in that stream occurs at some unique place and time, and yet the stream as a whole flows in a continuous, sequential manner, over time. The interface between the patient's behavior stream and the hospital's delivery system is fundamental to the understanding of a hospital. The planners and the agents of a hospital's delivery system assume that their environmental provisions and their role performances are intimately intertwined with patient behavior; if this was not so, there would be no reason to create systems of rehabilitative care. This means that a careful look at patient behavior and its environmental linkages will tell us a great deal about how a hospital system is functioning; that is, patient behavior is an important criterion of hospital performance and effectiveness.

Rehabilitation of persons with spinal cord injuries thus represents a fruitful arena within which to study the microecology of human behavior, for several reasons. First, the aftermath of spinal cord injury is an intensive microcosm of the ontogeny of behavior-environment relations. In a very real sense, the spinal cord-injured person is thrust back to an earlier developmental point because of a catastrophic loss. Second, since persons with spinal cord injuries spend relatively long periods in a hospital setting, working out problems of performance and adaptation within the rubric of goal-oriented programs, the period of hospitalization is a period of densely packed and evolving behavior-environment relations. Third, since the conceptions of behavioral ecology relate so closely to the idealisms of rehabilitation, and since so little has been known about the development of performance in relation to the environment in persons with spinal cord injuries, the rehabilitation profession needs research of this type.

Within the complex demands of rehabilitation, one of the most important problems is the assessment of how the patient is doing over time. Paradoxically, the principal methods developed over the years to assess performance reflect patient function in nearly static terms. Many traditional measures in rehabilitation evaluate a predetermined set of skills under relatively standardized conditions. Such measures emphasize performance on demand in a test situation over a short time interval. By the nature of their methodology, such techniques either measure capacity (or what a patient *can* do in response to a known, standard challenge), or they compress the important diversity of daily activities into impairment-ordered categories of such overgeneralization as to yield inadequate descriptors. Thus, these techniques fail to disclose accurately the dynamic quality and central concerns of the rehabilitation process, which are what disabled persons actually do (Anderson, 1975; Halstead, 1976; Halstead and Hartley, 1975; Katz and others, 1970; Sarno, Sarno, and Levita, 1973; Spencer, Baker, and Stock, 1975; Willems, 1976a; Willems and Campbell, 1975).

Finally, by the nature of the rehabilitation process, which compartmentalizes patient activity and assessment among a variety of team members, no one person or discipline is in a position to have firsthand information concerning how a patient performs during a twenty-four-hour period or even an eight-hour shift. Staff meetings, the patient's record, and even team rounds that include the patient generally provide a partial, static, point-in-time view of what is essentially a dynamic process. As a result of this fragmentation, there are major information gaps about how patients are actually performing. We believe that techniques that fill these gaps will improve patient care by tuning it more directly to patient performance. No one professional person's role spans the gaps or the type of behavioral assessment needed. On the clinical side, our work has been directed at these voids in patient assessment. We have applied the techniques of ecological psychology to the longitudinal assessment of patient performance as it relates to the settings of the rehabilitation hospital.

The Research Setting

In this section, we shall highlight some of the context, methods, and background of our research program, which is located at the Texas Institute for Rehabilitation and Research (TIRR) in Houston, Texas. Adults with spinal cord injuries (quadriplegics and paraplegics) comprise one of TIRR's major patient populations. TIRR provides the full range of services— surgery, nursing, physical therapy, occupational therapy, social work, vocational counseling, and out-patient clinics—and it enjoys a worldwide reputation as an excellent rehabilitation hospital.

Behavior Setting Survey. It is obvious that hopes, plans, and ideas regarding rehabilitation must be conceived by persons or groups of persons and that these plans and ideas must be updated and modified with some regularity. However, it should be just as obvious that the actual delivery of rehabilitation does not live at the level of ideas; it occurs at the level of real and organized arenas of activity and standard programmatic provisions mobilized by the hospital system. Second, the receiving of rehabilitation by spinal cord patients does not occur at the level of hopes and ideas; it consists of making sure that real patients become exposed to as many of the hospital's arenas of activity as possible in a timely and appropriate fashion. It is at these two levels—the hospital's meaningful units of activity and the patient's involvement in the activities occurring there—and at the linkages between the two that effective rehabilitation does or does not come about. Evaluation of the delivery of care and assessment of patient performance must therefore be addressed to both of those levels. In order to do that, the standard structure of the hospital environment in terms of activity arenas must be identified, described, and measured in a way that is relevant to the delivering and receiving of rehabilitative care.

It is for such reasons that we have used the *behavior setting* unit and two behavior settings surveys (Barker, 1968; Barker and Gump, 1964; LeCompte, 1972). The behavior setting is defined and measured in terms of location, physical environment, and patterns of behavior by occupants and its demarcation is based on the degree of interdependence of its component parts and its degree of independence of other settings. The behavior setting unit takes location and physical environment into account, but it is a much more "live" and behaviorally relevant unit than purely architectural units would be. For example, one of the behavior settings at TIRR (a ward setting) includes six architectural divisions (three bed areas, a nurses' station, the end of a corridor, and one bathroom). Yet it is *one* behavior setting, because the standing patterns of behavior and the flow of persons are common across the six architectural divisions and change beyond them. The importance of this to rehabilitation is that, when we measure the diversity of the environment to which a patient is exposed, this whole ward area is counted as one setting, and the patient is not counted as having entered a new setting (a new arena of activity) until he actually leaves this whole complex and enters the main corridor, which has its own patterns of behavior.

A behavior setting consists of a combination of social behavior patterns embedded within a physical and temporal structure. The behavior setting unit has the following defining attributes: (1) a recurrent pattern of behavior and (2) a particular physical structure, occurring at (3) a specific time and place, with (4) a congruent relation between behavior and the physical structure. Both the behavioral and the physical components of behavior settings are necessary to their identification. The basic method of the behavior setting survey is to specify a place (the treatment environment of TIRR, in our case) and to document all the specific settings that occur there during a delimited span of time (a year in our case). Some occur once, and some occur more often. The growing list of possible settings is culled and reorganized by systematic techniques of rating and comparison, and the result at the end of the year is a list of behavior settings, each of which has a consistent, quantitative level of independence from the others. Then, by observation, through the use of informants, or by perusal of data such as minutes and work logs, investigators tabulate who actually participates in the settings, broken down into classifications by age, sex, professional category, and so on, as well as by what various persons do and how long they do it. Standing patterns of behavior (modal behaviors) and mechanisms of behavior (how the things get done) are also rated. The end product is an organized and differentiated picture of how the hospital subdivides itself into functional ecological-behavioral units. In order to avoid biasing factors in data collection, such as those that are often caused by staff turnover and seasonal fluctuation, a relatively long period of time is usually taken as a base period for a behavior setting survey. At TIRR, an entire twelve-month year was taken for each of the two behavior setting surveys. In the first survey, the period from July 1, 1968, to June 30, 1969, was used. In the second survey, the same period in 1971 and 1972 was used. We have found that once a setting survey and a setting list have been completed, only minor updating is necessary to keep the list in usable form. Once the list is completed, numerical codes for settings become a part of the system for performance assessment described as follows.

Developmental Work on Patient Observation. In order to develop procedures for direct monitoring of patient behavior, we conducted programs of observation of patients in 1968 and 1971. Our approach represents an extension of the *specimen record* technique (Barker and Wright, 1955; Wright, 1967). We observed twelve patients at TIRR in the summer of 1968 and fifteen patients in the summer of 1971, each for one full eighteen-hour day (from 5:00 a.m. until 11:00 p.m.). In both studies, the groups included all of the spinal cord-injured pa-

tients who were involved in the hospital's program of comprehensive rehabilitation and included mixtures of ages, sex, races,
and variations from early in treatment to predischarge.

A team of trained observers followed each patient continuously for 18 hours by rotating in 2-hour observational
shifts. Using a small, battery-operated cassette recorder, the observer dictated a continuous narrative description of the target
patient's behavior and enough of the immediate situation to add
intelligibility to the narrative. Few strictures were placed on the
observational process, but observers were instructed to dictate
clock time into the narratives in terms of minutes and fractions
of minutes. After typists had transcribed the narratives, observers proofed their own transcripts, and one editor screened
all of the transcripts for grammar, clarity, and consistency of
style. By this process, we obtained 12 18-hour protocols totaling 216 hours of patient time in 1968 and 15 18-hour protocols
totaling 270 hours in 1971.

Our analysis of the protocols (Willems and Vineberg,
1970) assumes that they capture and describe the sequential
behavior stream of a patient and that the events in that behavior
stream include things the patient did, things that were done to
him or with him, and periods during which the patient was idle
or passive. Our major coding unit, a *chunk,* demarcates a molar
event in the behavior stream of a patient that (1) can be readily
characterized by a single principal activity, (2) begins at a clearly described starting point, (3) occurs over time in a characteristic, sustained fashion, with all its essential accompaniments, and
(4) ends at a clearly described stopping point. The analysis is
designed to minimize the coder's inferential burden and to provide the means to retrieve systematic and quantitative information regarding the common, everyday behaviors of patients.
Examples of chunks are "watching television," "eating scheduled meal," "conversing with physician," "passive range of
motion—arms," "waiting," "transferring," and "reading magazine."

Chunks are marked on the protocols by means of marginal brackets. The information on each chunk is then transferred
to computer storage, with the following eight codes: (1) patient

identifying number; (2) where the chunk occurred, in terms of behavior setting; (3) starting time; (4) ending time; (5) numerical code for the kind of behavior; (6) who else, if anyone, was directly involved in the principal activity of the chunk, and how many persons were involved; (7) who instigated or initiated the chunk; and (8) the degree of involvement by the target patient in the principal activity, on a scale including active, passive, and resistive participation. Thus, for each chunk, it is possible to retrieve information regarding *who* did it, *what* kind of behavior it was, *where* it occurred, *when* it occurred, for *how long* it occurred, *who else* was directly involved in it or whether the patient did it alone, who *instigated* it, and *how actively* the patient was involved in its execution. When these measures are taken singly and in combination and when the overall distributions of chunks are considered, a great many analyses and descriptive statistics become possible.

Longitudinal Observations: Assessment of Patient Performance. Since 1973, we have been observing patients longitudinally as a step toward the goal of developing a longitudinal functional assessment system. In this phase, we gather behavioral data from patients throughout their hospital stays (an average of three months) and for twelve months beyond discharge, for a total period of about fifteen months per patient. For purposes of the present chapter, we will concentrate on the in-hospital observations.

The in-hospital phase of observation starts on the day a patient is admitted to TIRR. After fully informed and signed consent is obtained from the patient, trained personnel begin to observe him directly on a prearranged schedule. Ten ninety-minute observations are spaced across each week in such a way that all of the fifteen hours between 7 a.m. and 10:00 p.m. are observed during the week. Typed transcripts of the observations are coded with a system that has been modified from our earlier version on the basis of reliability assessments. More recently, in order to reduce the amount of time and effort required to generate information, we have developed a note chart form for the observations, to replace the dictation and typing steps (Crowley, 1976). Since observers' notes are now coded directly, the

turnaround time from an observation to available data on patient performance has been reduced two hours.

Throughout our program of research, we have tested reliability on 10 percent of the data each week. Intercoder agreement ranges around an average of 95 percent, and interobserver
agreement ranges around an average of 92 percent (Bailey,
1977; Dreher, 1975).

We have begun to test the simultaneous acquisition of
two types of instrument-based measures. The first is gathered
by means of a series of pressure-sensitive pads that are placed
under the patient's mattress and connected to a continuous
strip chart recorder in one of the hospital laboratories (Halstead, 1976). This device provides a sensitive, continuous recording of motility on the bed surface and, more importantly,
an exact measure of time out of bed. The second is gathered by
means of a set of mechanical odometers attached to the two
wheels of the patient's wheelchair (Alexander, 1977). These
odometers provide a measure of patient mobility. We have
tested the reliability of the odometers and the adequacy with
which periodic readings estimate total mobility. Data from the
bed monitor and odometers are then mapped onto the performance data to ascertain which observational measures are
approximated best, or estimated best, by the instrumented measures. These efforts are motivated by the potential saving in
time and effort that would come from using instrumented measures as much as possible to supplement or replace the more
cumbersome observational measures.

Illustrative Data

In order to exemplify some of the uses of the data, we
will present brief illustrations of (1) longitudinal patient assessments and (2) some eco-behavioral complexities in those
assessments.

Longitudinal Assessment. The observational monitoring
procedures just described yield twenty-nine measures of patient
performance on a regular, longitudinal basis. From these, we
have selected a smaller set of key indicators by means of consul-

tation with professionals in rehabilitation, selection procedures using cluster analysis and regression analysis (Alexander, 1977; Willems, 1975, 1976b), and analyses of predictive validity (using medical records and our measure of posthospital performance). Thus, for clinically related assessment of patient status and progress, we now focus on longitudinal measures of *independence* (self-instigated and unaided activities) and *mobility* (entries into hospital settings, wheelchair distance, and time out of bed). Once each week—or more often, when requested—the clinical staff uses these data as assessments of how well the patient is doing. The clinical staff has come to depend on these data as relatively holistic and continuous measures that are not available in any of the traditional indicators from the separate clinical services.

Figure 1 displays weekly measures of independence for one patient, a male paraplegic. Data points are proportions of performances (chunks) that the patient instigated himself and

**Figure 1. Weekly Proportions of Self-Instigated and Unaided Performance
by One Patient**

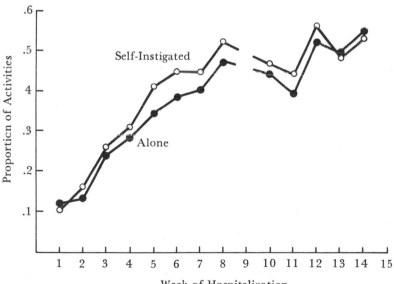

conducted without the direct aid of anyone else. Weekly information disclosed to the treatment staff that the patient displayed a period of rapid development from Week 2 to Week 6, after which he maintained a variable but high plateau until he was discharged. Weekly comparisons to normative data from other known cases indicated that this patient was doing very well and that his prognosis for posthospital adjustment was good.

Setting Dependencies. Within the context of such global measures and their acceptance into the clinical stream, we have rediscovered and documented a phenomenon that is central to ecological psychology; that is, the extent to which behavior depends on where it occurs. Before we present data on the links between patient behavior and behavior settings, some discussion of background is in order.

To the behavioral ecologist, *where* organisms are located is never unimportant or accidental because behavior and place concatenate into lawful, functioning systems (Barker, 1963a; Moos, 1973; Wicker, 1972; Willems, 1976a). "The correlation between site and activity is often so high that an experienced ecological psychologist can direct a person to a particular site in order to observe an animal exhibiting a given pattern of behavior" (King, 1970, p. 4). In the conduct of everyday affairs, we depend on location specificity in behavior for predictability and social order, and we often refer to departures from such correlations to label persons as being *crazy, sick, deviant,* and so on, and in need of help or control.

In their discussion of basic assumptions regarding the influence of the physical environment on behavior, Proshansky, Ittelson, and Rivlin (1970) argue that observed patterns of molar behavior in response to a physical setting persist regardless of the individuals involved. From their studies of persons in mental hospitals, the same investigators conclude that such intrasetting continuity of behavior often occurs even though inhabitants are cognitively unaware of the structural aspects of the settings. Barker (1968) also points out that place-behavior systems have such strong principles of organization and constraint that their standing patterns of behavior remain essentially the same, although individuals come and go. Wicker (1972) calls this "behavior-environment congruence." Barker (1968) calls it "behavior-milieu synomorphy" and argues that the appropriate units of analysis for studying such synomorphic relationships are *behavior settings,* whose defining attributes and properties he has spelled out in detail.

A clear example is found in the work of Raush and his colleagues in their studies of normal children and children diagnosed as hyperaggressive or disturbed (Raush, 1969; Raush, Dittmann, and Taylor, 1959a, 1959b; Raush, Farbman, and Llewellyn, 1960). By observing the children for extended periods of time in various settings and then examining the frequencies of various kinds of behavior by the children toward peers and adults, the investigators were able to demonstrate several aspects of place dependence. First, the interpersonal behavior of all the children varied strongly from one setting to another. Second, and perhaps most revealing, the place dependence of behavior was much stronger for normal children than for disturbed children; that is, the influence of the setting was greater for normal children. Finally, as the disturbed children progressed in treatment, the place dependence of their behavior came to approximate that of the normal children more and more.

Wahler (1975) observed two troubled boys periodically for three years in home and school settings. He found (1) that behaviors clustered differently in home and school settings, (2) that the clusters within each setting were very stable over time, and (3) that different patterns of deviant behaviors occurred in stable fashion in the two settings. Lichstein and Wahler (1976) observed sixteen behaviors of an autistic child and six behaviors of adults and peers for approximately six months. Observations were made in three different settings, and covariation of behaviors across time and settings was analyzed by means of cluster analysis. Again, the investigators found that the child's behavior was relatively stable across time within a given setting and that none of the child's behavior clusters appeared in more than one setting.

From the evolutionary standpoint, it makes sense to

argue that behavioral responsiveness to settings is selected for, because location-appropriateness of behaviors is crucial to adaptation in many settings (Sells, 1969; Skinner, 1971). The implications of such phenomena are widespread. Two that have become part of the behavioral ecologist's credo are, first, that behavior is largely controlled by the environmental setting in which it occurs and, second, that changing the environmental setting will result in changes in behavior. The third implication is related to methodology. This is the investigative problem of describing and classifying the types and patterns of congruence between behavior and environment and formulating principles that account for the congruence. This effort is important because it promises to contribute much to programs of environmental planning. To accomplish this goal, investigators must become more persistent in adding descriptions and codes for locations and context to their measures and descriptions of behavior.

Several of these principles are illustrated and elaborated by our program of research on persons with spinal cord injuries. First, when we look at distributions of patient behavior within different settings, we find that these profiles of behavior vary dramatically from one setting to another (LeCompte and Willems, 1970; Willems, 1972a, 1972b). Some behaviors that occur in one setting do not occur at all in others, and the relative frequencies and percentage weights of behavior show strong variation between settings. *What* patients do varies systematically from one setting to another. Both we and the clinical staff have come to expect this, and we take it into account in the assessments of patients.

Second, in addition to these topographical dependencies on settings, we find dependencies in the more dynamic aspects of patient behavior. From the observations, we extract behavioral measures of *independence* (that is, the proportion of performances that patients initiate and execute alone) and *zest* (that is, the proportion of performances that patients initiate and carry out actively). Because increases from very low rates in these measures reflect a relative normalizing of the patients' behavior repertoires, both relate closely to important goals of the hospital's treatment system. Many traditional, person-based theories of human behavior assume that independence and zest are largely a matter of individual motivation and thus should reflect a high degree of personal constancy across situations. What we find instead is that behavioral independence varies dramatically when patients move from one hospital setting to another. Table 1 illustrates this variation by settings from the

**Table 1. Characterization of Hospital Behavior Settings
in Terms of Patient Independence**

Setting	Rate of Patient Independence
Cafeteria	.64
Hallways	.48
Outside the Building	.30
Stations 1-3 (ward)	.30
Station 4 (ward)	.24
Occupational Therapy (OT)	.15
Physical Therapy (PT)	.08
Recreational Therapy (RT)	.02

Note: Proportion of performances patients initiate and execute alone.

day-long observations of twelve patients in 1968. Since these wide setting variations are based on data from all twelve patients, it is possible that the differences were produced by different patients who entered the settings at different rates. To test this alternative hypothesis, we calculated combined indices of independence for three settings (cafeteria, hallways, wards) and compared them to combined indices for a second set of three settings (occupational therapy, OT; physical therapy, PT; and rehabilitation therapy, RT) for each of the twelve patients. In the case of each patient, the results corroborated the patterns noted earlier. For every patient, the rate of independence dropped as he moved from cafeteria-hallways-ward to OT-PT-RT.

Third, we find in many cases that differences among settings account for more variance in patient performance than do differences among patients or other variables. Table 2 illustrates this phenomenon descriptively by displaying rates of zest

Table 2. Characterizations of Settings, Categories of Behavior, Involvements with Several Groups of Persons, and Individual Patients, in Terms of Patient Zest

Settings		Categories of Patient Behavior		Groups of Persons Involved with Patients		Individual Patients (Pt.)	
Cafeteria	.83	Eating	.68	Other patients	.60	Pt. 5	.52
Hallways	.52	Active recreational	.63	OT	.51	Pt. 12	.43
OT	.47	Conversing	.56	Nurses	.33	Pt. 4	.42
RT	.44	Transporting	.50	PT	.32	Pt. 10	.41
Outside	.36	Transferring	.39	Physician	.29	Pt. 6	.39
PT	.29	Exercise and performance training	.31	Aides and orderlies	.28	Pt. 2	.32
Ward 4	.29	Passive recreational	.24			Pt. 8	.24
Wards 1-3	.22	Nursing care and hygiene	.22			Pt. 11	.24
						Pt. 1	.20
						Pt. 3	.20
						Pt. 7	.18
						Pt. 9	.17
Range	.61		.46		.32		.35

Note: Proportion of performances patients initiate and carry out actively.

for settings, kinds of patient behavior, types of other persons involved in the behaviors, and individual patients from the same sample of twelve. Settings produced more variability than the other factors. It is also interesting to note that the settings and kinds of behaviors that were *accompaniments* of the rehabilitation process (cafeteria, hallways, eating, recreation) produced more zest than those settings and behaviors that were central to rehabilitation (OT, PT, transferring, transporting, exercising). Data such as these were used by the hospital staff as a basis for making several changes in the programs of the settings.

Fourth, and most interestingly, there are powerful variations among settings in the rate of growth and behavioral development displayed by patients. That is, patients show more goal-oriented change in some hospital settings than in others. To illustrate this phenomenon, Figure 2 displays proportions of behaviors that were self-instigated in three major settings by one patient (a quadriplegic) who was observed longitudinally throughout his hospital stay. On the abscissa, the patient's hospital stay is divided into thirds. Overall, this patient showed great improvement in his rate of self-instigated performance. However, the degree to which he displayed that progress depended strongly on where he was located in the hospital. This patient showed far more progress in OT than he did in the ward and PT. We find analogous setting dependencies in the cases of all patients, and we find them for the various aspects of performance; for example, rate of self-instigation, rate of performing alone (unaided).

Figure 3 shows the proportions of behaviors conducted without aid in three settings by another patient who was observed throughout her hospital stay. In this case, the abscissa of the figure divides the hospital stay into fourths. Because this patient was a paraplegic (lower level of spinal injury than the patient depicted in Figure 2), she was less impaired and displayed higher rates of performance. Overall, this patient showed a great deal of progress in unaided performance. She began at the highest level in the ward, but she displayed two-and-one-half times as much change in OT as in the ward.

In summary, not only do we find that persons perform

Figure 2. Proportion of Self-Instigated Performances to Total Performances by One Patient (a Quadriplegic) in Three Different Hospital Settings

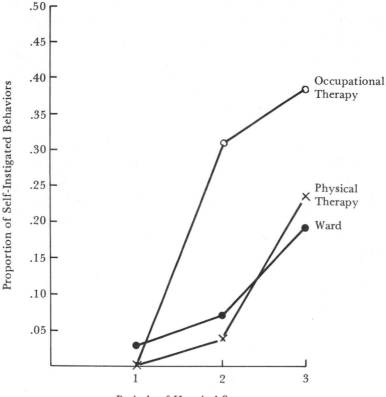

differently in different settings when we make simple comparisons between settings, but we also find that persons change in different ways and at different rates in different settings. When these central principles of behavioral ecology really soak in, they will affect human behavioral science in profound ways. One area that will be affected strongly is the area of human assessment. It will no longer be so tenable or defensible to assess *a person's* performance. Rather, we will have to assess performance by settings, simply because variations in settings produce variations in performance.

Figure 3. Proportion of Unaided Performances to Total Performances
by One Patient (a Paraplegic) in Three Hospital Settings

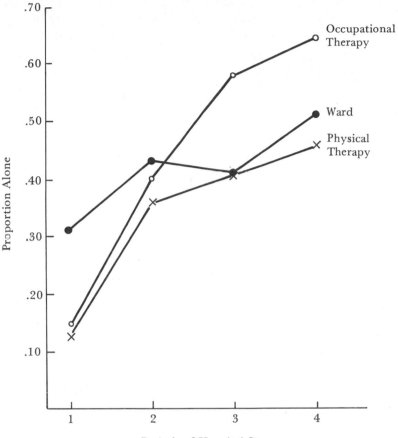

Closely related is the clear hint that many traditional approaches to diagnosis—judgments of what is wrong or how the client is doing—are far too narrowly defined, facile, and restricted. A case in point occurred when we began participating in patients' treatment teams in our program of research. Often, a staff member representing one service (for example, nursing) at patient rounds would offer a judgment of how the patient was doing that would be highly discrepant with the judgment of a staff member representing another service (for example, occupational therapy). Each assumed that he or she was giving a valid judgment of *the patient*. The interesting point here is that our data suggested in many cases that each staff member was responding to the patient's performance in a particular setting. In the case of the patient depicted in Figure 2, the staff member who reported that the patient was making excellent progress came from a setting (OT) in which the patient was indeed showing excellent progress, whereas the other came from a setting (ward) in which the patient was showing less progress. Fortunately, our data, which came from monitoring the patient wherever he went, clarified the complex picture of setting dependencies in the patient's status and progress and in staff judgments. Such intersetting complexities have now become part of patient assessment at TIRR.

One final issue deserves mention. For many types of behavioral problems and disabilities, the person is most dependent on ministration and intervention by the social and physical environment for survival and adaptation when the problem is most acute and severe. Thus, common sense and conventional social wisdom suggest (1) that the person's performance should show the most intersetting variability when he is "sickest" and (2) that the intersetting variability (setting dependency) should diminish as the person gets "better," perhaps because his performance comes more and more under the control of his own internal processes.

The findings of Raush, Dittmann, and Taylor (1959a, 1959b) suggest that just the opposite is the case for behavioral disturbances. That is, the more "normal" the disturbed boys became, the more differentiated their behavior became according to the disparate programs of the various settings they entered. Taken together, the data in Figures 2 and 3 support the conclusion of Raush and his group. Early in his hospitalization and a few days after his injury, Patient 33 (Figure 2) showed almost no intersetting variability in performance. As he got better, his behavior rapidly showed more variability among settings.

Patient 33 was a quadriplegic (broken neck), and his

impairment was very severe when he was admitted. One would expect that a person with less impairment would display more intersetting variability from the outset. Data from Patient 40 (Figure 3) suggest that this is the case. Patient 40, a paraplegic (broken back and lower spinal cord lesion than Patient 33), was less impaired at admission, and her performance displayed more variability among settings at the beginning of her stay in the hospital. Thus, there is growing empirical support for the two-part argument of the behavioral ecologist: (1) normal adaptation and adjustment is characterized by performance that matches the varied programs of the behavior settings that persons inhabit, and (2) reduction of impairment (that is, "normalizing" of adaptation and adjustment) means in part that the intersetting variability of performance will increase.

Concluding Comments

By means of a few discrete examples from an extended, ongoing program of research and development, we have tried to illustrate that the ecological perspective can affect a real-life problem of human performance. At the beginning of this decade, Odum (1971, p. 510) pointed out that "just how applied human ecology is to be developed and structured so that worthwhile goals can be achieved in the real world of society can be but dimly perceived at this point of history." We hope we have suggested that Odum's skepticism is no longer necessary. For the study of the microecology of human performance and for its bearing on problems of rehabilitation, we now have much more than dim perceptions—we have some articulated principles and guidelines, and we have some strategies for research and assessment on persons in institutional settings where ecological aspects of performance are central issues. Currently, the perspective and methods of our research program are being applied by other investigators in studies of mental retardation, hyperactivity, ambulatory care facilities, medicine wards in a general hospital, and spinal injury sections of Veterans Administration hospitals.

Part *3*

Studies in
Eco-Behavioral
Science

◆-◆◆-◆◆-◆◆-◆◆-◆◆-◆◆-◆◆-◆◆-◆◆-◆◆-◆◆-◆◆-◆◆-◆◆-◆◆-◆

Eco-behavioral science deals with the behavior-milieu entities we have called behavior settings. *The studies presented in Part Three deal with these entities and, via them, with human behavior, which is one of their essential components. This involves a shift of attention from designated persons, represented in Part Two, to the extraindividual behavior that implements the programs of behavior settings.*

Included are descriptions of behavior settings on both empirical and theoretical levels, investigations of the consequences for behavior setting inhabitants of different behavior setting attributes, methods of measuring certain dynamic properties and behavior outputs of behavior settings, procedures for measuring environmental extent and variety, and for assessing educational programs in terms of behavior settings.

191

Behavior Settings: Human Habitats and Behavior Machines

◆━◆◆━◆◆━◆◆━◆◆━◆◆━◆◆━◆◆━◆◆━◆◆━◆◆━◆◆━◆◆━◆◆━◆◆━◆

If a satellite with cameras for recording human behavior was positioned over any considerable portion of the world, it would show that human activities are by no means uniformly or randomly distributed over the earth but are clustered within relatively small, widely separated areas. These are towns (and settlements, villages, and cities). Outside towns and the roads connecting them, there are minor concentrations of human activity around farmsteads and other isolated habitations; otherwise behavior is sparsely distributed over the earth.

If the cameras were focused on a particular town, they would show again that human activities are not uniformly or randomly distributed but are concentrated in bounded regions. These are public behavior settings. Outside of these concentrations, there are much smaller clusters of behavior in private dwellings that line streets, but elsewhere behavior is spread thinly across towns. During a usual day in 1963 or 1964, there were 178 public behavior settings in Yoredale; 20.1 percent of the behavior of the town's residents within them occurred in the single behavior setting trafficways; 1.0 percent occurred in the behavior setting Hay's Garage, and the National Health Service Office accommodated 0.2 percent of the behavior. The same conditions obtained in Midwest where among the 146 loci of behavior in the town's public areas, 7.8 percent took place in trafficways; Weylin's Grocery Store encompassed 3.7 percent, and 0.3 percent of the behavior occurred in the setting county engineer's office.

Towns and behavior settings are easily seen and commonly reported. Most travelers describe the "life" of a country largely in terms of its towns, the behavior settings of the towns, and the behavior of the towns' inhabitants within settings. For example, in Dr. Alexander Hamilton's 1744 travel diary of a trip along the eastern seaboard of England's American colonies, the description leaps from town to town (Boston, Dedham, Wrentham, Providence, Bristol, Newport, . . .), each a unit of colonial life with only occasional mention of roadside inns and farmsteads. As Hamilton approached the town of Newport, Rhode Island, he described it (Bridenbaugh, 1948) as a unit with a few outstanding structures and regions: "The town of Newport is about a mile long, lying pritty near north and south. It stands upon a very levell spot of ground" with one long, narrow street and several branching lanes, one large market house, the town house, two Presbyterian meeting houses, one large Quaker meeting house, one Anabaptist meeting house, one Church of England, and the town's fort. But as a visitor within Newport, Hamilton described the town in terms of nine behavior settings as follows, with his behavior within them in the parentheses: White Horse Tavern (dining, "putting up" for the night), streets (walking about, sightseeing), Baptist meeting (attending church), rooming house and apothecary shop (lodging), coffee house (drinking coffee, spending evening with acquaintances), Hog's Hole, a shaded park area (gallantly "romping with the ladies"), Philosophy Club meeting (discussing with members), prison (conversing with prisoners), Little Rock, a park area (promenading with ladies). The behavior of Hamilton's associates is always described within the context of one of these behavior settings.

The prominence of behavior settings is exhibited, too, in the diary of Samuel Pepys. He describes his day (Latham and Mathews, 1970) in London on February 3, 1660 in terms of these behavior settings and his and other inhabitants' behavior within them: Harper's Tavern (drinking morning draught and hearing the news), St. James Park (playing on flagolette), guard chamber at White Hall (seeing prisoners), his office (paying soldiers), House chamber at Westminster (showing the chamber to visitors), Prior's Rhenish Wine House (purchasing wine and anchovies), Wilkinson's shop (bespeaking shoulder of mutton), White Hall (watching soldiers march), his home (dining with family and friends on shoulder of mutton), Palace Yard (hearing the news), Park (sporting with wife and friends).

If the satellite cameras were brought nearer with lens and film arrangements to penetrate the walls of particular behavior settings and to record movements within them, some of the internal arrangements would be revealed. It would not be difficult to focus on particular settings, for each is surrounded by a conspicuous wall or boundary zone. It would be found that the pattern of activity within each setting is stable and characteristic. The pattern within Weylin's Grocery Store in Midwest in the 1960s, for example, with the main current of the inhabitants and grocery carts flowing along the aisles between the shelves, past the checkout counter, and out the exit, is radically different from that within the county engineer's office, with a small stream of people moving into and out of one region (the secretaries' room) and a few of these branching off into a connected region (the engineer's private office).

Finally, if the cameras were lowered still more and focused on particular individuals, they would reveal that the behavior of persons who move between behavior settings conforms to the pattern prevailing in the setting they currently inhabit. Weylin's Grocery Store and the county engineer's office, for example, are not passive places where people assemble and behave in accordance with the intentions and abilities they bring to these settings; rather, these and other settings coerce their inhabitants. How do they do this? What are the properties of behavior settings?

Dictionary definitions reveal two properties. Behavior settings are mixes of physical and human components (they are eco-behavioral phenomena), and they are ongoing occurrences (they are programs of events). Here, for example, are definitions of two classes of behavior settings: A *grocery store* is a business establishment where foodstuffs are bought and sold by retail; a *hotel* is a house that provides lodging and usually meals, entertainment, and personal services for the public. According to these definitions, grocery stores are more than rooms, shelves, and foodstuffs; they are also standing patterns of customers buying and staff members selling. And hotels are more than bedrooms, dining rooms, lounges, and their furnishings; they are also ongoing programs of paying guests and serving hostelers. All other behavior settings involve human and nonhuman components in particular programs of events.

Two other attributes of behavior settings are variety of parts and interdependence of parts. Within Weylin's Grocery Store, some human components are young, some old; some buyers, some sellers; some male, some female; some butchers, some checkers; and the nonhuman components range from black pepper to refrigerators and fluorescent lights. In view of such variety, one can ask, What makes Weylin's Grocery Store a unitary phenomenon? Why do not its refrigerators and all other refrigerators in the town form an ecological unit? The answer is that each part of the store is dependent on every other part; the store functions as a unit. If the refrigerators break down, meat cannot be sold; if the checkout counter is blocked, customers cannot buy soup. It is the interdependence of the parts, rather than their similarity, that makes a behavior setting a unitary entity. The standing pattern of a behavior setting may involve very diverse occurrences, but stable, programmed forces within the setting enforce conformity by each of its human and non-human components to some phase of its diverse pattern. It is this conformity within a diversified, established pattern rather than uniformity of parts that makes a behavior setting a unit.

Related to interdependence of its parts is the fact that a

behavior setting is a self-governing entity with homeostatic control mechanisms that enforce, within limits, conformity of its diverse components to its standing pattern and level of functioning in the presence of internal and external disturbances. Weylin's Grocery Store enforces its characteristic pattern on its customers and staff; the customers do not enter a passive region but one that incorporates them into its ongoing program. A customer with the intention of quickly getting a can of soup for lunch, for example, finds that one door resists his entrance, while the other flies open at his approach; on gaining entrance, the one-way turnstiles require him to proceed to the right, away from the soups; the tide of other customers further opposes the most direct path, so he takes a longer way along the meat counter; here the friendly butcher urgently recommends to him a great bargain in chuck roast that he cannot resist; he insists, however, that the somewhat reluctant butcher cut the roast into two pieces and wrap it for his home freezer; at the one checkout counter in operation, he is delayed by a customer with a huge cartload of groceries; this troubles him greatly, and in his agitation he hoists the can of soup and packages of meat into the view of the clerk who signals him to proceed via the neighboring, unmanned, checkout counter; however, just as the automatic exit door is closing behind him, he is called back by the clerk for, in his haste, he has failed to sign the charge slip; so he must make a short loop back through the ever-eager entrance door to the checkout counter, to be released again by the exit door. Our customer is not a free spirit; the store exerts a claim over him.

Every behavior setting has an optimal complement of human components that varies with the prevailing standing pattern and level of functioning of the setting. The number may be precise, or it may cover a limited range. The behavior setting bridge game requires four human components, no more or less, whereas Weylin's Grocery Store in the 1960s operated smoothly with five employees and 150 regular customers, although it could function with both fewer and greater numbers, within limits.

Three characteristics of behavior settings are related to

their locations. Every behavior setting has a precise geographical and temporal locus. Weylin's Grocery Store exists in Midwest at 503 Delaware Street from 7:30 a.m. to 8:30 p.m. Monday through Saturday and from 8:00 a.m. to 12:00 a.m. on Sunday. Every behavior setting also has a boundary that completely surrounds it; this is frequently a wall with entrances and exits and properties that regulate the flow of human and physical components and influences across it. Weylin's Grocery Store, for example, excludes dogs at its entrance by the sign "No Dogs Allowed," and it insulates its interior space from the fluctuating outside temperature by the structure of its walls and by ventilating devices.

On a scale encompassing the whole world, behavior settings are small entities. Their spatial extents and populations in Midwest range from the setting telephone booth, 3 feet by 3 feet in area, with a single inhabitant at each occurrence, to the setting school football game, an area 400 feet by 500 feet in extent, with 600 inhabitants on some occasions. Most churches, schools, manufacturing concerns, government institutions, and many businesses consist of a numbers of behavior settings housed in one or a few buildings. For example, the county engineer's office in Midwest is a behavior setting located in the courthouse, along with a dozen other behavior settings. Behavior settings are human-sized units; they are the ecological units most proximal to people.

When it is remembered that almost all behavior within a town occurs within its behavior settings, it will be clear why they are so important. Although towns have many other parts (buildings, oxygen gas, institutions, social classes, industrial areas, families, organizations, for example), the topological position of behavior settings means that only they form the immediately circumjacent environments of the inhabitants. They intervene between a town's inhabitants and the wider environment via their selective boundaries and their coercive programs. In consequence, a town's inhabitants are almost always subject to influences residing in its behavior settings.

The effects of behavior settings are easily observed. They are clear in the case of visitors between Midwest and Yoredale, for example. Inhabitants of Yoredale who visit Midwest are quickly identified as foreigners, for many aspects of their behavior differ noticeably from those of Midwest residents. Likewise, visitors from Midwest are seen to be alien within Yoredale. However, if the visits are prolonged behavior differences diminish under the influence of the towns' settings. Natives of Midwest in Yoredale begin to walk more (and more vigorously) in its streets and sidewalks, to express their partisanship at its cricket games by discreet clapping rather than by wild cheering, to drive forthrightly on the left side of its streets, to accept without expressions of surprise meals served at 5 p.m. (tea) and 9 p.m. (supper), and, in general, to adopt the more leisurely pace of Yoredale's behavior settings. And Yoredale natives sojourning in Midwest begin to walk less (and less vigorously) in its trafficways, to raise their voices at basketball games, to drive bravely on the right side of the streets, to eat one evening meal, and to fit into the faster pace of Midwest's behavior settings. The new environments bend some features of the visitors' behavior to the different, prevailing patterns.

The influence of behavior settings is also evident in the case of particular inhabitants and particular settings. In the course of the customer's action to quickly get a can of soup, the behavior setting Weylin's Grocery Store imposes on him a roundabout spatial pathway to the soup by a system of one-way valves, ducts, and prevailing currents of inhabitant movement; it creates within him a new need for chuck roast by an input of information and social pressure; it frustrates his existing need for a fast lunch by a blockage of the escape channel due to temporary overload; and it detects and requires rectification of a defect in his behavior (failing to sign) by quality control inspection. Within behavior settings, there are pervasive forces that coerce both the human and nonhuman components to conform to the prevailing standing patterns.

On the other hand, when Weylin's Grocery Store admits an inhabitant, it does not gain a completely docile behavior setting component. The customer in our example alters the program of the meat department by insisting on special cutting and packaging of the roast, and he opens a bypass around the regular escape channel by his agitated signaling.

The powers of behavior settings and their inhabitants with respect to each other have special significance in view of another relation between them; behavior settings and their inhabitants are mutually dependent. Inhabitants are essential behavior setting components; behavior settings need people to implement their programs. Without the customer, butcher, and clerk in our example, or others like them, Weylin's Grocery Store would not be a behavior setting in the long run; it would decease and become like the remains of a gasoline engine lacking pistons and spark plugs. And a town's behavior settings are essential to its inhabitants; they need behavior settings for the satisfaction of their needs. Without Weylin's Grocery Store, or another setting like it, the food need of the person in our example would not be satisfied, and in the long run he, too, would decease. This reciprocal relation between behavior settings and people is fundamental; the behavior settings and inhabitants of a community have a symbiotic relation on which each is dependent for survival.

The symbiosis is not entirely harmonious. Although, in the example, the customer's behavior is in most respects favorable for Weylin's Grocery Store (promoting the smooth running of its program by helping reduce the oversupply of chuck roast, contributing to the financial requirements of the setting through purchases, and correcting the deviation from the prescribed sign-out program), his insistence on special services at the meat and checkout counters introduces minor disturbances into the programmed operation of the setting. And the store's program of operation is both favorable and unfavorable for the customer; he experiences the satisfactions of obtaining soup for lunch and meat at a bargain, but he also experiences frustration and annoyance at being delayed and recalled to sign. This disharmony arises because the needs of the behavior setting (for sales, for reducing inventory, for payment of accounts) are determined by economic and physical factors, such as prices, profits, and space for storage and display, whereas the needs of the customer (for soup, for quick service) are determined by psychological and physiological factors, such as plans for the day, blood sugar level, and hunger. The laws that determine the profit and loss of a store and those that determine the satisfactions and dissatisfactions of a customer are independent and incommensurate. The plans of a store's inhabitant and his blood sugar level do not enter the considerations that determine the selling price of chuck roast. This fundamental difference between behavior settings and their inhabitants may be stated in another way. People have two positions in behavior settings: They are components, and as such they behave in accordance with behavior setting requirements, but they are also inhabitants with unique needs and abilities, and as such they behave in accordance with the requirements of their own motives and perceptions.

However, both behavior settings and their human components have means of reconciling, within limits, their disharmonies and of maintaining the symbiosis so essential to both. Weylin's Grocery Store molds the urgent directedness of the customer's behavior to greater congruence with its own program of operation by its automatic doors, its one-way stiles, its partitions, the tides of its inhabitants, its aggressive butcher, and its alert clerk. And the customer modifies the rigid program of Weylin's Grocery Store to greater congruence with his own intentions by his insistence on special services at the meat counter and by his agitations at the checkout counter. Harmony is abetted, too, by the fact that behavior settings are not dependent on particular inhabitants nor inhabitants on particular settings. People with unsatisfied needs in one setting exchange it for others that are more adequate, and behavior settings with recalcitrant inhabitants replace them with others that are more suitable. Weylin's Grocery Store did not need the actual customer, butcher, and clerk described; another purchaser of soup, seller of meat, and cashier would have been satisfactory. And the customer did not need the setting Weylin's Grocery Store; another grocery store would have been adequate. This contributes greatly to the harmonious and stable symbiosis of a community's settings and its human components.

Behavior settings are richly complex phenomena; they have many other attributes. But this is, perhaps, enough to show that they may be considered the behavior machinery of towns: They generate behavior (for example, buying chuck roast), and they regulate behavior (for example, leaving only by the "out" door). Within the public areas of a town, people, whatever their intentions and abilities may be, are components of behavior settings—of such eco-behavioral systems as ongoing arithmetic classes, lawyer's offices, worship services, court sessions, and drugstores—whose programs they do not make. This is a fundamental significance of behavior settings for the inhabitants of towns.

Dan D. M. Ragle
Roger G. Barker
Arthur Johnson

13

Impact of the Agricultural Extension Service on Midwest

◆◆ ◆◆ ◆◆ ◆◆ ◆◆ ◆◆ ◆◆ ◆◆ ◆◆ ◆◆ ◆◆ ◆◆ ◆◆ ◆◆ ◆◆ ◆◆ ◆

This study reports the impact of the Kansas Agricultural Extension Service (AES) on a single town from September 1963 through August 1964 and compares the data with those from an earlier survey, September 1954 through August 1955. Midwest is a rural trading, school, and government center located near the middle of Jefferson County, a county that contains approximately 400 square miles and is inhabited by 11,200 persons. At some time during the year of the study, one of every seven

Reprint, with minor editing, of Ragle, Barker, and Johnson (1967).

town residents was directly involved in Agricultural Extension Service activities within the borders of Midwest. The AES also brought in many more nonresidents. What follows is a description of what AES adds to the environment within which Midwest residents live their lives.

Methods and Concepts

The first question is "How is the environment of behavior to be identified, measured, and described?" The list of environmental facts relevant for behavior is endless. During the course of the larger study, we discovered a limited number of community parts that together encompass all the other facts about the town and hence constitute the environment of the town's inhabitants. These parts we call *behavior settings*. A 4-H Club food sale is an example of a behavior setting. Within its space-time boundary, the behavior of individuals conforms to the pattern characteristic of the setting. The persons who maintain and control the setting make a deliberate effort to ensure that this is so. At the food sale, customers do not sample the cake frostings (there is social pressure against it) nor sit on the tables (physical arrangements prevent it—the tables are covered with food). There are many objectively existing behavior settings that blanket the town; no behavior occurs outside of a behavior setting.

When the parts and processes of two or more settings are interchangeable, these settings belong to the same genotype. Two grocery stores, for example, could exchange stock, personnel, bookkeeping systems, and so forth, with little interruption in their operation. The number of behavior setting genotypes in a town is a measure of the variety of the town's environment.

A description of behavior settings and genotypes is a description of the environment a town provides for the behavior of its inhabitants. Members of the Midwest Field Station staff visited and observed all behavior settings that occurred in Midwest during each survey year. For each setting, a record was kept of the name and age of each person participating, each person controlling the setting, and a description of the spatial-temporal patterns of the setting. These direct observations were in addition to, and augmented, the normal records kept by the controlling agency, the AES, regarding the dates, duration of meetings, attendance, program, and so forth. The observations of the research staff added detail, but primarily the data reported here were in the possession of the leaders of the various AES settings.

Size and Variety of Environment

Midwest had 884 behavior settings during the survey year; of these, 45 (5.1 percent) were sponsored by AES. The town had 830 residents in 1964, and 118 of them (14 percent) inhabited the behavior settings controlled by the AES. These behavior settings were also populated by over 400 nonresidents. Total population of AES behavior settings during the year 1963-1964 was over 500 persons.

The number of behavior setting genotypes is a measure of the environmental variety a town presents to its inhabitants. It is analogous to indicating the diversity of a farm property by reporting that it has three kinds of fields (for example, plow land, timber, and pasture) and also lakes and streams. Midwest had 198 different behavior setting genotypes in 1964, and, of these, the 45 AES settings were represented in 21 (10.6 percent). Eight of the town's genotypes (4 percent) occurred only in connection with AES behavior settings. The size dimensions of the AES behavior settings may be summarized and interpreted as follows:

1. There were 401 occurrences of AES behavior settings in Midwest during the survey year, or 7.7 during an average week. Five of these were occurrences of the AES office, so during most weeks there were about 3 other AES behavior settings in town.
2. AES behavior settings functioned for a total of 2,366 hours during the survey year, or 45.5 hours per week. The AES office was open 40 hours per week, leaving 5.5 hours as the mean weekly duration of other settings.

3. One hundred and eighteen town residents occupied the AES behavior settings for 7,018 hours, or 59.4 hours per year per person on the average. When the office time of the 3 employees is omitted (because most of their office time was not devoted to Midwest activities), town residents who inhabited AES behavior settings spent 4,013 hours in them, or about 34 hours per year per person, that is, 40 minutes per week.

We can draw the following conclusions from the 1964 data. If the program of the Agricultural Extension Service were eliminated from Midwest,

- The town's size in terms of behavior settings would be reduced by 5 percent.
- Its size, in terms of daily occurrences of behavior settings, their duration, and their person-hours of occupancy, would be reduced by less than 1 percent.
- Midwest's environmental variety would be reduced by 4 percent.
- The number of settings in almost 11 percent of its genotypes would be reduced.
- Eight genotypes (containing 17 settings) would be completely lost to the town.
- There would be almost 8 fewer behavior setting occurrences per week, lasting 45.5 hours.
- Fourteen percent of Midwest's inhabitants not professionally connected with the AES would have about 34 hours per year each to spend in other behavior settings.
- Four hundred nonresidents would have about 5,400 hours for AES activities in other towns, or for allocation to other activities.

Changes Between 1954-1955 and 1963-1964. Changes in the size of Midwest and in the contribution of the AES to the town over a nine-year period are reported in Table 1. These data show that the town increased on all dimensions by amounts varying from 1 percent (hours of duration) to 53 percent (number of behavior settings). If the office time of the staff is

Table 1. Dimensions of Midwest and of the Agricultural
Extension Service, 1954-1955 and 1963-1964

Dimensions	1954-1955	1963-1964	Percent change 1954 to 1963
Midwest			
Population of town	715	830	+16
Number of genotypes	171	198	+16
Number of settings	576	884	+53
Daily occurrences of settings	49,562	53,258	+ 7
Hours duration of settings	283,656	286,909	+ 1
Person-hours occupancy of settings by town residents	928,240	1,118,802	+21
AES			
Number of genotypes	20	21	+ 5
Number of settings	46	45	− 2
Daily occurrences of settings[a]	129	151	+17
Hours duration of settings[a]	310	326	+ 5
Person-hours occupancy of settings by town residents[b]	3,426	4,013	+16

[a]AES office omitted.

[b]AES staff office time omitted.

omitted for both years, when the change is assessed, the estimated person-hours for town residents in Midwest AES behavior settings increased from 3,426 hours in 1954-1955 to 4,013 hours in 1963-1964 (16 percent increase).

The data indicate that the Agricultural Extension Service in 1963-1964 contributed about as much to the size of the town's environment as it did in 1954-1955, but that relative to the town's size in 1963-1964, it contributed fewer behavior settings and genotypes. The increase in person-hours of occupancy of the AES settings was not accompanied by an increase in number of settings and genotypes as it was in the town as a whole. Thus the AES was, in terms of the farm analogy, tilling the same number and variety of fields as it did in 1954-1955, but tilling them somewhat more intensively. The town, however, was working a greater number of more varied fields for more person-hours of time, but spending less time in each field.

Content of the Environment

What does the Extension Service contribute to Midwest as a place to live? Data show that, aside from the county AES office (which we shall not consider here because of its county-wide rather than local relevance), the chief contributions of the AES to Midwest in 1963-1964 were (1) *business and discussion meetings* of committees and boards of the AES and related agricultural associations; (2) *cultural-educational-recreational meetings* of AES homemaker units and 4-H Clubs; and (3) *AES classes* in agronomy, animal husbandry, cooking, club and class leadership, general home economics, floriculture, and sewing. These three categories accounted for about two thirds of all AES behavior settings, about 90 percent of their occurrences, and about 80 percent of the person-hours that AES settings were occupied. Five settings involved displays and competitions of the results of educational undertakings (style revue, judging competition, crafts day, speaking contest) and should perhaps be included with the classes. There were three purely recreational behavior settings (theater party, ice cream social, and swimming party), one sale to raise funds by an AES activity (4-H Club food sale), and one community service setting (solicitation of funds for a children's charity).

In brief, in 1963-1964 the AES provided environmental enclaves in Midwest for transacting the business of organizations devoted to advancing agriculture as a way of life and as a business and for giving information and skills relevant to modern rural living and to farming business. Some of the settings were tempered, so to speak, with recreation; but recreation per se was minor by all measures; this was also true of community service.

Comparison of 1954-1955 and 1963-1964 data reveals that business meetings increased on all measures; for example, there were twenty-six occurrences of organization business meetings in the earlier survey year and sixty in 1963-1964. Cultural-educational settings, on the other hand, decreased on most measures. It would appear that settings concerned with organizational problems of the AES and associated organizations increased, that settings with cultural-educational content held constant or decreased, and that purely recreational behavior settings became very minor in extent.

We also approached the question of *what* rather than *how much* the AES contributed to Midwest, by rating behavior settings on eleven attributes called *action patterns*. For example, we asked to what degree a behavior setting fosters recreation. If the behavior occurring in a setting involves play and enjoyment primarily, the setting receives a high rating on the action pattern "recreation." A behavior setting may receive a high rating on more than one action pattern; for example, a handicraft exhibition may be high in recreational and in esthetic activities. Data in Table 2 show that the contribution of the AES to the town

Table 2. Number of Behavior Settings with High Ratings on
Action Patterns Expressed as Percents of Values for All Settings
and for AES Settings in Midwest, 1963-1964

Behavior Settings	Percent of Behavior Settings	
	AES[a]	Midwest[b]
Education (formal teaching in class)	44.4	16.3
Social (interpersonal interaction)	100.0	85.3
Personal appearance (dressmaking, grooming)	8.8	2.6
Nutrition (preparing and/or consuming food)	11.1	5.9
Government (direct government involvement)	8.8	7.8
Physical health (medical attention)	0.0	2.3
Esthetics (artistic activities)	4.4	8.5
Business (exchanging goods and services for profit)	2.2	7.1
Professionalism (paid leaders)	24.4	33.6
Recreation (play, enjoyment)	6.6	23.4
Religion (worship)	0.0	15.5

[a]Percent of 45.

[b]Percent of 884.

environment did not duplicate that provided by the town as a whole. Relative to the town, the AES overemphasized behavior settings where certain action patterns were prominent, and it underemphasized settings where other action patterns were prominent.

According to this evidence, the AES enriched the environment of the town in 1963-1964 with settings in which activities devoted to education, social interaction, personal appearance, nutrition, and government were prominent. Compared to the town as a whole, it added fewer settings in which activities devoted to religion, recreation, professionalism, esthetics, and physical health were prominent. If the AES had been removed from Midwest, the loss to adult education would be particularly severe, for the AES was, aside from the churches, the only regular source of adult education settings.

Inhabitants of the Environment

The AES settings in Midwest are open to all town residents, as members or visitors. It is justifiable, therefore, to ask to what degree subgroups of the town's population actually entered and inhabited these parts provided by the AES. We have asked if people who inhabited AES behavior settings had the same age distribution as did the population of the town and, if not, which ages were more and less represented in AES settings.

The data reported show that in both 1954-1955 and 1963-1964, children to the age of nine years constituted a smaller percent of the population of AES settings than of the town population. In both years, children nine to twelve years old contributed two and three times more than their proportionate share of AES inhabitants. In 1954-1955, adolescents (twelve to eighteen years) made up more than their proportionate number of AES inhabitants by a factor of 3.7; in 1963-1964, however, adolescents had become underoccupiers of AES behavior settings, comprising only 38 percent of the expected number of inhabitants of AES settings. In both years, adults (eighteen to sixty-five years) were present in AES settings in the same proportion as in the town population, but persons sixty-five years or older underoccupied AES settings in 1954-1955 at 24 percent of the expected rate.

Some of the sources of changes in the age composition of the inhabitants of AES settings are apparent. The decline in adolescent participation was due in part (1) to the removal of

some 4-H Club activities from Midwest to another town where
the 4-H Club fairground was located and (2) to a great increase
in competing activities in the school (for example, a greater
number of more varied athletic and musical events) and in the
community (for example, bowling and golf).

It should be emphasized again that changes in participation in AES settings in Midwest do not mean that these were
county-wide changes. In fact, there is some evidence, not included here, that the number of rural adolescents participating
in AES activities in town did not decline and that the transfer
of 4-H Club settings from Midwest to other towns in the county
was accompanied by an increase in county-wide participation.
In fact, eighteen of the thirty all-county behavior settings at the
4-H Club fairground in another town were attended by Midwest adolescents. Nevertheless, the changes within the town are
important for Midwest as an environment within which the
town's adolescents live.

It appears that the older people of Midwest have filled an
occupancy gap in AES behavior settings caused by the decline
in adolescent attendance. Part of this greater participation by
older people was due to the fact that the AES homemakers
units retained their aging members without experiencing a corresponding increase in the membership of younger women. This
lower recruitment appears to derive from the fact that more
women were working outside their homes in 1963-1964 and
perhaps also from a lesser tolerance for young children in settings that are essentially for adults. If the latter is true, it may
be part of a general, cultural urbanization of Midwest over the
period of the study.

Summary

In 1963-1964, the Agricultural Extension Service made a
substantial contribution to the behavior environment of Midwest. It provided 5 percent of the behaviorally relevant parts of
the town, and some of these parts (such as agronomy classes
and club officer training classes) were provided only by AES.
The parts of the town that were established and maintained by

AES were predominantly for education, especially adult education, and for carrying on the business of groups formed to advance rural life and farming. The AES settings not only enlarged the behavior opportunities of the town's inhabitants but also provided contacts with the outside world by bringing both lay and professional people into the town and by providing opportunities and channels of communication with settings within the county, state, and nation.

From 1954-1955 to 1963-1964, (1) AES settings maintained their attraction for town residents (hours of attendance increased in almost exact proportion to the increase in the town's population); (2) the total number and variety of AES settings did not increase as they did in the town at large; (3) however, settings concerned with the advancement of agricultural business and rural life increased, while those concerned with education and recreation decreased; (4) fewer town adolescents spent time in AES settings in 1963-1964 than in 1954-1955, and more people over sixty-five years of age spent time in AES settings.

This study illustrates a method that should be useful for surveys made by county-based agencies. This example of use of the method does have some limitations; it deals with only part of a county-wide system and so cannot give a complete picture of the impact of AES on Midwest. Also, it measures quantity rather than quality of participation. From what has been reported, however, it is clear that the analysis of the AES via its behavior settings contributed to the understanding of the actual functioning of the agency in one town and county.

As an example of the usefulness of the data reported here, when this report was first prepared, the Jefferson County AES agents noted the underoccupancy of adolescents in AES settings. A special effort was then made, with the cooperation of the Midwest school system, to provide two special settings of interest to adolescents and preteens: two forty-five-minute programs on bicycle safety for fifth- and sixth-grade students, and four one-hour grooming classes for high-school girls. These two settings involved 145 separate pupils, both town and out-of-town, most of whom were not involved in any other 4-H Club activity. A third activity, the "4-H TV Action Program" for third- through eighth-grade pupils, were actively promoted throughout the county, obtaining voluntary enrollments of 53 percent of all eligible county residents, and 152 out of 233 (65 percent) eligible Midwest school pupils, again both town and out-of-town. A behavior setting analysis for the year 1966-1967 would indicate that the underoccupancy of town adolescents in AES settings that occurred in 1963-1964 was being remedied.

This chapter's report indicates that the AES program is a significant part of Midwest and of Jefferson County, and that the data gave AES agents a basis from which to evaluate their performance and thus increase their effectiveness.

Roger G. Barker   *14*

Theory of
Behavior Settings

We seek some degree of lawfulness in the links between entities
that function according to laws that are conceptually incommensurate. The question is "Are there theories that can account
for some of the consequences of the interaction of behavior settings and their human components, in view of the fact that
these entities operate in accordance with laws as different as
those that govern business profits and thermostats on the one
hand and those that govern human perception and motivation
on the other? Specifically how do humans enter in a systematic,
derivable way into the structure and processes of behavior settings while these entities continue to operate by their own in-
commensurable laws?"

    Reprint of part of article entitled "Ecology and Motivation" in
Jones (1960, pp. 1-50).

Thing and Medium

I believe we can find some help here in a remarkable paper by Heider ([1926] 1959), written over thirty years ago but only recently brought to the attention of the general psychological public. In this paper, entitled *Thing and Medium*, Heider anticipates some of the concepts of cybernetics and information theory and applies them to certain psychological problems in ways that are still ahead of the time. Heider considered the problem of perception at a distance within the ecological sector of Brunswik's unit (1955). He tried to distinguish the *physical characteristics* of the objects of perception and of the processes that mediate between them and the perceiving organism. Heider pointed out, as is still largely true, that only processes at the receptor surface and within the organism had previously been considered.

Heider noted that distal objects in the ecological environment, at the origin of the perceptual unit, have different physical properties from the entities that intervene between these objects and the proximal stimuli on the receptor surface. He called the former objects *things* and the latter entities *media*. Things are *internally* constrained; they are relatively independent of external events for their forms and for the distribution of energy within them. A stone is an example of an object with strong thing characteristics; its firm, strong unity seems to issue from its own intrinsic nature. *Media*, on the other hand, are to a high degree *externally* constrained; they are relatively dependent on external events for the form and energy characteristics they exhibit. The pattern of light rays reflected from a stone is an example of a manifold of entities with high medium character; the pattern of the light is determined in some way by the extrinsic, alien stone. The second differentiating feature of thing and medium is that things are unitary events; their parts are *interdependent*. A change in one part of a thing causes a change in the next part and is in turn caused by a change in a previous part. The variety they can exhibit is limited by internal arrangements. But *media* are composite events; their parts are independent; every change in each part is caused separately from the outside. The variety a perfect medium can exhibit is not limited; it is completely docile to outside influences.

With these characteristics, things become centers of the causal texture of the world, and their influence is carried in the form of *spurious thing units* (to use Heider's term) by media whose forms and processes are molded by things. It is the stable, but imposed, spurious thing units that make it possible for a medium to represent a thing at a distance.

It is important to note, however, that each *single* part of even the most docile medium has its own structure and dynamics; thus light has its own unique reflection characteristics with respect to a stone. A single quantum of light represents itself rather than the stone from which it is reflected. However, a *manifold* of light rays, each reflected independently of the next ray, but with the same index with reference to the surface of the stone, does *as a pattern* represent the stone. Other things being constant, the number of parts of a set of entities, its differentiation, is directly related to the medium quality of the set. A single building block has poor medium qualities; a set of fifty blocks is a better medium; and five hundred building blocks is much better yet—it is a medium by means of which many different structures can be built.

We begin here to get a glimpse of a lawful relationship between phenomena on incommensurate conceptual levels that is more than an empirical probability. The laws governing the behavior of stones and light cannot now be subsumed within the same system. But the consequences of their interaction are univocally lawful, and beyond this some of the conditions determining this lawfulness begin to appear. Perception of things is possible because the same spurious medium unit is imposed on the light manifold by the thing every time they meet, and this spurious unit, in turn, has an unequivocal impact on the medium of the receptor system at the periphery of the organism, which is governed by still other laws. To function in this way, these different but coupled manifolds must all have the properties of media.

The physical sciences are replete with instances in which small entities on one level provide the medium for quite different phenomena on other levels, while continuing to function according to their own laws. A jet of gas issuing under pressure from a puncture in a container has its own characteristics of velocity and diameter, yet the gas molecules within the stream continue to behave according to their own laws; for example, according to the law of thermal agitation.

Every entity stands between phenomena on its outside and on its inside that belong to different orders of events from the entity itself and from each other. An entity forms the outside of the coupled phenomena within it, and it, along with other entities, forms the inside of superordinate entities. The entity is linked to both of these alien realms in two ways: as medium, when it is constrained in the variety it exhibits by the other level, and as thing, when it constrains the other level. In these terms, *environment* refers to phenomena (1) on the outside of an entity (2) that are coupled with the entity (3) by incommensurate laws that (4) constrain the entity (have the relation of thing to it) or (5) are constrained by the entity (have the relation of medium to it). Parallel statements can be made about phenomena on the inside of an entity.

These inside-outside couplings are matters of empirical fact: The patterning of words when a speaker speaks ideas (and the constraint on his expressed ideas by the words at his command), the patterning of cells within a developing embryo (and the restrictions on embryonic organization by the degree of cell differentiation), the patterning of people at a ball game (and the influence of the people on the game) are readily observed. Can we do more than describe the end terms of these couplings, that is, the inputs and the outputs, and the probability that certain outputs will follow certain inputs? Can we achieve concepts that will impose some necessity on these couplings?

Let us return to the glimpse we had of this possibility via the ideas of thing and medium. Docility is a characteristic of a medium: It is inert, exhibiting neither driving nor resisting forces. To the degree that a medium exhibits resisting forces when outside forces act on it, it is a poor medium; to the degree that it is the locus of driving forces when it encounters other entities, it is not a medium. A thing is in these respects the opposite of a medium; it contains driving forces, and it is patterned. It bends light, forms sentences, organizes cells, distributes people. These are attributes possessed in greater or less degree by phenomena on all levels. So although we may be unable to discover the means by which the pattern of forces from a thing on one level impresses itself on a medium on a different level (for example, how an idea is transformed into words), still, if the docility of the medium can be measured *on its level,* and the force issuing from the thing can be measured *on its level,* it may be possible to explain in *some* degree consequences that occur across unbreachable boundaries.

People: Media of Behavior Settings

Six features of the relationship between people and behavior settings must now be mentioned.

First, people are part of the inside manifold of behavior settings.

Second, of all the attributes of settings, people are the sine qua non. In emergencies, a setting can operate without some of its usual paraphernalia, but it must have people. They are the essential medium by which it functions. Nonetheless, although essential, people are anonymous; they are equipotential; their individuality is irrelevant to behavior settings. People in this respect are not different from the other behavior objects of the setting. If the functions of people can be more effectively carried out by machines, people, as we know so well, are replaced. Paradoxically, within behavior settings people are both essential and expendable, but if all the people of a setting are replaced by machines, the setting ceases to exist, and the equipment becomes an adjunct of another setting.

Third, each quasi-stationary level of a setting has its optimal population requirements. The Castle Cinema in Yoredale does very well with an audience of one hundred, a cashier, and a projectionist; the seventh grade in Midwest functions best with twenty-two pupils and one teacher. With a great many more people or fewer people, these settings exhibit signs of malfunctioning.

Fourth, of all the equipment and paraphernalia of a setting, people are among the most immediately malleable and adjustable. Rooms do not readily expand, tables do not hurry, and typewriters do not make speeches. But people quickly spread out or crowd together, speed up or slow down, write or talk. They have the greatest medium qualities of all the parts of behavior settings.

Fifth, different behavior settings on the same level of functioning, and therefore with the same optimal population requirements, actually differ greatly in population. Seventh-grade classes vary in population from two—a teacher and a pupil—to sixty or more. And there are wide fluctuations from time to time in the population of the same setting while it operates at the same quasi-stationary level. The Castle Cinema sometimes has 12 paying customers and sometimes 250. Behavior settings are frequently overpopulated or underpopulated, in terms of their momentary quasi-stationary levels.

Sixth, these five features of the relation between people and behavior settings emphasize the position of people as the media of behavior settings. However, no medium is perfect, and the imperfections can reside in any of its attributes or in a combination of them. Not all of the consequences of the different sources of imperfection are understood at the present time. But we can make a beginning, and for this purpose it is fruitful to distinguish dynamic and structural aspects of media.

The relative adequacy and inadequacy of a medium can reside in its dynamic characteristics. According to the theory we have presented, a thing is the origin of forces that in some way bear on the elements of the medium and cause it to take on characteristics of the thing. Every medium resists these forces to a greater or lesser degree because of internal constraints within elements and/or interdependencies between them. A measure of the medium quality of a particular medium relative to a particular thing is the amount by which the strength of the driving forces from the thing exceed the resisting forces of the medium. When this difference is zero or negative, the "medium" ceases to be a medium: The idea is not expressed (the words cannot be found), the clay is not shaped (it is too hard), the fingers do not grasp (the hand is too weak). While such a blocked thing-medium system continues, there is pressure on the medium and counterpressure back on the thing. In this case, a frequent consequence, via feedback loops, is an increase in the driving forces from the thing, or a decrease in the resisting forces of the medium. I press harder on my recalcitrant pen, and the ink and the words flow; I moisten the clay, and the shape appears.

The relative adequacy and inadequacy of a medium can reside also in its structural characteristics. An adequate medium assumes the form of a thing, and form has requirements so far as number of parts is concerned. A set of four straight sticks cannot assume the form of a hexagon, but it can represent a rectangle. A 900-word vocabulary may express exactly a customer's grocery order, and 9,000 words will not improve it, but 900 words will produce a more distorted version of Hamlet than a 9,000-word vocabulary.

Dynamic and structural attributes of media are inter-related in complex ways. In some cases, parts and energy are interchangeable, and relative deficiency of parts can be compensated for by increased energy expenditure. In other cases, energy will not take the place of parts: No amount of force will make four sticks represent a hexagon; an American with a limited French vocabulary will not speak more fluently if he puts more energy behind the words he does know and shouts.

Despite these and other unknown complexities, the fundamental features of thing and medium allow us to make some general derivations of the consequences of particular types of couplings between a thing and a medium. So we turn to behavior settings to discover how dynamics and structure are involved in the couplings between them as things and people as media.

Behavior Settings: Locus of Opportunities and Obligations

It will be of value first to change our viewpoint from behavior settings per se to the individual inhabitants of behavior settings.

A behavior setting is a place where most of the inhabitants can satisfy a number of personal motives, where they can achieve multiple satisfactions. In other words, a behavior setting contains opportunities. Furthermore, different people achieve different clusters of satisfactions in the same setting. The unity of a behavior setting does not arise from similarity in the motives of the occupants. In the behavior setting "football game," for example, the quarterback will experience a complex system of social-physical satisfactions, depending on what kind of a person he is; his mother in the bleachers will at the same time have quite a different set of satisfactions; and the coach will have still others. But unless these and other inhabitants of a football game are at least minimally satisfied, they will leave, or will not return on another occasion, and the setting will cease. In other words, a setting exists only when it provides its occupants with the particular psychological conditions their own unique natures require. Heterogeneity in the personal motives of the individual inhabitants of a setting contributes to the stability of the setting.

Behavior settings impose obligations on their occupants, too. These obligations are consequences of the intrinsic structure of behavior settings. If the inhabitants of a setting are to continue to attain the goals that bring them satisfactions, the setting must continue to function at a level that each occupant defines for himself in terms of his own satisfactions. Every occupant of a setting is, therefore, faced with three routes: One is the immediate, direct route to his goals; the others are toward operating and toward maintaining the setting so that his goals and the routes to them will remain intact.

The strengths of these sets of forces are controlled by feedback from the setting's quasi-stationary level of functioning. When an occupant of a behavior setting sees that this level *threatens* to decline and thereby to reduce the valence of the goals it provides him or to increase the resistance of the paths to these goals, an increase occurs in the forces along the routes that operate and maintain the setting. The amount and direction of the increase depend on the degree of the perceived threat and on the person's perception of its sources and the most promising ways of countering the threat.

It is the result of such adjustment circuits that keeps a

setting on a quasi-stationary level or moving toward a more satisfying level for the inhabitants. Sometimes, of course, the forces along the maintenance routes are too weak, and the setting deteriorates.

The Interface of Behavior Settings and People

We are ready now to bring together behavior settings, people, and the concepts of thing and medium by way of this question: Are there necessary consequences for people where their behavior occurs in a behavior setting with less than the optimal number of persons to serve as media for the setting in its current homeostatic state?

The point must be reemphasized that we are considering people on two levels: (1) as fixtures and paraphernalia by means of which a behavior setting functions, that is, as parts of an extraindividual behavior entity that is subject to behavior setting laws and (2) as individuals, subject to psychological laws.

From the general relations between thing and medium we have discussed, we would expect certain modifications to occur in both individuals and behavior settings when the population of a setting is reduced below the optimum. We can derive the nature of these modifications in this particular case from the characteristics of behavior settings we have considered. The property of homeostatic level means that behavior settings are strongly self-determined, that they therefore provide a coercive environment for their interior elements, that they stand as clear-cut things to the media within them. The optimal population requirement of each homeostatic level means that there are feedback circuits that connect the *number* of people in a setting with the state of the setting. The *opportunities* and *obligations* of behavior settings refer to details of the couplings by means of which particular individuals are constrained by the setting; it is these that particularly concern us here.

We can subsume opportunities and obligations under the concept of behavior setting *claim,* meaning thereby all the forces acting on individual members of a setting to enter and participate in its operation and maintenance in particular ways.

Let us see how behavior setting claim operates in the particular case in which we are interested, namely, when the differentiation of the internal medium of the setting is reduced below optimum, that is, when the number of people is less than optimal for the level on which the setting functions.

The homeostatic mechanism of the setting ensures that a reduction in personnel, within certain ranges, does not change the absolute number of opportunities or obligations the setting contains. The opportunities and the obligations are therefore shared by fewer people. The consequence is clear: the average valence per person is greater along both the direct and the maintenance routes of the setting. In general, then, the forces of the setting on its inhabitants increase in strength. This amounts to an amplification of the theory of thing and medium as it applies to behavior settings; namely, the media of behavior settings (people) are of a sort that are able to compensate via increased energy for decreased parts. Our first conclusion is that one consequence of reduction in personnel of a setting below its optimal level is increased behavior setting claim (forces to participate) on the remaining persons.

There are other consequences. Under the conditions we have defined, essentially the same complex of events and forces must find their points of application on fewer persons: There are, to use F. Allport's term, fewer junction points or encounters, but there are the same number of forces and events. Each point is the junction of more of these. This means that the same persons are pressed in multiple directions; they now must do more things. On an eight-man baseball team, with the center fielder missing, the left fielder has to cover left field and part of center field; likewise, the right fielder must cover part of center field as well as his own territory. The second baseman and/or shortstop must play deeper than normally in order to compensate partially for the gap left in center field, and the other infielders must adjust slightly, too, so that the infield is not vulnerable to slow hits. The behavior of almost every member of an eight-man baseball team will exhibit greater effort than when the full team plays, and it will be more versatile, too; that is, it will cover more territory and more positions. There will be secondary consequences, too, such as greater tension.

The primary communication channel by which these changes occur is via the people's perception of their greater opportunities and their recognition of the threat that the reduced population carries for all their opportunities. Cognition of the relation between opportunities and obligations is essential. The inhabitants of a setting need not comprehend the setting as a phenomenal unit, but they must experience a threat to their own goals, and they must comprehend some, at least, of its sources, sources that are in fact a part of the behavior setting even if not so recognized. A strong secondary feedback channel arises from the fact that most settings include more than one member. The perceptions mentioned do not involve only a single person but involve all members of the setting. *One direction of most of the inhabitants' maintenance forces is toward getting others to act along maintenance channels, too. These interlacings of obligations strengthen greatly the total claim of an underpopulated behavior setting* and homogenize, so to speak, the source of its forces.

The consequence for individuals who inhabit undermanned settings in comparison with those who inhabit optimally manned settings can be summarized as follows. First, the strength of the forces acting on the individual inhabitants of the undermanned settings will be stronger. Second, the range of direction of these forces will be greater. It is interesting to note what this means in terms of the three attributes of high medium quality, namely, lack of internal constraint within the elements of the medium, lack of interdependency with neighboring elements, and number of elements. In the case of behavior settings, we are suggesting that when number of interior elements declines, thereby reducing overall medium quality, modifications are instigated that in effect restore medium quality via the other attributes: The internal constraint of the elements becomes less effective under the increased strength of driving forces, and the interdependence of the elements is increased by the greater range in the directions of the forces acting on them.

These consequences follow, of course, only within a limited range of population decrement. At some point, the homeostatic level cannot be maintained, and the behavior setting is modified in the direction that is more appropriate for the medium; it becomes smaller, simpler, and so forth, while yet retaining the essence of the setting. And if the population declines below the minimum necessary, the setting ceases to function.

It is clear why in this case there is a close coupling between a behavior setting and its incommensurate inside phenomena: The setting constrains the *individuals* within it to behave appropriately; it uses them as media; but the people in toto, via their overall attribute of number (an attribute that does not apply to any single one of them), constrain the setting.

The primary derivations regarding the consequences for individual inhabitants of undermanned behavior settings have many phenotypic expressions, and there are numerous feedback loops and crisscrossing of influence. It is impossible to predict all of them. We shall list under each of the primary consequences some of its particular manifestations, with examples, and make a few comments on them.

First, the behavioral consequences of the greater claim of undermanned setting on individual occupants are as follows:

- Greater effort. Greater individual effort can take the form of "harder" work or longer hours. The greater effort is directed both toward the primary goals of the setting and along the maintenance routes. When the assistant yearbook editor leaves with no one available for replacement, the editor proofreads all the galleys, instead of half of them.
- More difficult and more important tasks. There is in most settings a hierarchy of tasks with respect to difficulty and importance. The inexperienced sophomore has to take the lead role in the play when the experienced senior becomes ill.

The primary sources of these changes have been identified. They are greatly enhanced in social behavior settings by the individual's perception of increased rate of work by others and by increased social pressure from others. One maintenance route for all members is to encourage and indeed to force others to work hard also. These ramifications of influence increase still further the strength of the claim; they also generalize the claim of a setting so it becomes a property of the whole setting.

Second, the behavioral consequences of greater range in the direction of the forces acting on individual occupants are as follows:

- Wider variety of activities. Each occupant is called on to fill more positions and play more roles in the setting. The director of the small choir also plays the organ. This primary resultant has many ramifications and manifestations; it involves perception as well as overt behavior. The person sees himself as suitable for previously "inappropriate" tasks. It involves people as well as nonsocial situations. The person has to meet and interact with a greater proportion of the total variety of people present.
- Less sensitivity to and less evaluation of differences among people. This will usually be in the nature of ignoring differences previously noted and exhibiting increased tolerance of those rated. It is a direct manifestation of the greater variety in the direction of forces; under their influence, not only does the person see himself as suitable for new roles but he also sees others as more widely suitable. Undoubtedly the increased strength of the behavior setting forces aids this process too. Recalcitrant media (the self and others) become more docile. Here we enter the field of values, at least on a functional level. When essential personnel are in short supply, it is necessary to "accept" those persons who are available and can do the job.
- Lower level of maximal performance. By reason particularly of the demands of great versatility, which introduces interfering skills, but also because of the greater effort and longer hours, with consequent fatigue, the maximal level of a person's achievement in any particular task is reduced. The soloist of the chorus who is also conductor, organist, and librarian is less able to excel in one of these tasks than if he were able to devote all of his time to it. This tendency may be enhanced in a social setting where an individual's performance requires others' support, as is often the case; it is easier to pitch a superlative ball game if the fielders can catch the ball.

Third, the behavioral consequences of the joint influence

of greater strength and greater range in the direction forces are as follows:

- Greater functional importance within the setting. With increasing scarcity of population, the people who remain become ever more essential. A stage is sometimes reached where everyone is a key person; this happens when everyone in the setting is in one or more essential jobs, with no substitutes available.
- More responsibility. In striving to maintain the setting for his own personal reasons, the individual in a setting where population is scarce is also contributing something essential to the other inhabitants of the setting, who may have quite different interests and motives. A high school student wants to study second-year Latin, and, by doing so, ensures for Sue and Joe and Mary, who want the class too, that it will be held. He, and all the others, achieve "Latin plus appreciation." Responsibility is experienced by a person when a behavior setting and what others gain from it depend on him. This in most cases amounts to adding a new set of social goals to the setting or to increasing the valence of an existing set.

    Both functional importance and individual responsibility are attributes experienced by a person himself and by his associates. They do not occur to so large a degree in optimally populated settings and do not occur at all in overpopulated settings. A setting that is truly optimally populated does not burden itself with essential personnel; people are too unreliable. Substitutes, vice-presidents, committee members in excess of the quorum requirement, a second team—these are regular features of optimally populated settings.
- *Greater functional self-identity.* A change occurs from preoccupation with "What kind of a person am I?" and "What kind of a person is he?" to "What has to be done?" and "Who can do this job?" This is a major shift. It is closely related to the importance and variety of jobs to be done, but it is grounded also in well-established perceptual laws. A functionless person—and many such people necessarily exist in an overpopulated setting and to some degree in an optimally

populated setting—has only personal attributes and *potential* functions (for example, abilities, aptitudes). The only functional relations he can have are the interpersonal ones of being liked or not being liked, of being judged and evaluated by others, and by himself. Thus the answer to "What kind of a person am I (or is he)?" becomes of central importance; it creates a highly personal and egocentric situation. Here, too, the person is in the position of a figure against an undifferentiated background, where small differences are clearly seen. Individual differences become important, and the innumerable ways of sorting and classifying people become prominent.

But a person with a function, as is necessary in an undermanned setting, is more than a person; he is a person in a complicated behavioral context, and he is judged within this context. Fine discriminations as to the kind of person he is are difficult to make. There is less possibility and need for classifying functioning people with respect to the kind of people they are. The question becomes "Is the job coming off?" If it is an important job and is coming off, the person takes on the value of this achievement no matter what "kind of a person" he is. Personality analysis (by self and others), including subtle testing, sorting, and classifying people, is a feature of overabundantly populated settings.

• *Lower standards and fewer tests for admission.* A baseball game of two members can scarcely maintain the semblance of the setting, although it occurs in this emasculated form in Midwest, with a batter-catcher and the pitcher-fielder. The claim of such a setting on potential participants is very strong indeed, so strong that it will accept, solicit, even impress a five-year-old player or a parent into the setting. We are all familiar with the change in personnel policies when the prime sources of labor are withdrawn from settings, as during a war. Age, sex, and ability tests for admission to settings are changed, and the formerly rejected members are welcomed: Women operate lathes, sixteen-year-olds supervise work crews, and retired professors are reprieved. The lower selectivity of behavior settings relatively deficient in occupants is closely related to the greater range of direction of the forces operating on them.

- *Greater insecurity.* Under the pressure of engaging in more difficult and more varied actions, a person in an underpopulated setting is in great jeopardy of failing to carry through his tasks. To his personal uncertainty is added that which arises from lack of reserves in the behavior setting as a whole. The latter amounts to increased dependence on every other person carrying through his assignments.
- *More frequent occurrences of success and failure.* The underpopulated setting, by providing a situation where high aspirations (in relation to ability) are encouraged in important actions but encouraged without authoritative coercion, provides a place for the flowering of success experiences and also of failure experiences. The underpopulated setting is one where self-esteem and social status can both flourish and also wither. The degree of the success and of the failure a person achieves is related to his evaluation of the importance of the setting in which the experience occurs.

General Significance of Behavior Setting Theory

If our argument is correct, it provides a bridge between two empirically linked but conceptually incommensurate levels of phenomena. In terms of it, predictions that are more than probability statements based on empirical observations can be made about the behavior of the inhabitants of behavior settings: Members of settings with less than optimal personnel *have* to be more energetic, more versatile, more insecure, and so forth than members of settings with optimal populations. These are not nomothetic laws of the behavior of individuals, but they involve much more than correlations between attributes of environment and attributes of behavior.

Roger G. Barker
Phil Schoggen

15

Measures of Habitat
and Behavior Output

◆━◆◆━◆◆━◆◆━◆◆━◆◆━◆◆━◆◆━◆◆━◆◆━◆◆━◆◆━◆◆━◆◆━◆

Habitat Measures

The problem of measuring the size of the habitat of molar actions is a perplexing one. Its solution requires an understanding of the relations between molar actions and their environmental supports. We consider some of these relations in this chapter.

Urbs and Centiurbs: Habitat Extent

A list of the behavior settings occurring during a year in a town or part of a town is a roster of its habitat regions. Three direct enumerations of the extent of this habitat are (1) the

Adapted from Barker and Schoggen (1973, pp. 22-48).

number of settings in the roster, (2) the sum of their days of occurrence, and (3) the sum of their hours of duration. The single measure of habitat extent we have called *urb* (and *centi-urb*, 0.01 urb) is based on these three enumerations and will now be explicated.

Relations Among Number, Occurrence, and Duration of Behavior Settings

On Tuesday, October 22, 1963, between 10 and 11 a.m., there were 148 behavior settings in Yoredale (YD) and 126 settings in Midwest (MW). In YD there were two places for banking behavior (compared with one in MW); there were seven places for hallway behavior (four in MW), four places to engage in beauty shop behavior (one in MW), and three places to place bets (none in MW). This ratio, in general, holds true; the mean number of behavior settings occurring in Midwest in an average hour in 1963-1964 was 88 percent of the number occurring in Yoredale.

But the story is different for a yearlong period. During 1963-1964, 884 behavior settings occurred in MW and 758 in YD; that is, by the year, in 1963-1964 the number of behavior settings in MW was 117 percent of the number in YD.

These data are surprising and confusing; they raise some fundamental questions. Is there a basic temporal interval for enumerating behavior settings? Are years more basic for this purpose than days; are days more basic than hours? Is there, in fact, a univocal measure of the extent of the environment? Some examples reveal the generality of the situation from which these questions arise.

First, an institutional example. A philanthropist endows a number of display galleries in four museums and fills them with art treasures. These permanent exhibits amount to 13, 15, 18, and 22 percent of the exhibit galleries in the fortunate museums. The museum directors, for administrative reasons, place restrictions on the days the galleries are open to the public. Counting each day a gallery is open to the public as one gallery-day, it turns out that the philanthropist's galleries are open for

4.5, 5.0, 3.6, and 7.0 percent, respectively, of the museums' total gallery-days. But the galleries, when open, are not always open for full days, so that the philanthropist's galleries account for 0.7, 0.9, 0.8, and 1.7 percent of the museums' total gallery-hours. The question is: What is the extent of the philanthropist's contributions to these museums?

To the museum directors, who see themselves as conservators of art treasures, he contributed 13 to 22 percent of their collections. But to museum visitors, the philanthropist contributed 3.6 to 7 percent of the exhibits; for, wandering freely through the open galleries on their occasional visits, they would find these proportions of the galleries acknowledging his gift. And to museum guards, the philanthropist's gifts account for 0.7 and 1.7 percent of their work hours. So there are three answers to the question: The philanthropist contributed 13 to 22 percent of the museums' resources, he contributed 3.6 to 7 percent of the museums' daily accessible exhibits, and he contributed 0.7 and 1.7 percent of the gallery-hours of operation. Is one of them truer than the others? Are there ways to combine them into a single measure of extent of museum environment?

Here is a biological example. Tidepools are important ecological features of the shore environment. Like behavior settings, some tidepools are year-round, continuous fixtures, while others have limited durations. Tidepools that are not continuous may be reconstituted each day by the tides, or they may be reconstituted only occasionally, during periods of conjunction of high tides and winds; they then last for varying times. A tidepool, like a behavior setting, has an identity that can be specified by spatial-temporal coordinates; it can be denoted by pointing; it can be examined and reexamined. One can enumerate precisely those present during any period of time: 45 minutes, 7 hours, 13 days, 9.5 months, and so forth. But what period? One might find the following numbers of tidepools on two shore areas: (1) total number of pools during a year—884 in Area 1 and 758 in Area 2; (2) mean number of pools during random days—146 in Area 1 and 178 in Area 2; (3) mean number of pools during random hours—33 in Area 1 and 37 in Area

2. In this conjectural example, the 1963-1964 data for the behavior settings of Midwest (MW) and Yoredale (YD) have been used; they are in fact data that might be duplicated on a shore region. It is obvious that the different measures of tidepool extent would have different consequences for different animal species. Measure 3 indicates that both areas are meager habitats for rapidly migrating birds; neither area is rich in pools for short-time visitors, but Area 2 is more favorable for them than Area 1. Measure 2 shows that both areas have more extensive tidepool environments for slower migrants, or for long-time residents that are daylong feeders, and that Area 2 is more extensive than Area 1. But for the staff of a permanent marine laboratory, Size Measurement 1 is salient; over the seasons, Area 1 is richer in tidepool collection sites than Area 2.

These examples show that our discovery that MW and YD are of different relative extents when their behavior settings are enumerated by the hour, day, and year is not peculiar to them. This equivocal relation occurs in all cases where the rate of recurrence of the entities enumerated is not the same in the localities compared. We conclude, therefore, that the same enumerating time interval must be used when comparisons are made and it must be chosen for its relevance to the problem under consideration. So the question arises, What is the relevant interval for determining the extents of MW and YD as habitats? Some fundamental facts about human action are relevant to this question.

Temporal Relations Between Behavior and Behavior Settings

Our concern is primarily with molar behavior. In the present connection, it is of great importance that molar actions extend over varying lengths of time. "Doing the family shopping" may continue for an hour, while "getting married next June" extends for months. Intentions (Lewin, 1951), plans (Miller, Galanter, and Pribram, 1960), and cognitive maps (Tolman, 1932) are stable states that have been postulated to account on the organism side for the elementary fact that behavior occurs in units that persist over time. A molar action takes place within behavior settings that are at hand during its time span, and our investigations show that the number of settings at hand varies with the duration of the span. "Doing the family shopping" occurs within a smaller time span and smaller habitat (number of behavior settings) than does "getting married next June." If we knew the durations of the molar actions that occur in MW and YD, these would provide the needed temporal frames for determining the extents of the towns' habitats.

We have some bases for estimating the durations of molar actions, for they are governed by the segments into which time is divided by clocks and calendars, by sunrise and sunset, by noon whistles and the six-o'clock news. Time in MW and YD is marked off by hours, days, weeks, months, and years as clearly as space is marked off by inches, feet, and miles. Engagement books, diaries, programs of organizations and institutions, and schedules of events are ubiquitous in both towns, and they are almost all segmented by hours, days, months, and years. In consequence, the actions of the inhabitants of MW and YD, their plans and intentions, are arranged in terms of hourly, daily, monthly, and yearly periods as inevitably as they are arranged in accordance with the towns' spaces and their temperatures, precipitations, and terrains.

However, another elementary attribute of molar behavior attenuates for individual actions the coerciveness of these imposed time intervals: Molar behavior is goal directed. When environmental circumstances change, alterations occur in the molar actions underway so that they usually maintain their goal directions until they are completed. An important environmental change is the periodic termination and initiation of the behavior settings of a community. Molar actions have a special property that maintains their directions under these circumstances, namely, flexible duration. If the behavior setting grocery store shows signs of terminating its daily occurrence at 5:30 instead of the expected 6 p.m., the action of "doing the family shopping," which usually continues for an hour, is either telescoped and completed before 5:30 or extended into the next day, when grocery store again occurs. In either case, "doing the family shopping" continues and is completed; the absence of grocery store between 5:30 p.m. and 8 a.m. the next day is not crucial. Most molar actions have this flexibility, and it makes their completion independent, to some degree, of the temporal schedules of the behavior settings they require for their completion. This means that a behavior setting is almost equally at hand for many molar actions if it occurs this hour, this day, tomorrow, or on following days.

Although the relative frequencies of molar actions of different durations are not known with precision, it seems probable on the basis of general observation, that the behavioral present, the time interval within which intentions are carried out, is distributed with about equal frequency around the modal intervals *during this hour, during this day,* and *during this year.* On this basis, the most general single measure of relative habitat extent is one that weights equally the number of behavior settings that occur within these three periods. When we do this for MW and YD in 1963-1964, we find that MW has 1.17 as many behavior settings per year as YD, it has 0.82 as many settings per day, and it has 0.87 as many settings per hour. The mean of these ratios, which weights them equally, is 0.95. For a sample of molar actions centering with equal frequency on completion *during this hour, during this day,* and *during this year,* there are 95 percent as many behavior settings at hand in MW as in YD.

Standard Town. In order to make general comparisons of habitat extent across towns and years, we require a common base. For this purpose, we have created a hypothetical standard town whose dimensions in terms of number of behavior settings per year, mean number per day, and mean number per hour are the means of four values: MW in 1954-1955 and in 1963-1964 and YD in 1954-1955 and in 1963-1964. These values for the standard town are (1) behavior settings per year, 680.5; (2) mean behavior settings per day, 151.0; (3) mean behavior settings per hour, 34.1. We have called the standard town with these dimensional values an *urb.* The dimensional values of the towns, of parts of the towns, and of individual behavior settings are reported in terms of percentages of the urb values. Here, as an example, are the dimensional values and extent in *centiurbs* (cu) of MW's habitat in 1963-1964: (1) behavior settings per year as percentage of urb, 100 (884/680.5) equals 130.0; (2) mean behavior settings per day as percentage of urb, 100 (146/151) equals 96.7; (3) mean behavior settings per hour as percentage of urb, 100 (32.6/34.1) equals 95.6; extent in centi-urbs (mean of Items 1, 2, and 3) equals 107.4. By the same process, we find that the extent of YD's habitat in 1963-1964 was 112.8 cu.

Many combinations of the dimensional values sum to the same habitat extent. Relatively few behavior settings per year may be compensated as far as habitat extent is concerned by relatively many per day or per hour, and vice versa. This is an aspect of behavior habitat reality; it is in accord with the fundamental nature of molar action (flexible means and stable goal direction); and it is in accord with the fundamental nature of the human habitat (particular parts present and absent on regular or irregular schedules).

Habitat Extent as a Measure of Resources for Molar Actions. Many kinds of molar actions occur only within particular kinds of settings: Sentencing a man to jail takes place only in settings of the district or county courts (not in grocery stores or worship services); getting a haircut occurs only in barbershops (not in business meetings or basketball games); filling a tooth is performed only in dentists' offices (not in garages or at dances). Where this relation holds, molar actions for which there are no appropriate settings do not occur: Cricket is not played in MW—there is no behavior setting cricket game; Latin is not taught in YD—there is no setting Latin class.

Because of this relation between behavior settings and molar actions, number of behavior settings is a more important component of the extent of the habitat of molar actions than is number of behavior setting occurrences or number of hours' duration. This is obvious when one considers the more limited behavior resources of the twelve monthly occurrences of the single Midwest recreational setting Bridge Club II in comparison with twelve occurrences of a wider sample of recreational settings: three meetings of Bridge Club II, High School Home Economics Club Christmas Party, Old Settlers' Pet Parade, Garland Lanes Bowling Exhibition, American Legion Auxiliary Card Party for March of Dimes, Married Couples Bridge Club Meeting in March, elementary school operetta, tractor pulling contest, Women's Bridge Club III May Meeting, Women's Bridge Club IV September Meeting. In terms of centiurbs, the twelve monthly occurrences of Bridge Club II have a habitat extent of 0.06 cu, and the twelve settings (including three Bridge Club II Meetings) have a habitat extent of 0.50 cu. According to the centiurb measurement, the opportunities to set goals and attempt to achieve satisfactions (molar behavior resources) are 12 percent as great in the former case as in the latter. Measurement of habitat extent by centiurbs weights an additional behavior setting 365 (or 366) times greater than an additional occurrence of an existing behavior setting, and it weights an additional behavior setting 8,760 (8,784) times greater than an additional hour of an existing setting.

Measurement of habitat extent in terms of centiurbs is a measure of the at-handness of habitat supports and coercions for molar actions; it is a temporal-spatial proximity measure. The larger the centiurb measure of habitat extent, the greater the number of molar behavior opportunities and requirements within the normal time perspective—that is, the greater the number of goal possibilities and obligations immediately at hand.

Genotypes: Habitat Variety

Similarity of parts has no place in the identification of a behavior setting; interdependence is the sole criterion. However, settings identified on the basis of degree of internal interdependence may have greater or less similarity. Weylen's Grocery and Reid's Grocery are more similar in standing pattern than Weylen's Grocery and Hooker's Tavern. Similarity of standing patterns provides a basis for the meaningful classification of settings into similar categories or genotypes.

The degree of behavior setting similarity that we have adopted for establishing a genotype is, essentially, the lowest degree of pattern similarity compatible with the exchange of major components between settings. The standing patterns of Pearl Cafe and Gwyn Cafe in Midwest are sufficiently similar that major components (staff, equipment, kitchens) could be transposed without appreciably disturbing the functioning of either setting; these behavior settings, therefore, belong to the same genotype. Exchange of major standing behavior pattern components would not be possible between Gwyn Cafe and the Midwest State Bank; they therefore belong to different behavior setting genotypes.

A description of the genotypes of a town portrays the varieties of standing patterns within its environment, and the number of genotypes in a town is a measure of its habitat variety, of the diversity of molar behavior resources and the range of molar behavior opportunities.

Habitat Claims: Human Components of Habitats

Behavior settings have internal structural and dynamic arrangements. One important feature of these arrangements is the power different parts of a setting exercise over it. This ranges from parts with virtually no power over the setting (such as the part "sidewalk superintendents" occupy in the setting high school construction project) to those with control over the entire behavior setting (such as the part occupied by the single teacher of the setting fourth-grade music class). We have called this dimension of behavior settings the *penetration dimension,* and we have identified seven zones of penetration, from Zone 0, the most peripheral zone and the one with least power, to Zone 6, the central and most powerful zone of penetration. Attributes and the nomenclature of the penetration zones are described in Table 1.

Habitat Claims for Human Components. The behavior settings that comprise the towns' habitats specify human components for certain loci (slots, positions) within them. These are habitat claims for human components. The honorary secretaryship of YD's Agricultural and Horticultural Society meeting is such a habitat claim; this position requires an appropriate human component, one with the necessary knowledge and

Table 1. Penetration Zones of Behavior Settings: Their Functions, Power, Habitat Claims, and Human Components; Examples of Implemented Habitat Claims (Behavior Output)

Penetration Zone	Functions	Power	Habitat Claims	Human Components	Behavior Output
6	Control and implementation of program and maintenance circuits	Direct control of entire setting	Single leaderships	Single leaders	Claim leader actions: club president presiding at meeting
5	Control and implementation of program and maintenance circuits	Direct, but shared, control of entire setting	Multiple leaderships	Multiple leaders	Claim leader actions: team captain conferring with coach
4	Joint control (with Zone 5 or 6) and implementation of subsystems of program and maintenance circuits	Direct, shared control of part of setting	Factorships	Factors (functionaries, assistants, and so on)	Claim factor actions: church organist playing for worship service
6-4	Control and operation of program and maintenance circuits	Direct control of entire setting	Habitat claims for operatives; positions of responsibility	Operatives	Claim operations or claim operator actions (responsible actions): lawyer or his secretary answering query of client
3	Implementation of major goal and emergency maintenance circuits	Indiréct control of most of setting	Memberships	Members (customers, clients, and so on)	Claim member actions: store customer making purchase
2	Implementation of minor goal and emergency maintenance circuits	Some influence on part of setting	Spectatorships	Spectators (audience, invited guests, and so on)	Claims spectator actions: parade viewer watching parade
1	No functions	Almost no power	None; neutral places	Onlookers (loafers, and so on)	Claim onlooker actions: infant accompanying mother in grocery store
0	Recruiting and dissuading potential inhabitants	Region of influence external to setting	None; potential places	Potential inhabitants	Potential guest reading invitation

skills, in order to become operational. Habitat claims are stable structural and dynamic features of a town's habitat.

Claims for operatives. Penetration Zones 4, 5, and 6, the operating zones, are particularly important. Their human components, the *operatives,* are the most immediately essential inhabitants of a behavior setting; they man its program and maintenance circuits, where they are responsible for maintaining the setting as a structural unit and operating its program. This responsibility entails power over the setting, but it also involves coercion by the setting, for, along with the greater power of the more central penetration zones over a behavior setting, there is greater power over the inhabitants. Behavior setting operatives are more strongly constrained by the homeostatic controls of the settings they implement than are members, spectators, or onlookers. The strength of the forces acting on the chairman of a meeting, the proprietor of a store, or the preacher in a worship service to enter the setting and behave in accordance with its program are greater than those on the typical member, customer, or parishioner. The more central the penetration zone, the more essential is each inhabitant to the occurrence of the setting. In behavior settings of the genotypes baseball games, business meetings, and attorneys' offices, for example, larger proportions of their claims for operatives than of their normal complements of members and spectators must be filled for adequate functioning on any occasion.

Operatives fill positions of responsibility within behavior settings; they are the human components of the habitat claims that are most crucial for the normal operation of settings, and these habitat claims are located within stronger force fields than other habitat claims. In psychological language, the inhabitants of the operating zones of behavior settings carry out important and difficult actions; they are important, hard-working people; they control the setting and are controlled by it. They are the setting's most responsible inhabitants. The number of habitat claims of a behavior setting for operatives is the number of positions of responsibility that must be filled (operatives that must be present) for the normal occurrence of the setting. For example, Presbyterian Church Worship Service in MW requires twenty operatives (one minister, one organist, twelve choir members, two ushers, two candle lighters, and two greeters). In 1963-1964, YD had 7,764 habitat claims for human components within its operating zones—that is, habitat claims for operatives. If all of YD's behavior settings were to occur simultaneously, it would require 7,764 human components to operate the town's habitat.

Claims for Members and Spectators. By no means are Penetration Zones 2 and 3 unimportant. In the long run, their components are the sine qua non of behavior settings; without them, a setting is like a kindled fire without a supply of fuel. Furthermore, they, along with operatives, man the maintenance circuits in emergencies; when behavior settings of a town's habitat are less than optimally habitable, the homeostatic controls of these settings pressure the inhabitants of all the penetration zones into the maintenance circuits. A town with relatively few inhabitants per centiurb falls below its optimally habitable state relatively frequently, and, when it does so, pressures per available component toward maintenance circuits are relatively great. On the average, therefore, the inhabitants of such towns are more important to its survival as a human habitat than are the inhabitants of towns with high inhabitant/centiurb ratios.

Penetration Zone 0. Penetration Zone 0 is the region surrounding a behavior setting within which the forces of the setting operate to impel people and materials into it or to repel them from it. Zone 0 is the zone of *potential* inhabitants. It is the region where advertisements urging attendance circulate, and where warnings such as "No Minors Allowed" are posted; it overlaps with Zones 1 to 6 of other behavior settings. For example, if a client in the YD behavior setting Blackett's Ladies' Hairdresser reads a notice on the counter stating that the annual Church of England Jumble Sale is being held and is soliciting attendance, the client is simultaneously in Zone 3 of Blackett's Ladies' Hairdresser and in Zone 0 of Church of England Jumble Sale.

Authority Systems: Intersetting Power Relations

A behavior setting may have power over a number of other settings or over no other setting. In MW, the behavior set-

ting elementary and high school board meeting has authority
over 227 other behavior settings ranging from elementary
school principal's office to sixth-grade hike; this constitutes one
authority system, a multisetting authority system. At the other
extreme, Burgess Beauty Shop has authority over no other setting. This also constitutes one authority system, a single-setting
authority system.

Authority systems are grouped into five classes on the
basis of the following characteristics of the *controlling* or *executive* setting: *Private enterprises* include all settings under the
control of behavior settings operated by private citizens in order
to earn a living; *churches* comprise those settings that are controlled by central administrative settings of churches; *government agencies* embrace all behavior settings managed by executive settings of town, county, state, or federal governments,
excluding school-controlled settings; the authority system
schools covers the settings under the aegis of executive settings
operated by private or public educational agencies (town, district, county, state, or national school boards or committees);
voluntary associations comprise all settings other than those in
the first four classes. Each behavior setting of a town occurs in
only one authority system; the five classes of authority systems
control all public behavior settings of a town.

Output Measures

A behavior setting inevitably produces behavior appropriate to it because the inhabitants are parts of the machinery
of the setting functioning according to its programs of operation. If the behavior settings barbershop, dentist's office, cricket
game, and Latin class are present in a town, hair cutting, tooth
filling, cricket playing, and Latin teaching inevitably occur. If
the action pattern religion is an attribute of the standing pattern
of a behavior setting, religious actions are among the actions of
its inhabitants (in the same way, a factory with facilities and a
program for manufacturing phosphate fertilizer actually produces phosphate fertilizer when it is in operation). However, the
habitat characteristics of a behavior setting where the action
pattern religion is present (and of the facilities and program of a

phosphate factory) do not reveal the amount of output of religious actions (or of phosphate fertilizer); they reveal only the programmed kind of output.

We present four measures of behavior output: person-hours, claim operations, leader acts, and leaders.

Person-Hours of Behavior

The inhabitants of a behavior setting act continuously in accordance with its standing pattern; therefore, the sum of the times all inhabitants spend in it is a measure of the amount of behavior with the attributes of its standing pattern. This sum for a survey year is the person-hours (P-H) of behavior it produces. This is the most comprehensive measure we have used. For example, in MW in 1963-1964, the 830 inhabitants inhabited the town's public behavior settings for 1,125,134 hours. This time can be partitioned among classes of inhabitants (children, adults, aged), among genotypes (worship services, funerals), and so forth, for many analytical purposes. For example, 27,000 (2.4 percent) of the MW hours occur in behavior settings where the action pattern religion is prominent. Of special importance for the analysis and presentation of the data are the person-hours of behavior generated via all inhabitants; this is the *gross behavior product* of the town (GBP). The person-hours generated via the residents of the town constitute the *town behavior product* (TBP).

Claim Operations

A claim operation is a unique combination of a *particular behavior setting, a specific habitat claim in Penetration Zones 4 to 6* of the setting, and *a particular human component* implementing the claim. For example, if in a Presbyterian worship service (behavior setting) the pulpit (habitat claim) is filled by Pastor George Smith (human component), a claim operation occurs. Claim operations such as this keep towns habitable for worshippers, shoppers, pupils, golfers, taxpayers, diners, and so on, for they implement the programs of behavior settings and maintain them in operating condition. The number of claim operations is a measure of the essential operations a town's habitat requires of its human components; it is a measure of the responsible, important, and difficult actions a town's inhabitants perform in the process of operating and maintaining the settings of the town as a human habitat. Claim operations implement habitat claims in all *operating* zones of behavior settings: in zones of single leaderships (in Zone 6, for instance, bank presidencies), in the zones of multiple leaderships (in Zone 5, for instance, joint proprietorship of stores), and in the zones of functionaries (in Zone 4, for instance, office clerkships).

Leader Actions

A town's output of leader actions comprises (1) all claim operations in Penetration Zones 5 and 6 and (2) all claim operations in Penetration Zones 3 and 4 of *executive* settings (behavior settings that control other settings—for example, Yoredale Rural District Council Meeting). These actions guide the town's operation and maintenance as a human habitat at the highest levels of responsibility. Persons who engage during a year in one or more leader actions are leaders.

Measurement Issues

The problem of measuring the size of the habitat of human molar actions has been a perplexing one. Perhaps because of its ease of measurement and the fact that actions often have spatial parameters, physical space has been widely reported, with the implications that it is coordinate with habitat size. But the size of the habitat must involve an environmental variable that is positively related to molar behavior possibilities, and amount of physical space is not so related. The behavior opportunities of a lone traveler imprisoned by a desert of vast spatial extent are surely not much greater than those of a prisoner in solitary confinement in a six- by nine-foot cell. It is true that the habitat of action always has a geographical locus and a physical milieu and that it always has temporal extent. How these attributes combine to form the habitat is a problem to be solved by theories and concepts grounded on empirical observation. The way they are combined in the centiurb measure of habitat extent is determined by a particular theory of molar action. This theory and the operations based on it require evaluation and validation.

Paul V. Gump **16**

Big Schools,
Small Schools

◆◆◆◆◆◆◆◆◆◆◆◆◆◆◆◆◆◆◆◆◆◆◆◆◆◆◆◆◆◆◆

Today many forces are pressing small communities to merge
their schools into larger systems. These communities are resisting the pressures. Claims and counterclaims are raised, but there
is little appeal to suitable evidence. Much evidence that is cited
bears on only one side of a necessarily two-sided issue. Such evidence pertains to facilities and curriculums; it usually does not
deal with the other side of the picture: what the effects of various
kinds of schools are on the students. No one knows how life is
different for the young persons who pass through the doors of the
large and small high schools. Most evidence being offered does not
tell us which educational arrangements produce more learning in
English, more development of social skills, more enthusiasm for
productive activity. Any research on how well institutions do

Reprint of Gump (1965). A detailed account of methods and findings is presented in the book *Big School, Small School* (Barker and Gump,
1964).

245

their job must include the results of the institutions' efforts, not just a survey of their offerings.

The research to be reported here provides evidence on one kind of results produced by large and small schools. The research was designed to answer a question of the effects of size on institutions and on their inhabitants. The research was not devised to answer political and educational issues; however, its results do have implications for such issues.

It must also be clearly stated that the evidence to be presented is not sufficient to answer all important questions regarding the effects of large and small schools. The evidence relates primarily to the effects of size on: (1) the variety of instruction, (2) the variety of extracurricular offerings, (3) the amount and kind of students' participation in school affairs, and (4) the effects of participation on the students.

Variety of Instruction. Do larger schools offer more varied instruction? The simple and direct answer to this question is yes. But, like other simple answers, it is true only with important qualifications.

The research investigated thirteen schools in eastern Kansas that varied in enrollments from 35 to 2,287. We found a total of thirty-four kinds or genotypes of academic and commercial classes in these schools. In this analysis, English for freshmen and English for sophomores, for example, were included in one genotype, whereas English and Public Speaking were categorized as different genotypes; Algebra I and Algebra II were in classes of the same genotype, Algebra I and Geometry I were in different genotypes.

It was possible to arrange eleven of these schools in size groups so that each group was approximately double the size of the preceding group. One can then see how much variety of instruction increases as schools become larger. Figure 1 displays this arrangement. The fact that as schools get bigger they also offer more is clear from Figure 1. It is equally clear that it takes a lot of bigness to add a little variety. On the average, a 100 percent increase in size yielded only a 17 percent increase in variety. Since size increase, by itself, pays relatively poor dividends, it might be well for educational planners to consider

Figure 1. High School Size and Variety of Instruction
(for Each School Size, Number of Schools, Median Number of Students,
and Median Number of Class Genotypes)

		Schools	Students	Genotypes
Distribution of Schools by Size		Very Small (2)	40 ▌	12.5 ‖‖‖‖‖‖‖‖‖
		Small (2)	88 ■	13.5 ‖‖‖‖‖‖‖‖‖
		Moderate (2)	185 ■	16.5 ‖‖‖‖‖‖‖‖‖‖‖
		Large (2)	339 ■	21.5 ‖‖‖‖‖‖‖‖‖‖‖‖‖‖
		Larger (1)	945 ▬	23 ‖‖‖‖‖‖‖‖‖‖‖‖‖‖
		Largest (2)	2105 ▬▬	28.5 ‖‖‖‖‖‖‖‖‖‖‖‖‖‖‖‖‖‖‖

other maneuvers for increasing the richness of the small school's curriculum.

A second qualification to the assertion that larger schools offer more variety bears on the implications of the word *offer*. One is likely to think that because the school has more different kinds of courses, the average student in it takes a wider range of courses. But there is real doubt about this. For a particular semester, students in four small schools actually averaged slightly *more* kinds of classes than did students in the largest school. It is misleading to extrapolate directly from what an organization offers to what participants experience. Not all parts of a large organization are equally available to all inhabitants; furthermore, large segments of these inhabitants may not use what is theoretically available. Certain students become "specialists" and find more opportunities for their specialty in the larger school. This was true, for example, of some students particularly interested in music in the large school. It would also be true for students interested in mathematics or art. The answer to "which is better?" depends on what one seeks: more opportunity for "specialists" or more breadth of academic experience for the general student body.

Number of Extracurricular Activities. Do larger schools offer more out-of-class activities or settings? This question may appear irrelevant to those who insist that activities outside the classroom are unfortunate interferences with the "real business" of education. But such affairs are not irrelevant to the students. And other research suggests that engagement in school affairs is one excellent predictor of whether students stay on to finish high school. A school's athletic events, its plays and concerts, its money-raising drives, its clubs, and its library and cafeteria are all part of the institution even if they are outside class. Within such settings, a variety of participation and leadership experiences are possible. Later on the meaning of participation in this nonclass area of school will be illustrated.

Since a careful examination of participation opportunity and of actual participation requires a good deal of effort, this study focused on the junior classes of one large school (enrollment 2,287) and four small schools (enrollment average 110). Investigators made a complete inventory of all nonclass behavior settings in each school. Perhaps some flavor of this area can be conveyed by a short list of such settings:

Student Council meetings	Junior class play
Basketball games at home	Band concert
Varsity dance	Principal's office
Junior Red Cross rummage sale	Scholarship assembly
Cheerleader tryouts	Christmas assembly
Library	Cafeteria

For the three-month period under test, the large school provided 189 such settings open to juniors, and the small schools averaged 48.5. Again it is clear that more is offered at the large school. However, one must look at the results of the offerings: How much were these offerings used and by whom?

Participation in Extracurricular Activities. Do students from the large or small schools participate more in out-of-class settings? After the investigators had made complete lists of all the schools' settings, they asked the junior students to indicate which of these they had attended over the previous three months. The *number* of participations was slightly larger in the big school; the *variety* of participation was clearly larger in the small schools. For example, students at the large schools would go to more affairs, but the affairs often were of the same kind. The large-school student might go to a number of musical settings; the small-school student went to fewer musical settings but also to athletic settings. A second finding was that the large school developed a sizable minority who attended very few affairs—often only the required ones, such as assemblies. This tendency of the big school to have a definite proportion of students who do little or nothing in their school's activities appears in other places in the study and will be referred to again.

Leadership Experience. Do students from the large or small schools get more experience in important, essential, or leadership participation? This question is perhaps more crucial than any other in the investigation. It is important to know what students did in these settings, not just whether they were there or not. It surely makes a difference whether one is an audience member or an actor at a play, a member or a chairman at a meeting, a customer or a salesman for a money-raising enterprise.

Almost every setting has positions for people who help make it go, who are relatively essential for its existence. In this research, such people have been labeled *operatives.* Student operatives at an athletic event are the players, the cheerleaders, the concession sellers, and so forth; members sit in the stands and watch. In a library, those who advise readers and keep books and records are operatives; those who read and study are members. Although operatives in a setting may have different degrees of importance, any operative is very likely to have responsibility, to be important in the activity of that setting. Operatives are needed. If a member drops out of a setting, it usually is not too damaging; if an operative quits, some readjustment is necessary. It is important to note that "being needed" when one is an operative is a fact of life in the activity; it is not simply a good feeling one may get because people are nice to one. One could predict that operatives get different satisfactions from their participation than do members; that operatives feel a sense of worth and obligation. Furthermore, since operatives are likely to be in the center of action, they may experience more challenge than do members.

What are the chances in large and small schools that students will become operatives in their schools' settings? The large school had 794 juniors and provided 189 settings; the small schools averaged 23 juniors and 48.5 settings. There were fewer settings per student in the large school; one might expect the large school settings to be relatively crowded, the small school settings to have fewer students. This expectation is correct: In the large school there were 36 juniors in the middle setting; in the small school, there were 11.

In any setting, if there are many people, the chances of any one becoming an operative are less than if there are only a few. If there are 300 juniors at a class play, the chances of any one being an actor, musician, or stagehand are less than if there are 23. In the latter case, it is likely that *all* will be operatives, whereas in the 300-person setting, perhaps 50 or 75 will be called to perform as operatives while the rest watch the play.

Since each student reported on what he did in each setting, it was possible to check the prediction that more small-school students would become frequent operatives. Results were clear-cut: During the three-month period, the average large-school junior was an operative in 3.5 settings. For the same time period, the average small-school junior was an operative in 8.6 settings.

Perhaps almost as impressive was the fact that 28 percent of the large-school juniors had not performed as an operative in *any* setting, compared with only 2 percent of the small-school juniors. Again the large school tended to produce that sizable minority of students who experienced much less benefit from their school's offerings; these were the "outsiders."

Knowledgeable and sensitive people in the big schools are aware of this problem; they have tried various measures to counteract the effects of big populations. However, the effects of size are coercive, one is working against powerful arithmetic. If there are many people in an institution, there are likely to be many people in its settings. These many people must share a

limited number of places for operatives. The way this works is
shown in Figure 2.

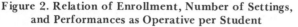

**Figure 2. Relation of Enrollment, Number of Settings,
and Performances as Operative per Student**

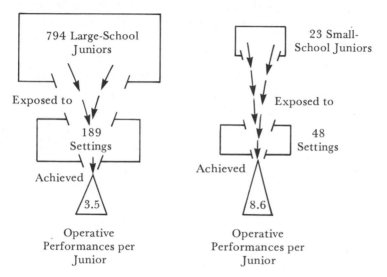

From Figure 2, it can be seen that if a great many students are available for comparatively few settings, the average
operative rate is low; when few students are available for comparatively many settings, the average operative rate is high. (It
might also be added that this trend is true for large and small
schools that are not so extremely different in size; differences
are not so extensive, but they are quite clear.)

Differing Satisfactions from Extracurricular Activities.
Do juniors from large and small schools get different kinds of
satisfactions from their out-of-class experiences in school? It has
been established that the small school yields markedly more
operative experiences than does the large school. It has been
suggested that being an operative is a significantly different experience than being a member. Therefore one might expect
juniors in the small schools to report different satisfactions for
their nonclass experiences than those reported by juniors from

the large school. Accordingly, this investigation measured student satisfactions. Essentially, students were asked, "What did your experiences in the settings mean to you—what did you get out of your participation?" Students responded with gratifyingly rich and frank statements of their experiences. Their answers were categorized and tabulated. As would be expected, there were certain kinds of satisfactions that were frequent in schools of both sizes. For example, the out-of-class satisfactions often mentioned by both groups were related to opportunities to "learn about" such matters as debate, parliamentary procedure, topics discussed in clubs, places and people contacted on field trips, and so on. Both groups also mentioned satisfactions having to do with novel experience or "change of pace." Students enjoyed banquets that helped them meet new people, plays in which they could "be somebody else for a change," and so forth. The richness and frequency of such answers created the conviction that these out-of-class events were important parts of life in both the large and small schools.

Differences in satisfactions were also prominent: The *small-school students* mentioned the following types of satisfactions significantly more often than did the large-school students.

- Increase in competence: "Football gets you into good physical shape," "Acting in the play gave me more confidence," "Going on trips with the team helps you learn how to adjust yourself to different surroundings," and "I learned how to get along with other people better."
- Challenge, competition, and success: "This magazine subscription sale gave me a chance to see whether or not I'm a good salesman. I now believe that I am," "I like tough, hard competition, and in basketball I usually get it," and "It was a lot of work organizing the dance, but we all thought it was worth it."
- Belonging to an action group: "In the play, our class worked together as a group, which I enjoyed very much," and "I like being active with a group of fellow students."

Satisfactions more common with *large-school students* were the following:

- Vicarious or "secondary" pleasures: "I like to watch a good, suspenseful game," "It was very interesting to hear the ideas and arguments of the debaters," and "I enjoyed listening to the orchestra at the dance."
- Belonging to crowd or school: "I like the 'companionship' of mingling with a crowd at games," "Pep rallies give you a feeling of school spirit."

From this sample of findings, one senses that satisfactions in the small schools are more related to improvement of one's capacity, to challenge and action, to close cooperation among peers, and to "being important." Large-school satisfactions tended to be more passive; that is, they were derived from somebody else's action. These satisfactions were also connected with belonging to "something big."

With the data, it was also possible to determine why the patterns of satisfactions differed in the two sizes of schools. It was demonstrated that most of the differences came about because the small-school student had many more experiences as an operative. When students in the large school were able to perform as operatives, they achieved many of the same satisfactions as did the performers in the small school. Unfortunately the "facts of life" in the large school do not allow for nearly as many operative experiences per student.

Obligation to Support Activities. Do large or small school students feel more obligation to support their schools' activities and affairs? To answer this question, Willems (1964) interviewed two kinds of students: the regular and the marginal. The word *marginal* here means those youth whose capacity, knowledge, and background make them relatively unsuited for academic success. Members of this group do poorly on IQ tests, have low grades, and have mothers and fathers who often did not finish high school. The "dropout rate" for such students is often quite high. The word *regular* here simply means students with fewer such academic handicaps. Both classes of students in both sizes of school were interviewed. Willems asked what might cause them to participate in various out-of-class settings. A frequent element in their response was that of responsibility or obligation. Students would often say that they would participate because they were needed, that they had a job to do, that friends or teachers were depending on them.

Two types of comparisons were made for this responsibility element. First, regulars and marginals were combined together, and then small-school replies were compared to large-school replies. The result was that small-school students averaged 5.5 responsibility answers, while large-school students averaged 2.0 responsibility answers. Second, regular and marginal students within each school were compared. The result was that marginal students in the small schools gave *just as many* responsibility answers as did regular students, while marginal students in the large school gave only *one fourth* as many responsibility answers as did regular students.

When one thinks about "instilling a sense of civic responsibility" in our youth, these results should be considered. Here is evidence that the small schools, with their real need for students' participation, are offering experiences that may be quite valuable. This is responsibility learned in action, not out of books. It may also be significant that whether a person is marginal in the sense of being involved in the enterprises around him depends not only on his talent and background but also on how much he is needed by these enterprises. The large school again seems to have produced its group of "outsiders." Its academically marginal students are also socially marginal. This did not happen in the small school. The investigators do not want to be misunderstood. The large-school personnel is not to blame for this. Conscientious administrators and teachers worked diligently to include the marginal student. And there was no campaign afoot among the students to see that large groups of marginal students were left out. The problem is that, as institutions get larger, "selection into" and "selection out of" begins to work automatically.

If the schools are to benefit the students, they are going

to have to keep them. There is accumulating evidence that the dropout rate in the larger schools is significantly higher than in the small ones. And this tendency for people to drop out or to be absent as institutions get larger seems to be true for institutions besides the high school. It is true for Rotary Clubs, for mining crews, for textile workers, for airline workers, and so on. The old saying, "The bigger the better!" is of dubious worth.

What, then, are some major findings of this investigation? First, the larger the school, the more the variety of instruction offered. However, it takes an average of a 100 percent increase in school size to yield a 17 percent increase in variety. Furthermore, there is no clear evidence that the greater variety in the large school results in the average student experiencing a broader range of academic classes.

Second, students in the larger school participate in a few more out-of-class activities than do students in the small school. On the other hand, students in the smaller school participate in more different *kinds* of settings (genotypes).

Third, students in the small school participate in over double the number of performances as operatives as do students in the large school. The chance to be essential, to gain an active or demanding role in activity comes much more often to the average small-school student.

Fourth, students in the smaller schools experience different kinds of satisfaction in their out-of-class activity than do large-school students. The small school yields satisfactions of developing competence, of meeting challenges, of close cooperation with peers. The large school yields more satisfactions that are vicarious and that are connected to being a part of an imposing institution.

Fifth, students from the small schools report more sense of responsibility to their school's affairs. Furthermore, academically marginal students in the large school are particularly lacking in reported sense of obligation to their school's enterprises. They appear to be social "outsiders." The marginal students in the small school, however, are just as likely to reveal responsibility attitudes as are the regular students.

Problems of school size cannot be solved by this or by

any other single program of research studies. However, it seems clear that the small high school has advantages for one important phase of high school life. The large school may offer a great deal, but the offering tends to be used by only part of the students. Although opportunities in the large school seem great, the small school does a better job of translating opportunities into actual experiences for the total student body.

If the small school has some advantages, how can the relative disadvantage of limited instruction offerings be overcome? Up until now, the major solution has seemed to be making the small school larger by consolidation. What this comes down to is the movement, by bus, of many bodies to one central spot. This may be an unnecessary and even old-fashioned solution. Today a veritable revolution in educational practices is occurring: There are taped courses, television lectures and demonstrations, traveling teacher specialists, and self-instructional machines and programmed books. Once we free ourselves of old molds and assumptions, it might be possible sometimes to bring education to students instead of always bringing students to education.

Finally, we need more "two-sided" research on the questions: (1) What are schools like? and (2) What are students getting out of their schools? Such investigations are more costly and more difficult, but they are the only kind that answer the crucial questions—questions that must be answered if we are to use research to improve education.

Importance of Church Size for New Members

◆◆◆◆◆◆◆◆◆◆◆◆◆◆◆◆◆◆◆◆◆◆◆◆◆◆◆◆◆◆◆

This study examines the relationship between church size and two measures of its import for new members: (1) their assimilation into church activities and (2) their support of churches' activities in comparison with long-established members.

The principal data were obtained from members of a small United Methodist Church (338 members) and from a comparable large church of the same denomination (1,599 members). Both churches were located in metropolitan Milwaukee, Wisconsin. More complete descriptive data on the churches and evidence that the activities of the small church are undermanned relative to the large church are presented in another publication (Wicker, 1969b).

Prepared for this book on the bases of data reported in Wicker (1969c) and Wicker and Mehler (1971).

Assimilation of New Members

According to behavior setting theory, the need for additional personnel in the activities of the small, undermanned church has a number of consequences. It leads to behavior directed toward seeking out potential members and making them feel welcome and even obligated to participate. Newcomers are drawn into the relatively large number of positions of responsibility available to them. Increased participation leads new members to meet and interact with many of the church's members and officers. And new members themselves recruit others to participate. In contrast, the large church, with its larger pool of available personnel to carry out its activities, has less need to recruit new members, and newcomers in this situation feel less welcome and obligated to participate. There are fewer positions of responsibility open to the new members, and they are less likely to serve in them; their acquaintance with other members and officers is less intimate, and they feel little pressure to recruit others.

Participants and Procedures

In each church, membership records were used to identify all married couples who had joined the church between three and one half and thirty months prior to the investigation. Persons who had participated in a study conducted a year earlier were not included. There were thirty people in the small church and eighty-one in the large church who met the criteria. Thirty persons were randomly eliminated from the large church, leaving fifty-one in the sample.

The members were first contacted by a personal letter from their church pastor; questionnaire data were obtained in group meetings at the churches or individually at members' homes. Questionnaires were completed by twenty-six members from the small church (87 percent of those contacted) and by forty members in the large church (78 percent). The difference in participation of the members of the two churches does not approach significance. The average length of membership for the small-church participants was 15.0 months, compared to

17.8 months for the large church. The two samples were highly similar in average age, number of children, sex distribution, percentage who had attended another church in the two years prior to joining the present church, reported attendance at the previous church, responsibilities held in previous church, and satisfaction with previous church.

Questions dealt with the following: demographic variables (age, sex); involvement in and satisfaction with the church that the member previously attended (if any); rating of importance of various factors in choosing a church; beliefs about differences in large and small churches; and a series of questions to measure assimilation into the church. Six of the assimilation questions dealt with three activities common to both churches: church choir, social clubs for married couples, and the women's or men's organization. For each of the three activities, members were asked how frequently (1) they had been invited to join or attend, (2) other members had offered to accompany them, (3) they had attended, and (4) they had asked someone else to attend. Also, for each of the three activities, members indicated on four-point scales how welcome they felt and the extent to which they felt obligated to participate. For these questions, responses were summed across the three activities. An additional index of felt obligation was obtained from members' responses to questions about whether they felt they should help by teaching a children's church school class, working in other church activities, being an officer in a church organization, and making a monetary pledge to the church. The index was the number of affirmative responses to the four questions. Finally, a general question about assimilation was the following: "To what extent do you feel a part of, or close to, this church and its members?" A six-point graphic rating scale was provided.

The questionnaire contained a list of all the activities that had occurred in each church during the fifteen-week period preceding the testing sessions. The members checked the activities they had attended, indicated the number of hours spent in each, and noted whether they had held a major responsibility (leader category), a minor responsibility (worker), or merely attended (member).

The members were given a list of some other members of

their church, and were asked to indicate if they (1) recognized the name, (2) knew the person personally, and (3) addressed the person by his first name. Each list contained the names of lay officers in the major positions of the church along with names of randomly selected church members. For the small church, twelve officers and seventeen other members (5 percent of the membership) were listed. For the large church, sixteen officers and eighty other members (also 5 percent of the membership) were named. The same functions were served by the officers listed for the two churches; the large church had more specialized offices in several cases. A preliminary correlational analysis indicated that the assimilation measures were positively correlated, with the highest coefficients in the .80 to .90 range. It was therefore decided to treat the various measures as items in an overall test of assimilation of new members by calculating composite scores on which group comparisons would be made. Scores on each of the twelve assimilation measures listed in Table 1 were converted into standard scores. Composite assimi-

Table 1. Mean Scores on Assimilation Measures

Measure	Small Church	Large Church
Number of invitations to join or attend three activities	5.7	5.5
Number of offers to take members to three activities	3.0	1.4
Frequency of attendance at three activities	4.7	1.6
Number of times member has asked others to attend three activities	2.8	.8
Felt obligation to participate in three activities (larger number indicates greater felt obligation)	6.6	5.4
Felt obligation to support four church activities ("yes" answers to four questions)	2.7	2.0
Sense of belonging to the church (1 = not at all a part, 6 = very much a part)	4.2	3.6
Number of church officers known personally or addressed by first name	5.1	1.6
Number of church members know personally or addressed by first name	1.0	2.6
Number of activities attended	3.6	2.8
Number of hours spent in activities	16.5	14.1
Number of activities in which the member was a worker or leader	2.0	.8

lation scores were obtained by summing across the twelve standard scores for each member. A t-test and a two-by-two analysis of variance were employed to compare the new members of the large church and the small church.

Results. Group means for the twelve assimilation measures are shown in Table 1. Means for members of the small church are higher than corresponding large church means for eleven of twelve measures. The single exception is number of church members known personally or addressed by the first name, and this result is somewhat ambiguous, since members of the small church were given a much smaller list of names (seventeen, compared to eighty for the large church). The composite assimilation score for new members of the small church is significantly higher than the score for new members of the large church.

The results support the hypothesis derived from behavior setting theory that assimilation is facilitated in organizations whose activities are relatively undermanned.

Support of Church Activities

This part of the study is concerned with two questions: (1) Is there a difference in the degree to which new and long-established members support church activities? and (2) Is the difference, if any, related to church size? Behavior setting theory does not bear directly on these questions; however, answers to them will contribute to the understanding of settings and organizations.

Participants and Procedures. A previous study of church members who were selected without regard to length of membership (Wicker, 1969b) provided a source of data on long established members with which to compare the present data on new members. The participants of the earlier study who had been members for thirty months or less when they provided data were assigned to the new-member cateogry, leaving in the established group only persons who had been members longer than thirty months. The numbers of participants (*N*) and the mean lengths of membership in years (*M*) for the various groups are as follows: small church new members: $N = 30$, $M = 1.3$; large church, new members: $N = 37$, $M = 1.4$; small church, established members: $N = 18$, $M = 7.4$; large church, established members: $N = 33$, $M = 11.8$.

New and established members were compared on three measures of their participation in church activities (Items 1, 2, and 3, Table 2), on Sunday service attendance, on pledges and contributions. A limitation of the comparisons is that the measures on most of the new members (all except those from the earlier study) were obtained one year after the same measures on the established members. The single exception is data on members' pledges, which are for the same period. Both churches are relatively stable, however. Degree of participation was secured by questionnaire, frequency of members' attendance at Sunday worship service was determined from church records (in each church a sign-up sheet is passed along the pews during each service), and the amounts of money pledged and contributed to the church by the member and his or her spouse (a combined figure for both) during the fiscal year in which the study was conducted were obtained from church records.

Results. Data are reported in Table 2. They show that (1) for each measure, greater support is shown by members of the small church; (2) new members are less supportive than estab-

Table 2. Comparison of New and Established Members
in a Large Church and a Small Church

	Small Church		Large Church	
Measure	New members	Established members	New New members	Established members
1. Number of activities attended	5.5	10.2	3.4	7.5
2. Number of kinds of activities attended	4.6	6.4	2.4	4.7
3. Number of activities in which the member was a worker or leader	2.8	4.6	1.1	2.8
4. Sunday worship service attendance	19.9	26.2	14.1	14.5
5. Pledged contribution	$173	$258	$145	$141
6. Actual contribution	$126	$187	$109	$109

lished members—they attend fewer and a narrower range of activities, serve in fewer positions of leadership, and attend worship service less often; and (3) for none of the measures is the interaction of size of church and length of membership significant, suggesting that the differences between new and established members' support for church activities is the same in the large church and the small church.

Discussion. The finding that members of the small church (both new and established members) are more supportive of its activities than these classes of members of the large church is consistent with earlier research supporting behavior setting theory (Baird, 1969; Barker and Gump, 1964; Wicker, 1968, 1969a, 1969b; Willems, 1967). But the finding that new members of both the large and the small churches are less supportive of church activities than established members is a new discovery, and it will require further research to account for it. As a beginning, several possibilities come to mind for exploration. New and established members may not be equivalent with respect to motivation: It is certain that not all new members remain to become established members; some drop out from lack of interest, so the established group does not include these less-motivated persons. Or perhaps new members have less complete knowledge of the opportunities and requirements of church programs than do established members, and their relative ignorance is a barrier to involvement. It is possible that new members are more widely dispersed geographically than established members, thus meeting greater obstacles to church participation. But the cause may not lie wholly in differences in new and established church members; it may lie to some degree in the church programs. Position of responsibility may be reserved for tried and true (established) members, or the strength of pressures to participate may increase with length of membership. (See Wicker and Kauma, 1974, for further discussion of some of these points.)

The finding that the difference in support of church activities by new and established members is not related to church size is a new discovery, too. This means that, although new members of the small church are more involved in church activities than new members of the large church, both are about equally less involved than the established members of the churches. This may mean that new members select churches of the size that make demands most consistent with their willingness to expend effort. Perhaps prospective church members know they will be called on to work harder in a small church and select or avoid it according to their preference. In fact, data relative to this were assembled, but their indications are ambiguous and are not reported here; they are important for persons interested in further research and are available in the more extensive paper by Wicker and Mehler (1971).

Conclusions

This research has verified with new data a previous discovery about organizations differing in size and manpower, and it has made three new discoveries. It has verified, again, the prediction from behavior setting theory that a small, relatively undermanned organization elicits greater involvement from its members in its ongoing activities than a large, more adequately manned organization. The new discoveries are as follows: (1) in accordance with undermanning theory, the assimilation of new members is facilitated in the undermanned organization relative to the optimally manned one; (2) also in accordance with theory, the effects of undermanning occur in connection with both new and established members; and (3) new members are less supportive than are established members of both the undermanned and the optimally manned organizations.

Roger G. Barker
Phil Schoggen

18

Behavior-Generating Machines: Models Midwest and Yoredale

◆•◆•◆•◆•◆•◆•◆•◆•◆•◆•◆•◆•◆•◆•◆•◆•◆•◆•◆•◆

The behavior settings of Midwest (MW) and Yoredale (YD) are predominantly of the same varieties; most of them could be interchanged with little disruption in their operations. Although there are some differences in the extents of equivalent settings, some differences in their ongoing programs, and some differences in the characteristics of the people who inhabit them, the towns are so similar with respect to the settings that instigate and regulate the behavior of their inhabitants we can consider them to be two models of the same behavior-generating machine, the MW and YD models. The models produce behavior

Adapted from Barker and Schoggen (1973, pp. 400-415, 443-445).

by their human components that differ in important ways, some of which can be explained by behavior setting theory. Other differences, although clearly residing in the towns' setting systems, involve attributes and interrelations that have not been identified and disentangled.

Specifications and Behavior Outputs

In Figure 1, we present schematic sketches of the models with specifications. Here we see that Model MW has 37 percent fewer human components than Model YD to implement behavior settings that are only 5 percent less extensive and habitat claims that are 33 percent more extensive. In accordance with behavior setting theory, the output of Model MW per human

Figure 1. Great American-English Behavior-Generating Machine

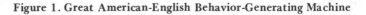

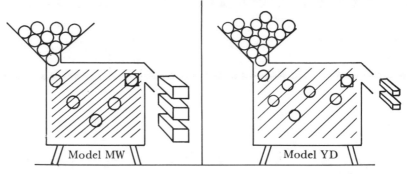

Key

Symbol	Measure	Specifications	
		Model MW	Model YD
	Habitat Extent	107 cu	113 cu
	Habitat Claims for Operatives	10,220	7,764
	Input: Human Components, Town	830	1,310
	Behavior: Output per Unit Input		
	a. Mean Person-Hours (P-H)	1,356	1,089
	b. Mean Claim Operations (CO)	8.0	3.2
	c. Mean Leader Acts (LA)	1.8	0.7

component is greater; it is 25 percent greater in person-hours of behavior, 150 percent greater in claim operations, and 157 percent greater in leadership actions.

Consequences for Children

The MW and YD models have important implications for the child-rearing systems of the towns insofar as the towns' public habitats are involved in child rearing. Evidence that they are thus involved is shown by the amount of time children spend in public settings. For example, of the approximately 5,110 waking hours per child per year for children nine through eleven years old, about 38 percent is spent in public settings by Midwest children and about 30 percent by Yoredale children.

The influence of the MW and YD models on the way children are reared is so clear we have characterized their consequences as the Melting Pot System and the Enlightened Colonial System, respectively, for reasons that will be apparent from data we shall present for children under twelve years. But first we shall describe the systems.

Melting Pot System of Child Rearing. According to the Midwest system, children are best prepared for adulthood by participating in a wide variety of the town's settings. Natives of Midwest think it is of particular benefit to children to undertake tasks that are important and difficult for them before they can discharge the tasks with complete adequacy. Educational settings are important in Midwest education, but they are thought to be most effective if children participate along with adults in other community settings too. "Doing your part" is especially valued, even if "your part" cannot be carried out with great effectiveness.

Midwest children are in the position of an underdeveloped minority; but this minority, according to the Midwest system, becomes acculturated by processes that occur during interaction with the superior majority within integrated settings. Segregation, even for the alleged purpose of achieving eventual equality and mutual acceptance, is generally believed in Midwest to be not only wrong but ineffective. When a solicitous "foreigner" seated behind a family at a church service offered to remove the fussing infant and care for him outside, the mother responded, "When do you think he will *learn* to behave in church if you take him out?!" Egalitarianism is a central value in Midwest, and it is also looked on as a method for reducing differences (for teaching children appropriate behavior in church worship services).

Enlightened Colonial System of Child Rearing. According to the Yoredale system, children are best prepared for adulthood by removing them from the general, public settings and placing them in specially arranged and reserved children's settings under the direction of experts who, over a period of time, are able to prepare the children for entrance into the life of the community. In the Yoredale system, children are not welcomed into some community settings, because they do not have requisite skills and attitudes to take their places smoothly.

In terms of the Colonial System metaphor, Yoredale children are also an underdeveloped minority, but Yoredale adults are the responsible bearers of a higher culture with the responsibility of acculturating the pagan tribes among them. As underdeveloped people, children are permitted to take part in few of the privileges and responsibilities the town reserves for adults, because children lack the necessary skills to participate successfully in them and because they lack the values to appreciate adult privileges and opportunities. However, the underdeveloped people of Yoredale (the children) are carefully placed in segregated reservations (Scout troops, schools, Sunday Schools) under benevolent administrators (masters), where as subordinate and relatively powerless candidates they are prepared for the good life of adulthood. According to Yoredale values, differences between people of various classes, cultures, educational levels, vocations, and ages should be respected and even encouraged; but mobility toward the circles of the elect should be accomplished outside these circles, and admissibility to them should be demonstrated before admittance is allowed. This is called *realism* (a "good" word) in Yoredale, and its opposite is termed *egalitarianism* (a "bad" word).

Children and Adolescents in the Melting Pot and on the Reservations. The different child-rearing systems of Midwest and Yoredale are by no means fully implemented in the towns. However, their imperfectly realized, multiple, and often compensating and reinforcing trends bring very different influences to bear on children. Furthermore, the theories that support the systems are not univocally approved within the towns, and there is considerable tension within each town between those who approve and those who disapprove of each system in its pure form. Finally, there is evidence of change; Yoredale's new comprehensive school involves some elements of the Melting Pot System. Nevertheless, it is not possible to divorce the children from the towns' overall eco-behavioral systems, and, as long as inhabitants have the functional differences as habitat components that we have discovered, it seems inevitable that the Melting Pot and Enlightened Colonial systems will remain.

The general differences between the towns in habitat extent, habitat claims, and human components hold for their children: Children are in shorter supply in Midwest than in Yoredale. Midwest's 159 and Yoredale's 220 children have similar numbers and kinds of public settings for satisfying their similar needs via consummatory activities; they have about equal opportunities to ride bicycles, skip rope, take music lessons, view parades, play hopscotch, go to parties, and so on. But within Midwest there are 10,220 difficult and important positions (habitat claims) to be filled in the process of maintaining and operating the town's habitat, compared with 7,764 in Yoredale. This has a variety of consequences for children; we shall now consider some of them.

The Pied Piper Index. Evidence that the children of the towns do, in fact, live and behave in accordance with the Melting Pot and Enlightened Colonial systems is provided by differences in their functional importance and power in the towns' behavior settings. Children inhabit eighty centiurbs of Midwest's habitat and eighty-four centiurbs of Yoredale's, amounting to 74 percent of each town's habitat, but within these equal proportions of the towns' total habitats Midwest children engage in more claim operations per child: playing in city band concerts, assisting in household auction sales, collecting tickets at the Parent-Teacher Association Carnival, running a lawn mower for the city park volunteer work group, carrying the Capital City paper route, reciting at the mother-daughter banquet, acting as secretary of the Jolly Juniors' 4-H meetings, and so forth. According to the Pied Piper index, the functional importance of children in maintaining and implementing the programs of the towns' habitats is 1.7 times greater in Midwest than in Yoredale. The loss *without replacement* of a single average Midwest child would leave .034 percent of the town's total claim operations without implementation; the loss of one Yoredale child would leave .020 percent of the town's claim operations without implementation (.034/.020 = 1.7). Midwest children are more important and more powerful by a factor of 1.7; they are truly less expendable than Yoredale children; this is the kernal of the difference in the towns' public child-rearing systems.

Children as Benefactors and Beneficiaries. Settings can be sorted with respect to the classes of inhabitants who implement their programs as operatives and the classes who participate in their programs as users (members, customers, and spectators). The relation between operatives and users within behavior settings is universally one of more power versus less power; and for the present analyses behavior settings have been selected where operatives, in addition to being more powerful, are benefactors of the users. Yoredale's Church of England Juniors' Sunday School class is an example of a setting implemented by adult and adolescent operatives (the teacher and her assistants) for the benefit of the child members; here, the teacher and her assistants are operatives (with more power) and benefactors; the children are users (with less power) and beneficiaries.

We have selected two categories of behavior settings for analysis. In one category children are operatives and benefactors, and other age groups are users and beneficiaries. Examples are the elementary lower school operetta in Midwest, and Methodist Sunday afternoon anniversary program in Yoredale; in these settings, children as performers (program operatives) benefit (entertain, exhilarate, refresh) adolescents, adults, and aged persons as members of the audiences. In the other category adolescents, adults, and aged are operatives and benefactors, and the children are users and beneficiaries. Examples are Anita Kelly piano lessons in Midwest and the county primary school playground in Yoredale; here, adults as teachers and custodians (program operatives) benefit (educate, entertain) children as pupils. Only a minority of the habitats of both towns have these particular operative-beneficence properties; about 80 percent of the habitats of both towns benefit all age groups equally.

We expect that in Midwest's Melting Pot System the category of behavior settings where children are powerful benefactors will be more extensive and their behavior outputs greater than in Yoredale's Enlightened Colonial System. These expectations are strongly supported. On the average, Midwest children spend 21 hours per year and Yoredale children spend 1.5 hours per year in behavior settings where they—that is, members of their age group—benefit members of other age groups. Behavior settings where these arrangements are built into the program constitute about one in fifty of the settings at hand for residents of Midwest, which exceeds such arrangements in Yoredale by a factor of ten. Furthermore, the benefactions of Midwest children have greater impact than those of Yoredale children. Midwest adolescents are beneficiaries of children in this way for a total of 40.2 hours per person, whereas Yoredale adolescents are beneficiaries for 1.5 hours; Midwest adults are beneficiaries for 11.4 hours per person, whereas Yoredale adults are beneficiaries for 1.3 hours; and Midwest aged are beneficiaries for 1.2 hours per person, whereas Yoredale aged are beneficiaries for 0.5 hours.

It is clear that Midwest's Melting Pot System of child rearing installs children in positions of relative power and worthiness in more of its habitat than does Yoredale's Enlightened Colonial System and that the adolescents, adults, and aged of Midwest transact more behavior as beneficiaries (customers, spectators, guests) of children than the adolescents, adults, and aged of Yoredale.

The expectation that the category of behavior settings where children are passive recipients of the benefactions of others would be more extensive and productive in Yoredale is less clearly supported by the data. Settings where these relations occur are more extensive in Yoredale than Midwest as expected (20 and 17 centiurbs of habitat, respectively), but Midwest children spend more time in these settings than Yoredale children, contrary to expectation (828 and 638 hours per child, respectively). Midwest's children appear to have the best of the two systems: more of the satisfactions of both benefactors and beneficiaries.

Interactions of Adults and Children. According to the data of Chapter Seven ("Social Actions of American and English Children and Adults"), the actions of adults to the children of Midwest and Yoredale accord closely with their positions in the two child-rearing systems. Adult actions that are more pervasive in Yoredale than in Midwest are those of an enlightened colonial administrator of primitive peoples—dominating, disciplining, punishing, showing impatience, and devaluing them, but at the same time valuing and providing opportunities for them. And adult actions that are more pervasive in Midwest than in Yoredale are those of a participant with less able associates: influencing, managing, and being friendly with them. Similarly, the actions of children toward the adults of the towns are congruent with their positions. Children behave as supervised colonials more widely in Yoredale: They are more pervasively helpful and polite to adults but they also more widely resist adults than they do in Midwest. In Midwest, children are the friendly associates of adults more pervasively than in Yoredale.

Freedom of Movement for Children. An essential feature of the Melting Pot System is freedom to participate in behavior settings to the maximum of the child's ability, and essential in the Enlightened Colonial System are reserves where attendance is either required or prevented. Differences in freedom of movement, therefore, provide another test of the proposition that the children of Midwest and Yoredale live and behave in accordance with the Melting Pot and Enlightened Colonial systems. We expect greater areas of free movement with greater output of free behavior and smaller areas of coerced movement with smaller output of coerced behavior in Midwest than in Yoredale.

The relevant data consist of the extent of two categories of behavior settings and the participation of children within

them. The first category consists of behavior settings that encourage, are neutral to, or discourage the attendance of children. These settings constitute regions of relatively free movement for children: Large parts of them impose no restrictions or
coercions, and where restrictions and coercions are imposed
they are not absolute and can be breached by determined children. Within these regions, the needs of children are dominant
in determining the settings they inhabit. The second category
consists of behavior settings that require or prohibit the attendance of children. These settings constitute reserved areas of
the towns: The required settings are reserved for children
(under the control of older persons), and the prohibited settings
are reserved for older persons (free from intruding children).
Within these regions, behavior setting forces are dominant in
determining settings inhabited by children. The data bear out
our expectations. The areas of free movement are 9 percent
more extensive for Midwest than for Yoredale children (eighty-
four and seventy-seven centiurbs, respectively), and the reserved
areas are 34 percent less extensive in Midwest than Yoredale
(twenty-four and thirty-six centiurbs, respectively). Midwest
children spend 43 percent more time in the free areas than
Yoredale children (645 and 452 hours per child, respectively)
and almost the same amount of time in the reserved areas (575
and 564 hours per child, respectively).

   Spontaneity of Behavior. Finally, a fragment of evidence
of the operations of the two systems of child rearing is provided
by the data presented in Chapter Eight ("Behavior Episodes
of American and English Children"). It would appear
that the Melting Pot System, where participation to the maximum of the child's ability is favored, should generate more
spontaneous episodes and fewer pressured episodes than should
the Enlightened Colonial System, where benevolent administrators are in charge. The data show that this is the case; spontaneously initiated and terminated episodes constitute 48 (MW)
and 34 (YD) percent of all episodes, whereas episodes both initiated and terminated in response to pressure constitute 14
(MW) and 27 (YD) percent.

Unanticipated Differences

The MW and YD models of the Great Behavior-Generating Machine produce different amounts of behavior in general, and different amounts of behavior with particular qualities that are in accord with predictions from the theory of behavior settings; for example, the models produce different amounts of responsible, impatient, beneficent, and leadership behavior. The theory does not account for other differences, such as these: YD residents engage in 9.3 hours of large-muscle activity per week, on the average (walking, lifting, carrying, and so forth), whereas MW residents engage in 7.7 hours of such behavior; and YD residents transact 6.4 hours per week of behavior involving the hands primarily (writing, using hand tools, playing musical instruments, and so forth), whereas MW residents transact 10.0 hours of such behavior. We shall now consider some of the unanticipated differences in the MW and YD models.

Qualities of Behavior. If difference in the behavior produced by the two models were uniform across all kinds of behavior, MW's output of person-hours of behavior per human component would in all cases be 25 percent greater than YD's (its overall excess of behavior); the time spent in talking and in education, for example, would each yield a MW/YD ratio of 1.25. But this is not the case: The two ratios are, respectively, 1.03 and 2.36; MW exceeds YD less than expected in output of talking behavior and more than expected in output of educational behavior. Behavior with MW/YD ratios greater than 1.25 are (with the ratios in the parentheses): affective behavior (2.6), leadership actions (2.5), educational behavior (2.4), behavior concerned with civic affairs (2.2), manipulative behavior (1.6), church-connected behavior (1.5), and social behavior (1.5).

The YD model produces 80 percent as many person-hours of behavior per human component as the MW model, but this, again, does not hold for all kinds of behavior. YD/MW ratios of outputs are greater than 0.80 for behavior concerned with government agencies (1.5), with physical health (1.3), with nutrition (1.3), with large-muscle activity (1.2), with personal appearance (1.1), and with esthetics (1.0).

Habitat Inhabitant Bias. Behavior settings have inputs of material that they program and process and then emit in a changed state. The MW setting Chaco Garage takes in Mr. Jones' defective automobile in the morning, acts on it during the day, and emits it in a repaired condition in the evening. Likewise, it takes in as a human component of its operations Mr. Chaco (the proprietor) in a relatively clean and rested state and in a particular emotional and financial condition in the morning, puts him through a program of action (Mr. Jones' car demands dirty, tiring behavior), and ejects him in the evening dirty, tired, and possibly financially and emotionally altered. The MW and YD models of the Great American-English Behavior-Generating Machine are differentially selective with respect to inputs and outputs. We have studied the selectivity of the models for a variety of human components.

In 1963-1964, the mean yearly amount of behavior produced by public settings was 1,356 hours per human component by Model MW and 1,089 hours by Model YD. These constitute the best estimates available of the amount of behavior expected. However, if some classes of human components are biased against some settings or if the settings are biased against the components, the latter will engage in less than the expected mean amounts of behavior; that is, there will be a negative bias between components and settings. For classes of components with more than the expected amounts of behavior, the biases between components and settings will be positive. The deviation of the observed from the expected behavior is a measure of the setting component or habitat inhabitant bias.

In Table 1, the mean outputs of various classes of inhabitants are expressed as percentages of the expected outputs. The classes of each town are ordered in the table from the one with greatest negative habitat inhabitant bias to the one with greatest positive habitat inhabitant bias. We find, for example, that the mean output of MW's preschool inhabitants is 29 percent of the mean output of MW's inhabitants in general; the difference between 29 and 100 is a measure of the negative habitat inhabitant bias between the MW model and members of its preschool behavior setting components. Midwest's adolescent class, on the

Table 1. Bias Between the MW and YD Models and Classes
of Human Components, 1963-1964

	MW	Bias	YD	Bias
Negative Bias	Preschool	− 29	Gentry	− 15
	Infant	− 31	Infant	− 30
	Aged	− 35	Aged	− 38
	Negro	− 49	Preschool	− 48
	Social Class III[a]	− 85	Social Class I	− 6
	Female	− 89	Female	− 92
			Social Class II	− 96
	All Inhabitants	100	All Inhabitants	100
Positive Bias	Social Class II	+104	Social Class III	+106
	Male	+107	Male	+108
	Adult	+118	Adolescent	+112
	Younger School	+119	Adult	+123
	Older School	+142	Older School	+141
	Social Class I	+155	Younger School	+163
	Adolescent	+166		

[a]See footnote, Table 3, Chapter Six.

other hand, yields 166 percent as much behavior per member as its inhabitants in general; there is a positive bias between Midwest and its adolescents.

These deviation measures may be interpreted as the reduction in behavior output from the loss of a single, average class member stated as a percentage of the reduction due to the loss of a single, average human component. Loss of a preschool inhabitant would attenuate MW's behavior output less than the loss of any other class member and 29 percent as much as the loss of an average inhabitant; loss of an adolescent inhabitant would cost MW's behavior output more than the loss of a member of any other class, and two thirds more than the loss of an average inhabitant. As measured by their contributions to MW's total behavior output, infants are more expendable than adolescents.

In these terms, YD's most expendable inhabitants are its gentry, and its least expendable inhabitants are its younger school children; loss of a younger school child would cost YD in behavior output almost eleven times as much as the loss of a member of the gentry. MW's most expendable class of inhabitants are its preschool children, and its least expendable inhabitants are its adolescents; loss of an adolescent would cost MW in behavior output 5.7 times as much as the loss of a preschool child. The models differ most in their biases for Social Class I (MW's is positive, YD's negative; the difference in bias measures is eighty-nine), for adolescents (MW's is more positive than YD's; the difference in bias measures is fifty-four), for younger school children (YD's is more positive than MW's; the difference in bias measure is forty-four), and for Social Class III (YD's is positive, MW's negative; the difference in bias measures is twenty-one). Both models have negative biases for preschool, infant, aged, and female inhabitants and have positive biases for male, adult, younger school, older school, and adolescent inhabitants; MW is negative and YD positive to Social Class III, and MW is positive and YD negative to Social Classes I and II.

We have discovered the bases of some of these differences. MW's greater negative bias for preschool components is located almost entirely in behavior settings of the school authority system; these settings reject all preschool children as pupils, whereas Yoredale's schools claim preschool children at five years of age. The situation is reversed for adolescents. Behavior settings under the egis of Midwest's School authority system actively and successfully claim almost all the town's adolescents, whereas Yoredale actively ejects 27 percent of the town's adolescents during most daytime hours (it transports 25 percent of them to a government grammar school twelve miles distant), and another 15 percent actively reject the town's school settings for distant government and private schools.* But Yoredale is not altogether more negative to adolescents than Midwest. Yoredale's private enterprise authority system has a

---

*These arrangements were changed in 1971. Some Midwest adolescents were ejected for several half-days per week to a distant technical school. Yoredale's Secondary Modern School had become a Comprehensive School; therefore, more of Yoredale's adolescents attended school in town than did in 1963-1964; however, some Yoredale adolescents continued to be ejected to sixth-form or technical schools, and about the same number as formerly attended private schools.

greater positive bias for adolescents than does Midwest's; 17 percent of Yoredale adolescents are employed full-time within the town, and many continue as permanent inhabitants (as craftsmen, shop assistants, clerks, housewives, and so forth).

Some of the circumstances of Midwest's positive bias and of Yoredale's negative bias for Social Class I are revealed by other analyses. Midwest residents of Social Class I are especially attracted to or pressured into settings where there are programs with prominent governmental, religious, personal adornment, and business qualities; it is these settings that generate the surplus behavior of Class I Midwest residents. Class I residents of Yoredale avoid or are impeded from entering settings with educational, personal, adornment, manipulation, and gross motor attributes; it is these settings that generate the behavior deficits of Class I Yoredale residents. An important part of the deficit of Class I Yoredale residents is due to the habitat inhabitant bias between Yoredale's school authority system and adolescents; almost all Class I adolescents are among those that are ejected by or reject Yoredale's school settings.

Loci of Controls. Behavior settings differ in the extent to which their functioning is influenced by occurrences originating within the community and at different geographical distances from it. For example, crucial features of the program of the Yoredale behavior setting British Railways Freight Office and Delivery are subject to control from the national level by executive settings located outside of Yoredale, outside of the surrounding rural district, and outside of the surrounding dale region; its performers are appointed and its program is determined at a great distance from Yoredale. British Railways Freight Office and Delivery has, therefore, a low degree of local autonomy. On the other hand, the performers and program of the Yoredale behavior setting dramatic society reception are determined almost entirely by the executive setting dramatic society committee meeting, which is located in Yoredale; therefore the setting dramatic society reception has a high degree of local autonomy. The extent of a town's behavior settings that are locally autonomous is a measure of the degree to which its inhabitants control the environment in which they live.

We report two degrees of local autonomy: high and low. A behavior setting with *high* local autonomy is predominantly controlled from sources within the town or the circumjacent area with approximately a four-mile radius of the town; this embraces a governmental district in each case: Midwest's school district and Yoredale's rural district. The appointment of leaders, admission of members, determination of fees and prices, and establishment of policies and programs are controlled largely by sources located within the setting, the town, or this circumjacent area. A setting of *low* local autonomy is predominantly controlled from sources located at the state and national administrative centers (Midwest), or at the county and national centers (Yoredale).

High Local Autonomy. Model MW has greater local autonomy than Model YD. Behavior settings with high local autonomy are forty-seven centiurbs in extent and have 4,290 claims for operatives in Model MW; they are thirty-five centiurbs in extent and have 1,328 claims in Model YD. In consequence, the MW models generate 3.98 and the YD models 1.03 high-autonomy claim operations per human component. These are the mean numbers of responsible positions filled and implemented by town inhabitants without directives from outside the towns or the immediately surrounding districts.

Low Local Autonomy. Model YD is under much more control of distant authorities than Model MW. YD settings with low local autonomy are 35.7 centiurbs in extent and have 2,295 claims for operatives, whereas MW settings are 8.5 centiurbs in extent and have 500 claims for operatives in Model MW. The YD model produces 0.73 and the MW model 0.26 low-autonomy claim operations per human component.

The mean number of responsible positions filled and implemented in conformity with directives from a distance are fewer for both models than the number filled and implemented locally, but the difference is much greater for the MW than for the YD model. For MW, the locally autonomous claim operations per human component are 15 times greater than those implemented from a distance, and for YD they are 1.4 times greater.

Value of a Man and Power of the People. Midwest residents have greater power than Yoredale residents in two ways: They hold more positions of power as behavior setting operatives and leaders, and more of the settings in which they have power are of high local autonomy. These different degrees and loci of power have some paradoxical consequences.

Value of a Man. The loss of an average Midwest resident without replacement or compensatory adjustment reduces the operating efficiency of the town by a factor of .00056 because this removes 8 of the 14,249 essential claim operations (chairmen, clerks, choir members, cheerleaders, and so forth); this, in percentage terms, .056, is the Pied Piper Index. The loss of an average Yoredale inhabitant reduces the operating efficiency of Yoredale by a factor of .00027; its Pied Piper Index is .027. On the average, therefore, Midwest residents are more valuable than Yoredale residents by a factor of 2.07 as operatives of the towns' habitats. Although this is not a psychological finding, being no more psychological than the fact that buildings with fewer supporting beams per ton of weight place greater average burdens on their beams than those with more supporting beams per ton of weight, it has some important psychological resultants according to behavior setting theory: Relative to Yoredale residents, Midwest residents, on the average, are more important people, have greater responsibilities, have to accept lower standards of adequate performance, value concrete accomplishments more and general personal qualities less, are more insecure, are more versatile, and work harder. These are the psychological costs and benefits of being more valuable as habitat components.

The Pied Piper data mean that Midwest residents are less expendable than Yoredale residents, with the psychological consequences indicated, and that Yoredale residents are more redundant than residents of Midwest. Redundancy has psychological consequences too. The leadership data are especially relevant here. Undoubtedly, approximately the same proportions of the towns' inhabitants are able to do the difficult things that habitat claims for leaders entail. However, twice the percentage of Midwest residents are leaders; there are, therefore, more redundant leaders in Yoredale than in Midwest. In fact, from the data on leadership and population we find that 275 Yoredale inhabitants who were not leaders in 1963-1964 would have been leaders if its habitat had been similar to Midwest's with respect to human components and claims for leaders. Thus, many more able Yoredale residents experience the psychological consequences of being expendable, of not being important, of not having responsibilities in the operation and maintenance of the town. The consequences of this are in general the converse of those listed for Midwesterners. Yoredale residents, in comparison with Midwest residents, are on the average less important to the functioning of the town, have fewer responsibilities, have higher standards of adequate performance, value personal qualities more and concrete performance less, are more secure, less versatile, and do not work so hard. Another resultant is that the cultivation of leisure is a more common pursuit in Yoredale, and this may be one source of the more prominent esthetic and muscular qualities of Yoredale behavior. More Yoredale residents than Midwest residents have the time for flower gardening, countryside rambles, and long evenings at the pub. The Coronation Club, where many able inhabitants of Yoredale spend much time, has no counterpart in Midwest.

Power of the People. Residents of Midwest are not only more frequently than residents of Yoredale in powerful, responsible positions as operatives where they carry out the programs of the town's behavior settings; they also have complete control of more of the town's settings. Behavior settings with a high degree of local autonomy comprise 47 centiurbs (44 percent) of Midwest's habitat and 35 centiurbs (31 percent) of Yoredale's. Within the locally controlled habitats, there are 4,290 (42 percent) of Midwest's and 1,378 (18 percent) of Yoredale's claims for operatives. This means that Midwest residents have ultimate control of 34 percent more of its habitats than Yoredale residents do and of three times as many of its responsible positions. On the other hand, habitats with a low degree of local autonomy comprise 36 centiurbs (32 percent) of Yoredale's habitat and 8.5 centiurbs (8 percent) of Midwest's. Within the settings whose programs are controlled from a distance, there are 2,295 (29 percent) of Yoredale's claims for operatives and 500 (5 percent) of Midwest's. Remote authorities control 4.2 times as much of Yoredale's habitat and 4.6 times as many of its responsible positions as they do of Midwest's. The inhabitants of Midwest have final control of more of the important and powerful positions within the town, including their programs and personnel, than the inhabitants of Yoredale.

Power of Operatives Versus Power of Members. Having power over one's habitat, whether as operatives of behavior settings or as members of locally autonomous behavior settings, promotes interest and activity, whereas powerlessness of either kind breeds detachment and passivity. To the degree that residents of Yoredale are more powerless than residents of Midwest, they are more apathetic toward those aspects of the town's habitat they disapprove of. This is doubtless one factor behind the fewer person-hours of occupancy and fewer claim operations per town inhabitant in Yoredale than in Midwest.

In addition to this general resultant of the differences in the two kinds of power, there are some other and paradoxical consequences. Midwest residents have *immediate* power as operatives over more of the town's habitat than do residents of Yoredale; and they have *ultimate* power over more of the habitat as members of more behavior settings with high local autonomy. However, this greater ultimate power of Midwest residents diminishes the stability of the local base from which they wield their greater immediate power. The converse is true for Yoredale; how it occurs there may be indicated by a concrete instance.

The behavior setting trafficways has low local autonomy in Yoredale; it is under the control of a distant authority (the county council) with headquarters in the county hall, eighteen miles distant. The power of Yoredale residents over trafficways is limited in three ways: (1) as operatives, they are agents of the distant authority and have limited immediate power to change the street program they implement or to influence the authority's decisions; (2) this limited power of Yoredale inhabitants as operatives in turn limits the power of other Yoredale residents

to influence trafficways by directly pressuring the local operatives; (3) the ultimate power of Yoredale inhabitants via the
county council is attenuated by distance and by their small representation on it. These conditions render all residents of Yoredale, both trafficways operatives and users, more helpless and
more apathetic about the town's streets than are residents of
Midwest, for whom all these power conditions are reversed.

However, the very conditions that weaken the power of
Yoredale residents over the town's streets increases the stability
of the local base of the operatives' limited power; *their powerlessness enhances their security.* On the contrary, the greater immediate power and influence of Midwest trafficways operatives
attract from their fellow townsmen greater pressure on them to
alter inadequate street programs and policies and, in extreme
cases, to vacate their positions as operatives. Townspeople can
exert this pressure in two ways: directly, on the operatives, and
indirectly, via the local authority (the town council), which
they ultimately control. So we find that the very conditions
that strengthen the power of Midwest residents over the town's
streets weaken the local base of the operatives' greater power;
their powerfulness reduces their security.

These differences hold for many behavior settings of Midwest and Yoredale. The greater but more fragile power of
Midwest residents is an important factor in its greater habitat
erosion and accretion. More Midwest residents than Yoredale
residents have the power to make habitat changes (to initiate, to
discard, to alter settings), but their greater insecurity more
often retires them and rescinds the changes they have begun.
This is a manifestation of greater tension within Midwest between the operatives who at any moment are in charge of the
habitat and the other inhabitants who oversee the operatives. In both towns, there is continuing conflict between
those who wish to enhance the value of persons and the
power of the people, at the cost of tension, hard work, low
standards, and insecurity, and those who wish to decrease tension and effort and increase standards and security—to increase
efficiency—at the cost of the value of persons and the power of
the people.

Midwest and Yoredale as Human Habitats

According to our present understanding, the public environments that Midwest and Yoredale provide for their inhabitants consist of behavior settings of the same basic design but with differences in some details. One of the latter is the fewer and less adequate number of human components per setting in Midwest than in Yoredale. This structural difference in the towns has quite disparate and important consequences for the behavior and experiences of their inhabitants. Behavior setting control mechanisms compensate for Midwest's deficiency in human components by operating them differently and more intensively than Yoredale's greater number of components. As a result, the towns' behavior settings function on approximately the same level. The differential adjustments in the behavior of the towns' inhabitants by which this is accomplished are described for the undermanned (Midwest) and the more optimally manned (Yoredale) settings in Chapter Fourteen. In addition, the different numbers of human components provide the infrastructure of two dissimilar subsystems of child rearing that further differentiate the towns as habitats for children.

Our research makes it clear that behavior settings are complex entities whose workings we have only begun to understand. We do know that the settings of Midwest and Yoredale are differentially selective of classes of human components and that they generate behavior with different mixes of attributes, but the processes behind these and other differences await further study.

Roger G. Barker   19

Return Trip, 1977

◆◆◆◆◆◆◆◆◆◆◆◆◆◆◆◆◆◆◆◆◆◆◆◆◆◆◆◆◆◆◆◆◆◆◆◆◆

The towns I observed from the Illinois Central train in 1940 are still there and easily recognized despite some changes: Bypasses swing the highway around most of the towns, most have a few more inhabitants, all are spruced up (trim houses, clipped lawns, paved streets, new fronts to business buildings), and all have replaced the old technologies with 1977 developments (television antennae; single-story, flat-roofed school buildings with wide parking lots and flood-lighted football fields). But the changes in the towns are less dramatic than the change in my comprehension of them. In 1940 I only asked, "What do people do in these towns?" In 1977 I ask in addition, "What do these towns do to people?" In 1940 I looked on the towns as a psychologist; in 1977 I also see them as an eco-behavioral scientist.

The development did not come quickly. It was in part a product of the psychological data we collected on what people do, minute by minute, throughout their days. The discovery that the behavior streams of Persons A and B usually change similarly when they move between Locales X and Y (later identified as behavior settings) raised a problem: To what degree are people and to what degree are locales sources of behavior attri-

285

butes? Personal experience by no means pointed solely to people. I thought of how much I behaved in accordance with my own intentions and how much in accordance with the dictates of the towns and cities I inhabited. I did know that I could not have my favorite lunch in Carbondale in 1940, or even my second or third preferences; Carbondale's restaurants fed me pork chops, roast pork, or pork steak (the economy was depressed, and pork was plentiful and cheap in southern Illinois). After a week of living in a central city, I was physically exhausted by the behavior it required of me: walking great distances (a private car was impractical, taxis were uncertain, and both were too expensive), climbing (down to subways, up to elevated trains and overpasses), and standing (for traffic lights and elevators, in queue lines). I escaped with relief to the easy locomotor life my small home town allowed me. And there was the continuing concern from 1940: "If a town exercises such strong control over people within so small a part of its whole domain as a single highway, to what degree does it take overall charge of its inhabitants?"

Nevertheless, in 1940 I saw the towns as collections of people, each person a dynamic entity freely carrying out his plans within the environment the town provided, an environment that was beneficient with respect to some of his plans, deficient with respect to others, and resistant to still others, but an environment that, although frustrating and constraining to some extent, was a relatively stable, reliable ground for action. In 1977, I see the towns as assemblies of dynamic, homeostatic entities (drugstores, city council meetings, third-grade music classes, and so forth) where people are essential components (among other classes of components, such as drugs, a gavel, and music books). These are behavior settings, and within them people do not act in relation to a relatively fixed, dependable environment of benefits, deficiencies, and constraints, because stores, meetings, classes, and all other behavior settings have plans for their human components and armories of alternative ways of enforcing their plans. Although according to this new understanding, people are less free in the immediate present than in the older view, they are not diminished; quite the contrary. When people understand behavior settings and learn to create and operate them, they greatly increase their power by managing the environment that has so coercive an influence over them. And in the new view people are more important than in the earlier one: As essential parts of ongoing behavior setting enterprises that are larger than their personal undertakings, they have a hand in providing satisfactions (and dissatisfactions), not only for themselves and their immediate associates but for all others involved in the setting. As essential components of behavior settings, people have significance for more than those with whom they have direct contact.

The fundamental significance of behavior settings for the behavior sciences comes from their position within the topological hierarchy of entities ranging from cell, to organ, to person, to behavior setting, to institution (in some cases), and to community. Within this included-inclusive series, behavior settings are proximal and circumjacent to people (people are components of behavior settings), and behavior settings are proximal and interjacent to institutions and communities (they are components of institutions and communities). Although we have only the beginning of an understanding of behavior settings, we can see that enlightenment must move in two directions: inward to relationships between behavior settings and their human components and outward to relationships with institutions and communities. In both directions, there are important potential applications. People control their lives to an important extent (1) by creating and influencing the programs of the behavior settings of their communities and (2) by selecting, so far as possible, the settings into which they allow themselves to be incorporated. A person's greatest strength is at the boundary of a setting; once he "joins," he has to cope with much greater forces than those operating at the boundary. Knowledge of a community's behavior settings should be a strong weapon in the armory of those professionals who counsel individual persons.

Interior Relationships: Behavior Settings and People

Behavior settings are the concrete environmental units where people engage in behavior. People do not live in poverty or affluence, in the middle or the upper classes; they live in behavior settings. The terms *poverty* and *upper class* refer to some aspects of the actual settings people inhabit. Behavior within the settings where people live is influenced by three classes of variables: their physical properties, the number and character of their human components, and their programs. All three doubtless contribute to such global qualities as poverty and upper classness.

Physical Properties of Behavior Settings. The amount and arrangement of space, the number, location, and properties of entrances and exits, the illumination, temperature, and decoration, and the furnishings and equipment of behavior settings all contribute to their standing patterns of behavior. Paving the streets of the Illinois towns (behavior setting trafficways) doubtless contributed to the widely deplored speed with which the inhabitants drive their cars. The importance of the physical side of behavior settings is suggested by the significance for baseball games of the size, shape, and boundaries of the field and by the furor in the basketball fraternity caused by the proposal to increase the height of the basket. Manipulating the physical properties of behavior settings in order to influence behavior is the province of architects, engineers, and designers. Unfortunately, solid empirical evidence or promising theories to guide these professionals have been meager. In recent years, for example, many "open" schools have been built with very little knowledge of the consequences for children and teachers of behavior settings without boundary walls. However, our ignorance of the relations between the physical aspects of behavior settings and behavior is now well recognized, and many investigations are underway; these may provide a basis for new specialties, such as eco-behavioral architecture, engineering, and design.

Human Components of Behavior Settings. Behavior within a setting is influenced by the number and the characteristics of its human components. We are relatively well informed about some consequences of variation in number of human components, especially of fewer than the optimal number of human components, of the undermanning of behavior settings. Issues of greatest social importance are involved here, for in many parts of the world the balance is changing from scarcity or adequacy to redundancy of human components for behavior settings. In the United States, for example, in the days of the western frontier, people were at a premium to operate the established settings. People were valued in a nation of many undermanned behavior settings, and the characteristic syndrome of behavior on the frontier was in close accord with the derivations from theory of undermanning: busyness, hard work, versatility, self-confidence, self-esteem, responsibility, low standards, mutual support. Now the United States and many other societies are confronted with the problem of how to cope with redundant people. At the level of behavior settings and their interior relations with their human components, the answer is clear: Keep the number of people and the number of behavior settings in balance so that all available people are needed for behavior setting operation. This requires reducing the number of people or creating more behavior settings with fewer inhabitants per setting. Is the latter possible? In a crisis of declining supplies of gasoline, we place constraints on large automobiles. In a crisis of increasing numbers of people, can we place constraints on large behavior settings? Much of the answer to this lies in the external relations of settings with the institutions and communities of which they are parts.

We know very little about how the characteristics (as opposed to the number) of the human components of behavior settings affect their operation and thence rebound on the components. But we do know that variety is essential for the functioning of almost all settings. Even so specialized a behavior setting as a president's news conference requires not only the president and newsmen for its occurrence, but persons with the skills of audio engineers, guards, custodians, photographers, video specialists, and so forth. Just as physical components are as essential to behavior settings as human components, people with strong backs and skilled hands are as essential as those with intellectual and verbal abilities. When such human diversity occurs in behavior settings, the setting, itself, with its controls and interior forces produces a functional tolerance and appreciation among its human components.

Programs of Behavior Settings. The point of entry for most directly influencing behavior within settings is by way of its program of operation. When a teacher makes a new lesson plan, when a chairman changes the agenda of a business meeting, when the new owner of a store changes its policies, the standing patterns of behavior in the settings change appropriately: The pupils may do seat work instead of recitations, the members of the meeting may vote on Issue Y before they vote on Issue X, and the customers may have to pay cash rather than charge their purchases. But most program changes cannot be made easily. An established behavior setting is an interdependent, homeostatic entity in semistable equilibrium, and as such it is resistant to change. A change in program may require more space, rearranged space, and new equipment, and meet physical and perhaps economic resistance; it may require more or fewer human components and altered behavior and may face social and psychological opposition. And some resistance may come from the outside: Permission from a reluctant zoning commission may be required. Furthermore, because of the interdependence of behavior settings, changes in parts reverberate in unexpected ways through them, and a change in program may have unforeseeable consequences, some of which may be undesirable. Kounin (1970), for example, found that a school class program that involved publicly countering certain kinds of behavior deviation had consequences far beyond the disciplined person whose misbehavior the program was intended to correct.

It is sometimes easier to establish a new behavior setting than it is to change the program of an old one. Members of a church who become dissatisfied with its program and meet resistance to change may more easily withdraw and establish a new church with behavior setting programs that satisfy them. New interests, new social policies, new dilemmas, and new opportunities require new behavior settings. If one were to study the Illinois towns in detail, one would undoubtedly find that despite the continuity in their surface appearance great changes have occurred in their behavior settings since 1940. Midwest, a similar town in the same region of the country, consisted of 884 behavior settings in 1963-1964; 504 of these (57 percent) were newly established during the previous decade, amounting to 56 new behavior settings per year, on the average. And behavior settings continually cease to occur. There were 576 behavior settings in Midwest in 1954-1955; in the following decade, 215 of these (36 percent) vanished, amounting to 24 a year, on the average. Because the rate of accretion of behavior settings was greater than the rate of erosion, Midwest was more extensive as a human habitat in 1964 than in 1954. Less than half (43 percent) of its 1963-1964 behavior settings were as much as ten years old. During the decade, Midwest grew 53 percent in terms of behavior settings and 16 percent in terms of population, so here is one town that was not troubled with an increase in redundant inhabitants; over this period, it created for itself a habitat where people were in ever-greater demand as behavior setting components.

Communities renew themselves by changing the programs of their ongoing behavior settings, by discarding settings, and by creating new settings. Sarason (1972, 1974; Sarason and others, 1977) has elucidated important aspects of these processes. They are at the present time in the hands of practical persons: proprietors of stores, chairpersons, band leaders, classroom teachers, club presidents, community activists, and so forth. All are necessarily amateurs, some of them expert amateurs, because we do not yet have a science and an accompanying technology of behavior settings.

Whole-Part Relations

Eco-behavioral science and ecological psychology deal, respectively, with whole phenomena—namely, behavior settings—and with certain parts of the same phenomena; they do this in the way that some physical sciences deal with wholes (for example, bridge design) and other sciences deal with parts (steel, concrete) of the same structure. And just as some attributes of the physical parts when in place are determined by the structures into which they are built (their compression, temperature), and some attributes of the structures are determined by their component materials (endurance, vibration), some attributes of the human components of behavior settings are determined by the behavior settings into which they are incorporated (busyness, versatility), and some attributes of the behavior settings are determined by their human components (stability, functioning level). The "whole" sciences and the "part" sciences can be pursued independently; the forms and properties of steel and concrete can be investigated without reference to their use in bridges, and the dynamics of arches can be studied without reference to the use of steel and concrete in their construction. Nevertheless, the history of science reveals a continual enrichment of the sciences of wholes by the sciences of parts and vice versa. This is clearly shown in the work at the Midwest Psychological Field Station, where data of ecological psychology, the science of behavior setting parts, led to the discovery of the whole phenomena, behavior settings; and the inclusion of behavior settings in the study of problems of ecological psychology greatly explains the latter; studies reported in this book—namely, American-English and physically handicapped-nonhandicapped behavior differences and the assessment of physical rehabilitation in a hospital—are examples.

At the present stage of its development, the scientific rigor of ecological psychology is greatly increased by eco-behavioral science. Previously, it was impossible to satisfactorily identify and describe the environmental context of the naturally occurring behavior of persons under investigation. The best that usually could be done was to specify the geographical location and fragments of some of the social context. So in this respect ecological psychology was less rigorous than experimental psychology, which created and precisely described the environment (the experimental conditions) of the behavior it studied. Now, with the ability to specify the behavior settings in which actions occur, much more rigorous studies are possible. This greater rigor is exemplified by the ecological psychology studies reported in Chapters Seven, Eight, Nine, and Eleven.

Exterior Relations: Behavior Settings, Institutions, and Communities

Behavior settings are fundamental units for describing the habitat that an institution or community provides its inhabitants. On an elementary level, a simple listing of the settings and changes in the lists over time provides important information. In the decade between 1954 and 1964, the following behavior settings, among others, disappeared from the list of Midwest's settings—circus, cream collection station, dairy barn, farm practice class, ice depot, telephone exchange—and these new settings appeared—bowling games, kindergarten classes, self-service laundry, telephone kiosks, x-ray laboratory. When measures of the extents and properties of behavior settings are added, more meaningful data are obtained; the lists become equivalent, so far as human behavior possibilities are concerned, to a catalogue of the soils of a region, with their properties and extents, for plant growth possibilities. In 1963-1964, behavior setting programs with high concentrations of business behavior constituted 17.1 percent of Midwest's and 28.3 percent of Yoredale's total habitats, whereas settings with high concentration of religious behavior constituted 8.5 percent of Midwest's and 4.2 percent of Yoredale's habitat. When measures of the amount of behavior are included, the description of the town as a habitat for behavior becomes still more complete. Although Yoredale's business habitat was 74 percent greater than Midwest's, its behavior output via town inhabitants was only 48 percent greater; in fact, Midwest's business habitat produced 6 percent more business behavior per town inhabitant than Yoredale's. Midwest's business habitat was less extensive but more productive than Yoredale's.

None of the behavior settings in Midwest or in the towns along the Illinois Central Railroad stand alone; all are subject to controls from outside their boundaries. Some are subject only to prohibitions from the encircling town. The behavior setting Women's Afternoon Pinochle Club meeting can do as it pleases except set up its tables in the middle of Illinois Street, thus interfering with the operation of other behavior settings and the rights of persons who are not members. The program, components, and equipment of Women's Afternoon Pinochle Club meeting are its own business. But other behavior settings are less free. This is true, for example, of the setting high school Algebra I class meeting. Its physical properties (location, duration, equipment), its human components (members, teacher), and its program (teaching methods, topics to be covered) are imposed to a greater or less degree by the institution, the high school, of which Algebra I is a part. But Algebra I is by no means helpless. There is two-way interaction between the setting and the school, and forces from the school often elicit counterforces or resistance from the setting. This is the arena of business executives, school superintendents, city managers, management experts, community psychologists, and students of organizations.

The work at the Midwest Field Station identified and described the extents and behavior outputs of these five classes of institutions (there called *authority systems*): government institutions, school institutions, business institutions, church institutions, and voluntary association institutions. We confronted only one issue of general, theoretical importance, namely, the relationship between the size of institutions (in terms of number of inhabitants) and the manning of their constituent behavior settings. The data we assembled on schools and churches of different sizes and our general observation of other institutions and communities indicated to us that the component behavior settings of large institutions are, on the average, larger than those of small institutions and that undermanning is more prevalent among the settings of small institutions than of large ones. In view of our finding that in relatively small, undermanned settings more people have power and importance than in large ones, we asked if it is inevitable that large settings diminish their inhabitants in this way. Must the large, consolidated school we studied have large algebra classes, a large football game, a large cafeteria, and so forth, where hardly anyone is missed by the setting when absent, where, in fact, a crucial problem of classes, games, and services is the superabundance of people? We asked why the new school could not have three football teams and games, as the small schools in the separate towns had before consolidation. To most school officials, the question was ridiculous. Efficiency is the name of the school game, as it is of the business game, the government game, even the church game. The argument is that one pastor and ten lay representatives with modern technology (automobiles, word-processing machines, sound systems, audiovisual aids, and so forth) can run a unified 900-member church more effectively than six pastors and sixty lay representatives can run six 150-member churches; in short, a large church is more man-power-efficient and technically superior. The one big-church pastor can be more highly selected (more intelligent, more learned, more charismatic, more spiritual) than the six small-church pastors, and his assistants can be specialists (in youth work, in music, in counseling). But there is one more attribute of the large, more efficient, unified church: It greatly reduces the significance in church affairs of about 80 percent of the former powerful and important lay representatives and pastors and of an uncounted number of Sunday School teachers, committee chairmen, ushers, organists, secretaries, and choir members. The six churches provide many more people than does the large church with the opportunity to satisfy their needs to be competent and approved by carrying out essential operations in valued enterprises. We observed an instance of this during our studies of Yoredale when a new local government policy was instituted by consolidating a number of rural district councils into a single, large, and presumably efficient district government. This entailed sacrificing twenty-two of twenty-four local councilors with the evaluation, "you never will be missed," in fact, "we are better off without you." Beside depriving these people of important satisfactions, the change deprived local government of the talents and devotion of many able, responsible people.

The pressure of population, of technology, and efficiency against opportunities for people to be significant may be as great threats to survival as the pressure of population against food. The former threats are as salient, or more so, in "advanced" as in underdeveloped countries. The assertion that large, manpower-efficient, technically superior enterprises inevitably produce a better product more cheaply requires searching investigation. Modern transportation and communication makes it possible to share expertise among small enterprises; it would seem that three reading specialists can be transported between small schools more cheaply than the bodies of 600 students can be transported to the three reading specialists. And a frequent error in computing the costs of a manpower-efficient enterprise is to ignore the costs that are exported beyond its walls. A greater proportion of dropouts from a large school than from several small schools would amount to exporting problems and expenses to other institutions and settings (to courts, to jails, to counseling centers, to dole lines), problems and costs the community must meet. The science and art of reducing the size of machines without sacrificing their output has been spectacular in many cases; so we have efficient small electric motors, gasoline engines, clothes washers, television sets, pumps, generators, and so forth. There would appear to be a similar opportunity to contrive efficient, small behavior settings where people are important. Small is indeed beautiful to people who want to reduce the risk of being helpless and expendable.

Sometimes, during the life of the Midwest Psychological Field Station, it seemed that the research findings reduced the importance of people and increased the importance of the environment, but by the time of the return trip to the towns in central Illinois it was clear that eco-behavioral science enhances the power and importance of people to the degree that we understand and make use of behavior settings.

Chronological List of Midwest Psychological Field Station Publications and Theses

━━━◆◆◆◆◆◆◆◆◆◆◆◆◆◆◆◆◆◆◆◆◆◆◆◆━━━

1949

Barker, R. G., and Wright, H. F. "Psychological Ecology and the Problem of Psycho-Social Development." *Child Development,* 1949, *20,* 131-143.

1950

Barker, R. G., Wright, H. F., Nall, J., and Schoggen, P. "There Is No Class Bias in Our School." *Progressive Education,* 1950, *27,* 106-110.

Wright, H. F., and Barker, R. G. "The Elementary School Does Not Stand Alone." *Progressive Education,* 1950, *27,* 133-137.

1951

Barker, R. G., and Wright, H. F. *One Boy's Day.* New York: Harper & Row, 1951. Reprinted by Hamden, Conn.: Shoestring Press, 1966.

Barker, R. G., and Wright, H. F. "The Psychological Habitat of Raymond Birch." In J. H. Rohrer and M. Sherif (Eds.), *Social Psychology at the Crossroads.* New York: Harper & Row, 1951.

Barker, R. G., Wright, H. F., and Koppe, W. A. "The Psychological Ecology of a Small Town." In W. Dennis (Ed.), *Readings in Child Psychology.* Englewood Cliffs, N.J.: Prentice-Hall, 1951.

Schoggen, P. *A Study in Psychological Ecology: A Description of the Behavior Objects Which Entered the Psychological Habitat of an Eight-Year-Old Girl During the Course of One Day.* Master's thesis, University of Kansas, Lawrence, 1951.

Wright, H. F., Barker, R. G., Koppe, W. A., Meyerson, B., and Nall, J. "Children at Home in Midwest." *Progressive Education,* 1951, *28,* 137-143.

1952

Barker, L. S., Schoggen, M., Schoggen, P., and Barker, R. G. "The Frequency of Physical Disability in Children: A Comparison of Three Sources of Information." *Child Development,* 1952, *23,* 215-226.

1953

Newton, M. R. *A Study in Psychological Ecology: The Behavior Settings in an Institution for Handicapped Children.* Master's thesis, University of Kansas, Lawrence, 1953.

1954

Koppe, W. A. *A Study in Psychological Ecology: A Survey of the Behavior Settings of Midwest.* Doctoral dissertation, University of Kansas, Lawrence, 1954.

Schoggen, P. *A Study in Psychological Ecology: Structural Properties of Children's Behavior Based on Sixteen Day-Long Specimen Records.* Doctoral dissertation, University of Kansas, Lawrence, 1954.

1955

Barker, R. G., Schoggen, M., and Barker, L. S. "Hemerography of Mary Ennis." In A. Burton and R. E. Harris (Eds.), *Clinical Studies of Personality.* New York: Harper & Row, 1955.

Barker, R. G., and Wright, H. F. *Midwest and Its Children.* New York: Harper & Row, 1955. Reprinted by Archon Books, Hamden, Conn., 1971.

Wright, H. F., Barker, R. G., Nall, J., and Schoggen, P. "Toward a Psychological Ecology of the Classroom." In A. P. Coladarci (Ed.), *Readings in Educational Psychology.* New York: Holt, Rinehart and Winston, 1955.

1956

Ragle, D. D. M. *Children's Naturally Occurring Problems and Problem-Solving Behavior.* Doctoral dissertation, University of Kansas, Lawrence, 1956.

Simpson, J. E. *A Study in Psychological Ecology: Social Weather of Children in the Behavior Settings of Midwest.* Doctoral dissertation, University of Kansas, Lawrence, 1956.

Wright, H. F. "Psychological Development in Midwest." *Child Development,* 1956, *27,* 265-286.

1957

Barker, R. G. "Structure of the Stream of Behavior." In Proceedings of the 15th International Congress of Psychology, 1957.

Wiest, W. M. *Children's Situations in Communities Differing in Size as Revealed by a Projective Test of the Environment.* Master's thesis, University of Kansas, Lawrence, 1957.

1958

Dickman, H. R. *The Perception of Behavioral Units.* Master's thesis, University of Kansas, Lawrence, 1958.

Dyck, A. J. *A Study in Psychological Ecology: A Description of Social Contacts of Twelve Midwest Children with Their Parents.* Master's thesis, University of Kansas, Lawrence, 1958.

1959

Fawl, C. L. *Disturbances Experienced by Children in Their Natural Habitat: A Study in Psychological Ecology.* Doctoral dissertation, University of Kansas, Lawrence, 1959.

1960

Barker, R. G. "Ecology and Motivation." In M. R. Jones (Ed.), *Nebraska Symposium on Motivation.* Lincoln: University of Nebraska Press, 1960.

Barker, R. G. "Small High Schools (Letter)." *Science,* 1960, *131,* 1560-61.

Wright, H. F. "Observational Child Study." In P. H. Mussen (Ed.), *Handbook of Research Methods in Child Development.* New York: Wiley, 1960.

1961

Barker, R. G., and Barker, L. S. "Behavior Units for the Comparative Study of Cultures." In B. Kaplan (Ed.), *Studying Personality Cross-Culturally.* New York: Harper & Row, 1961.

Barker, R. G., and Barker, L. S. "The Psychological Ecology of

Old People in Midwest, Kansas and Yoredale, Yorkshire."
Journal of Gerontology, 1961, *16,* 144-149.

Barker, R. G., Wright, H. F., Barker, L. S., and Schoggen, M.
Specimen Records of American and English Children. Lawrence: University of Kansas Press, 1961.

1963

Barker, R. G. "On the Nature of the Environment." *Journal of
Social Issues,* 1963, *19* (4), 17-38. Reprinted in E. P. Hollan-
der and R. G. Hunt (Eds.), *Current Perspectives in Social
Psychology.* New York: Oxford University Press, 1967.

Barker, R. G. (Ed.). *The Stream of Behavior.* New York: Appleton-Century-Crofts, 1963. This book includes the following:

    Barker, R. G. "The Stream of Behavior as an Empirical
Problem," pp. 1-22.

    Barker, R. G., and Barker, L. S. "Social Actions in the
Behavior Streams of American and English Children,"
pp. 127-159.

    Dickman, H. R. "The Perception of Behavior Units,"
pp. 23-41.

    Dyck, A. J. "The Social Contacts of Some Midwest Chil-
dren with their Parents and Teachers," pp. 78-98.

    Fawl, C. L. "Disturbances Experienced by Children in
their Natural Habitats," pp. 99-126.

    Gump, P. V., Schoggen, P., and Redl, F. "The Behavior
of the Same Child in Different Milieus," pp. 169-202.

    Schoggen, M., Barker, L. S., and Barker, R. G. "Structure
of the Behavior of American and English Children,"
pp. 160-168.

    Schoggen, P. "Environmental Forces in the Everyday
Lives of Children," pp. 42-69.

    Simmons, H., and Schoggen, P. "Mothers and Fathers as
Sources of Environmental Pressure on Children," pp.
70-77.

    Simpson, J. E. "A Method of Measuring the Social Weath-
er of Children," pp. 219-227.

Barker, R. G., and Barker, L. S. "Sixty-Five and Over." In R. H.

Williams, C. Tibbitts, and W. Donahue (Eds.), *Processes of Aging.* New York: Prentice-Hall, 1963.

Willems, E. P. *Forces Toward Participation in Behavior Settings of Large and Small Institutions.* Master's thesis, University of Kansas, Lawrence, 1963.

1964

Ashton, M. *An Ecological Study of the Stream of Behavior.* Master's thesis, University of Kansas, Lawrence, 1964.

Barker, R. G. "Observation of Behavior: Ecological Approaches." *Journal of Mt. Sinai Hospital,* 1964, *31* (4), 268-284.

Barker, R. G., and Gump, P. V. (Eds.). *Big School, Small School.* Stanford, Calif.: Stanford University Press, 1964. This book includes the following:

Barker, R. G. "Community Size and Activities of Students," pp. 154-171.

Barker, R. G. "Ecological Units," pp. 11-28.

Barker, R. G. "The Ecological Environment," pp. 3-10.

Barker, R. G., and Barker, L. S. "Structural Characteristics," pp. 41-63.

Barker, R. G., and Hall, E. "Participation in Interschool Events and Extracurricular Activities," pp. 64-74.

Barker, R. G., and LeCompte, W. F. "Adolescents in the Towns of Midwest County," pp. 172-192.

Campbell, W. J. "Some Effects of High School Consolidation," pp. 139-153.

Gump, P. V., and Barker, R. G. "Overview and Prospects," pp. 195-202.

Gump, P. V., and Friesen, W. V. "Participation in Nonclass Settings," pp. 75-93.

Gump, P. V., and Friesen, W. V. "Satisfactions Derived from Nonclass Settings," pp. 94-114.

Willems, E. P. "Forces Toward Participation in Behavior Settings," pp. 115-135.

Willems, E. P. "Review of Research," pp. 29-37.

Gump, P. V. "Environmental Guidance of the Classroom Behavioral System." In B. J. Biddle and W. J. Ellena (Eds.), *Contemporary Research on Teacher Effectiveness.* New York: Holt, Rinehart and Winston, 1964.

1965

Barker, R. G. "Explorations in Ecological Psychology." *American Psychologist,* 1965, *20* (1), 1-14.

Chess, S. B. *Children's Requests in a Bedtime Context.* Master's thesis, University of Kansas, Lawrence, 1965.

Hall, E. *An Ecological Study of Parent-Child Influencing Behavior.* Master's thesis, University of Kansas, Lawrence, 1965.

Willems, E. P. "An Ecological Orientation in Psychology." *Merrill-Palmer Quarterly,* 1965, *11* (4), 317-343.

Willems, E. P. *Participation in Behavior Settings in Relation to Three Variables: Size of Behavior Settings, Marginality of Persons, and Sensitivity to Audiences.* Doctoral dissertation, University of Kansas, Lawrence, 1965.

Willems, E. P., and Willems, G. J. "Comparative Validity of Data Yielded by Three Methods." *Merrill-Palmer Quarterly,* 1965, *11,* 65-71.

1967

Barker, R. G. "Naturalistic Methods in Psychological Research: Some Comments on the Symposium Papers." *Human Development,* 1967, *10,* 223-229.

Barker, R. G., Barker, L. S., and Ragle, D. D. M. "The Churches of Midwest, Kansas and Yoredale, Yorkshire: Their Contributions to the Environments of the Towns." In W. Gore and L. Hodapp (Eds.), *Change in the Small Community.* New York: Friendship Press, 1967.

Bechtel, R. B. *Footsteps as a Measure of Human Preference.* Doctoral dissertation, University of Kansas, Lawrence, 1967.

Irving, J. J. *Student Response to the Classroom Behavior Setting: A Cross-Cultural Study.* Master's thesis, University of Kansas, Lawrence, 1967.

Ragle, D. D. M., Johnson, A., and Barker, R. G. "Measuring

Extension's Impact." *Journal of Cooperative Extension,* Fall 1967, *5* (3), 178-186.

Wicker, A. W. *Students' Experiences in Behavior Settings of Large and Small High Schools: An Examination of Behavior Setting Theory.* Doctoral dissertation, University of Kansas, Lawrence, 1967.

Willems, E. P. "Behavioral Validity of a Test for Measuring Social Anxiety." *Psychological Reports,* 1967, *21,* 433-442. Copyright, Southern Universities Press, 1967.

Willems, E. P. "Sense of Obligation to High School Activities as Related to School Size and Marginality of Student." *Child Development,* December 1967, *38* (4), 1247-1260.

Wright, H. F. *Recording and Analyzing Child Behavior.* New York: Harper & Row, 1967.

1968

Barker, R. G. *Ecological Psychology: Concepts and Methods for Studying the Environment of Human Behavior.* Stanford, Calif.: Stanford University Press, 1968.

Gump, P. V. "Persons, Settings, and Larger Contexts." In B. Indik and K. Berrien (Eds.), *People, Groups and Organizations: An Effective Integration.* New York: Teachers College, Columbia University Press, 1968.

Wicker, A. W. "Undermanning, Performances, and Students' Subjective Experiences in Behavior Settings of Large and Small High Schools." *Journal of Personality and Social Psychology,* 1968, *10* (3), 255-261.

1969

Barker, R. G. "Wanted: An Eco-Behavioral Science." In E. P. Willems and H. L. Raush (Eds.), *Naturalistic Viewpoints in Psychological Research.* New York: Holt, Rinehart and Winston, 1969.

Binding, F. R. S. *Behavior Setting Leadership in an American Community.* Doctoral dissertation, University of Kansas, Lawrence, 1969.

Gump, P. V. "Intra-Setting Analysis: The Third Grade Class-room as a Special but Instructive Case." In E. P. Willems and H. L. Raush (Eds.), *Naturalistic Viewpoints in Psychological Research*. New York: Holt, Rinehart and Winston, 1969.

Wicker, A. W. "Cognitive Complexity, School Size, and Partici-pation in School Behavior Settings: A Test of the Frequency of Interaction Hypothesis." *Journal of Educational Psychol-ogy*, 1969, *60* (3), 200-203.

Wicker, A. W. "School Size and Students' Experiences in Extra-curricular Activities: Some Possible Implications for School Planning." *Educational Technology*, 1969, *9* (5), 44-47.

1970

Botts, P. *An Exploratory Study of the Use of Still Photography as a Research Tool in Ecological Psychology*. Master's thesis, University of Kansas, Lawrence, 1970.

1971

Gump, P. V. "The Behavior Setting: A Promising Unit for Envi-ronmental Designers." *Landscape Architecture*, January 1971, *61* (2), 130-134.

Gump, P. V. "Milieu, Environment, and Behavior." *Design and Environment*, Winter 1971, *2* (4), 49ff.

Gump, P. V. "What's Happening in the Elementary Class-room?" In I. Westbury and A. A. Bellack (Eds.), *Research Into Classroom Processes: Recent Developments and Next Steps*. New York: Teachers College, Columbia University Press, 1971.

Olen, D. R. *Environmental Offerings and Students' Behavior in All-Boy, All-Girl and Coeducational Catholic High Schools*. Master's thesis, University of Kansas, Lawrence, 1971.

1972

Gump, P. V. "Linkages Between the 'Ecological Environment' and the Behavior and Experience of Persons." In W. M. Smith

(Ed.), *Behavior, Design, and Policy Aspects of Human Habitat.* Green Bay, Wisc.: University of Wisconsin Press, 1972.

James, E. V. *Environment and Behavior of Hospital Patients in Psychiatric and Medical Wards.* Unpublished doctoral dissertation, University of Kansas, Lawrence, 1972.

1973

Barker, R. G., and Schoggen, P. *Qualities of Community Life: Methods of Measuring Environment and Behavior Applied to an American and an English Town.* San Francisco: Jossey-Bass, 1973.

References

Alexander, J. L. "The Wheelchair Odometer as a Continuous, Unobtrusive Measure of Human Behavior." Unpublished master's thesis, University of Houston, 1977.

Allport, F. H. *Theories of Perception and the Concept of Structure.* New York: Wiley, 1955.

Allport, G. W. *Personality.* New York: Holt, Rinehart and Winston, 1937.

Allport, G. W. *Pattern and Growth in Personality.* New York: Holt, Rinehart and Winston, 1964.

Anderson, A. D. "The Reality of Restorative Care in Harlem's Municipal Hospital: The Patient as a Therapeutic Agent." *Archives of Physical Medicine and Rehabilitation,* 1975, *56,* 165-168.

Angyal, A. *Foundations for a Science of Personality.* New York: Commonwealth Fund, 1941.

Bailey, D. M. "Multidimensional Analysis of Reliability in Direct Observations of Human Behavior." Unpublished doctoral dissertation, University of Houston, 1977.

Baird, L. L. "Big School, Small School: A Critical Examination of the Hypothesis." *Journal of Educational Psychology,* 1969, *60,* 253-260.

Baldwin, A. L. *Behavior and Development in Childhood.* New York: Holt, Rinehart and Winston, 1955.

Barker, R. G. "On the Nature of the Environment." *Journal of Social Issues,* 1963a, *19* (4), 17-38.

Barker, R. G. (Ed.). *The Stream of Behavior.* New York: Appleton-Century-Crofts, 1963b.

Barker, R. G. *Ecological Psychology: Concepts and Methods for Studying the Environment of Human Behavior.* Stanford, Calif.: Stanford University Press, 1968.

Barker, R. G., and Gump, P. V. (Eds.). *Big School, Small School.* Stanford, Calif.: Stanford University Press, 1964.

Barker, R. G., and Schoggen, P. *Qualities of Community Life: Methods of Measuring Environment and Behavior Applied to an American and an English Town.* San Francisco: Jossey-Bass, 1973.

Barker, R. G., and Wright, H. F. *One Boy's Day.* New York: Harper & Row, 1951.

Barker, R. G., and Wright, H. F. *Midwest and Its Children.* New York: Harper & Row, 1955. (Reprinted by Archon Books, Hamden, Conn., 1971.)

Barker, R. G., and others. *Adjustment to Physical Handicap and Illness.* New York: Social Science Research Council, 1953.

Beals, E. W., and Cottam, G. "The Forest Vegetation of the Apostle Islands, Wisconsin." *Ecology,* 1960, *41,* 743-751.

Blatz, W. E., Chant, S. N. F., and Salter, M. D. "Emotional Episodes in the Child of School Age." University of Toronto Studies, Child Development Series, No. 9. Toronto: University of Toronto Press, 1937.

Bridenbaugh, C. (Ed.). *Gentleman's Progress: The Itinerarium of Dr. Alexander Hamilton, 1744.* Chapel Hill, N.C.: University of North Carolina Press, 1948.

Brunswik, E. "The Conceptual Framework of Psychology." *International Encyclopedia of Unified Science.* Vol. 1, Part 2. Chicago: University of Chicago Press, 1955.

Burton, A., and Harris, E. H. (Eds.). *Clinical Studies of Personality.* New York: Harper & Row, 1955.

Crowley, L. R. "Development and Assessment of an Alternative to the Narrative Observation." Unpublished master's thesis, University of Houston, 1976.

Dewey, J. *Psychology.* New York: Harper & Row, 1891.

Dickman, H. R. "The Perception of Behavior Units." In R. G. Barker (Ed.), *The Stream of Behavior.* New York: Appleton-Century-Crofts, 1963.

Dreher, G. F. "Reliability Assessment in Narrative Observations of Human Behavior." Unpublished master's thesis, University of Houston, 1975.

Friedman, F. *Dot for Short.* New York: Morrow, 1967.

Goodenough, F. *Anger in Young Children.* Minneapolis: University of Minnesota Press, 1931.

Gump, P. V. "Environmental Guidance of the Classroom Behavioral System." In B. J. Biddle and W. J. Ellena (Eds.), *Contemporary Research on Teacher Effectiveness.* New York: Holt, Rinehart and Winston, 1964.

Gump, P. V. *Big Schools—Small Schools.* Moravia, N.Y.: Chronical Guidance Publications, 1965.

Gump, P. V., Schoggen, P., and Redl, F. "The Camp Milieu and Its Immediate Effects." *Journal of Social Issues,* 1957, *13,* 40-46.

Halstead, L. S. "Longitudinal Assessment of Patient Performance as a Clinical Tool in Rehabilitation." Paper presented to the American Psychological Association, Washington, D.C., 1976.

Halstead, L. S., and Hartley, R. B. "Time Care Profile: An Evaluation of a New Method of Assessing ADL Dependence." *Archives of Physical Medicine and Rehabilitation,* 1975, *56,* 110-115.

Heider, F. *The Psychology of Interpersonal Relations.* New York: Wiley, 1958.

Heider, F. "Ding und Medium." *Symposion,* 1926, *1,* 109-157. (F. Heider and G. M. Heider, Trans.) *Journal of Psychological Issues,* 1959, *1* (3, entire issue).

Inselberg, R. M. "The Causation and Manifestations of Emotional Behavior in Filipino Children." *Child Development,* 1958, *29,* 249-254.

Isaacs, S. *Social Development in Young Children.* London: Routledge & Kegan Paul, 1933.

Jones, M. R. (Ed.). *Nebraska Symposium on Motivation.* Lincoln: University of Nebraska Press, 1960.

Jordan, T. E. "Research on the Handicapped Child and the Family." *Merrill-Palmer Quarterly of Behavior and Development,* 1962, *8,* 4.

Katz, S., and others. "Progress in Development of the Index of ADL." *The Gerontologist,* 1970, *10,* 20-30.

King, J. A. "Ecological Psychology: An Approach to Motivation." In W. J. Arnold and M. M. Page (Eds.), *Nebraska Symposium on Motivation.* Lincoln: University of Nebraska Press, 1970.

Kounin, J. S. *Discipline and Group Management in Classrooms.* New York: Holt, Rinehart and Winston, 1970.

Ladd, G. T. *Outlines of Descriptive Psychology.* New York: Scribner's, 1898.

Latham, R. and Mathews, W. *The Diary of Samuel Pepys.* Vol. I, 1660. London: G. Bell and Sons, 1970.

LeCompte, W. F. "The Taxonomy of a Treatment Environment." *Archives of Physical Medicine and Rehabilitation,* 1972, *53,* 109-114.

LeCompte, W. F., and Willems, E. P. "Ecological Analysis of a Hospital: Location Dependencies in the Behavior of Staff and Patients." In J. Archea and C. Eastman (Eds.), *EDRA-2: Proceedings of the 2nd Annual Environmental Design Research Association Conference.* Pittsburgh, Pa.: Carnegie-Mellon University, 1970.

Leeper, R. W. *Lewin's Topological and Vector Psychology: A Digest and Critique.* Eugene: University of Oregon Press, 1943.

Leeper, R. W. "Learning and the Fields of Perception, Motivation, and Personality." In S. Koch (Ed.), *Psychology: A Study of a Science.* Vol. 5. New York: McGraw-Hill, 1963.

Leighton, A. H. *My Name Is Legion.* New York: Basic Books, 1959.

Lewin, K. *Dynamic Theory of Personality.* New York: McGraw-Hill, 1935.

Lewin, K. *Field Theory in Social Science.* New York: Harper & Row, 1951.

Lichstein, K. L., and Wahler, R. G. "The Ecological Assessment of an Autistic Child." *Journal of Abnormal Child Psychology,* 1976, *4,* 31-54.

Miller, D. R., and Swanson, G. E. *Inner Conflict and Defense.* New York: Holt, Rinehart and Winston, 1958.

Miller, G. A., Galanter, E., and Pribram, K. H. *Plans and the Structure of Behavior.* New York: Holt, Rinehart and Winston, 1960.

Moos, R. H. "Conceptualizations of Human Environments." *American Psychologist,* 1973, *28,* 652-665.

Muenzinger, K. F. *Psychology: The Science of Behavior.* New York: Harper & Row, 1939.

Murray, H. A. "Preparations for the Scaffold of a Comprehensive System." In S. Koch (Ed.), *Psychology: A Study of a Science.* Vol. 3. New York: McGraw-Hill, 1959.

Odum, E. P. *Fundamentals of Ecology.* (3rd ed.) Philadelphia: Saunders, 1971.

Parsons, T. "An Approach to Psychological Theory in Terms of the Theory of Action." In S. Koch (Ed.), *Psychology: A Study of a Science.* Vol. 3. New York: McGraw-Hill, 1959.

Proshansky, H. M., Ittelson, W. H., and Rivlin, L. G. "The Influence of the Physical Environment on Behavior: Some Basic Assumptions." In H. M. Proshansky, W. H. Ittelson, and L. G. Rivlin (Eds.), *Environmental Psychology.* New York: Holt, Rinehart and Winston, 1970.

Ragle, D. D. M., Johnson, A., and Barker, R. G. "Measuring Extension's Impact." *Journal of Cooperative Extension,* Fall 1967, *5* (3), 178-186.

Raush, H. L. "Naturalistic Method and the Clinical Approach." In E. P. Willems and H. L. Raush (Eds.), *Naturalistic Viewpoints in Psychological Research.* New York: Holt, Rinehart and Winston, 1969.

Raush, H. L., Dittmann, A. T., and Taylor, T. J. "The Interpersonal Behavior of Children in Residential Treatment." *Journal of Abnormal and Social Psychology,* 1959a, *58,* 9-26.

Raush, H. L., Dittmann, A. T., and Taylor, T. J. "Person, Setting and Change in Social Interaction." *Human Relations,* 1959b, *12,* 361-379.

Raush, H. L., Farbman, I., and Llewellyn, L. G. "Person, Setting and Change in Social Interaction: II. A Normal-Control Study." *Human Relations,* 1960, *13,* 305-333.

Ricketts, A. "A Study of the Behavior of Young Children in Anger." *University of Iowa Studies in Child Welfare,* 1934, *3* (9), 159-171.

Sarason, S. B. *The Creation of Settings and the Future Societies.* San Francisco: Jossey-Bass, 1972.

Sarason, S. B. *The Psychological Sense of Community: Prospects for a Community Psychology.* San Francisco: Jossey-Bass, 1974.

Sarason, S. B., and others. *Human Services and Resource Networks: Rationale, Possibilities, and Public Policy.* San Francisco: Jossey-Bass, 1977.

Sarno, J. E., Sarno, M. T., and Levita, E. "The Functional Life Scale." *Archives of Physical Medicine and Rehabilitation,* 1973, *54,* 214-220.

Schoggen, P. "Environmental Forces in the Everyday Lives of Children." In R. G. Barker (Ed.), *The Stream of Behavior.* New York: Appleton-Century-Crofts, 1963.

Schoggen, P. "Environmental Forces in the Everyday Lives of Children with Physical Disabilities." *Mimeographed Report of Vocational Rehabilitation Administration Project #714,* 1964. Summary reported in G. N. Wright and A. B. Trotter, *Rehabilitation Research.* Madison: University of Wisconsin, 1968.

Sears, R. R., Maccoby, E. E., and Levin, H. *Patterns of Child Rearing.* Evanston, Ill.: Row, Peterson, 1957.

Sells, S. B. "Ecology and the Science of Psychology." In E. P. Willems and H. L. Raush (Eds.), *Naturalistic Viewpoints in Psychological Research.* New York: Holt, Rinehart and Winston, 1969.

Skinner, B. F. *Beyond Freedom and Dignity.* New York: Knopf, 1971.

Spencer, W. A., Baker, R. L., and Stock, D. D. "Basic Data Requirements: Individual Care and Internal Management of

Long-Term Institutions and Services." Paper presented to National Conference on Long-Term Care Data, Tucson, Arizona, May 1975.

Stern, W. *General Psychology.* New York: Holt, Rinehart and Winston, 1938.

Tolman, E. C. *Purposive Behavior in Animals and Man.* New York: Appleton-Century-Crofts, 1932.

Wahler, R. G. "Some Structural Aspects of Deviant Child Behavior." *Journal of Applied Behavior Analysis,* 1975, *8,* 27-42.

Warner, W. L., Meeker, M., and Eells, K. *Social Class in America.* Chicago: Science Research Associates, 1949.

Watson, J. B. *Behaviorism.* New York: Norton, 1924.

White, R. W. *Lives in Progress.* New York: Holt, Rinehart and Winston, 1952.

Wicker, A. W. "Undermanning, Performances, and Students' Subjective Experiences in Behavior Settings of Large and Small High Schools." *Journal of Personality and Social Psychology,* 1968, *10* (3), 255-261.

Wicker, A. W. "Cognitive Complexity, School Size, and Participation in School Behavior Settings: A Test of the Frequency of Interaction Hypotheses." *Journal of Educational Psychology,* 1969a, *60* (3), 200-203.

Wicker, A. W. "School Size and Students' Experiences in Extra-Curricular Activities: Some Possible Implications for School Planning." *Educational Technology,* 1969b, *9* (5), 44-47.

Wicker, A. W. "Size of Church Membership and Members' Support of Church Behavior Settings." *Journal of Personality and Social Psychology,* 1969c, *13,* 278-288.

Wicker, A. W. "Processes Which Mediate Behavior-Environment Congruence." *Behavioral Science,* 1972, *17,* 265-277.

Wicker, A. W., and Kauma, C. E. "Effects of a Merger of a Small and a Large Organization on Members' Behavior and Experiences." *Journal of Applied Psychology,* 1974, *59,* 24-30.

Wicker, A. W., and Mehler, A. "Assimilation of New Members in a Large and a Small Church." *Journal of Applied Psychology,* 1971, *55,* 151-156.

Willems, E. P. "Forces Toward Participation in Behavior Settings." In R. G. Barker and P. V. Gump (Eds.), *Big School, Small School*. Stanford, Calif.: Stanford University Press, 1964.

Willems, E. P. "Sense of Obligation to High School Activities as Related to School Size and Marginality of Student." *Child Development*, 1967, *38* (4), 1247-1260.

Willems, E. P. "The Interface of the Hospital Environment and Patient Behavior." *Archives of Physical Medicine and Rehabilitation*, 1972a, *53*, 115-122.

Willems, E. P. "Place and Motivation: Complexity and Independence in Patient Behavior." In W. J. Mitchell (Ed.), *Environmental Design: Research and Practice*. Los Angeles: University of California at Los Angeles, 1972b.

Willems, E. P. "Longitudinal Analysis of Patient Behavior." In W. A. Spencer (Ed.), *Annual Report of Research and Training Center No. 4*. Houston, Texas: Texas Institute for Rehabilitation and Research, 1975.

Willems, E. P. "Behavioral Ecology, Health Status, and Health Care: Applications to the Rehabilitation Setting." In I. Altman and J. F. Wohlwill (Eds.), *Human Behavior and Environment: Advances in Theory and Research*. New York: Plenum, 1976a.

Willems, E. P. "Longitudinal Analysis of Patient Behavior." In W. A. Spencer (Ed.), *Annual Report of Research and Training Center No. 4*. Houston, Texas: Texas Institute for Rehabilitation and Research, 1976b.

Willems, E. P., and Campbell, D. E. "Behavioral Ecology: A New Approach to Health Status and Health Care." In B. Honikman (Ed.), *Responding to Social Change*. Stroudsburg, Pa.: Dowden, Hutchinson and Ross, 1975.

Willems, E. P., and Halstead, L. S. "Quantifying Behavior and Physical Activity of the Handicapped and the Service System to Measure Outcome Effectiveness." Paper presented to the American Association for the Advancement of Science, New York, January 1975.

Willems, E. P., and Halstead, L. S. "Longitudinal Functional Assessment in Rehabilitation: Problem and Perspective." *Medical Care*, in press.

Willems, E. P., and Raush, H. L. (Eds.). *Naturalistic Viewpoints in Psychological Research.* New York: Holt, Rinehart and Winston, 1969.

Willems, E. P., and Vineberg, S. E. *Procedural Supports for the Direct Observation of Behavior in Natural Settings.* Houston, Texas: Texas Institute for Rehabilitation and Research, 1970.

Wright, H. F. *Recording and Analyzing Child Behavior.* New York: Harper & Row, 1967.

Index

317